Blackshirts in Devon

Blackshirts in Devon

Todd Gray

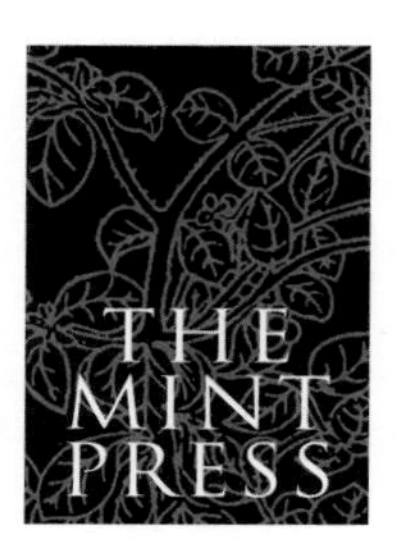

First published in Great Britain by
The Mint Press, 2006

ISBN 978-1-903356-46-3

Cataloguing in Publication Data
CIP record for this title is available from the British Library

The Mint Press
76 Longbrook Street
Exeter, Devon
England EX4 6AP

Typeset by Kestrel Data
Cover design by Delphine Jones

Printed and bound in Great Britain
by Short Run Press Ltd, Exeter

Contents

One of the greatest means of support for the Blackshirts in Devon came from the farming community. This photograph illustrates a dispute at Whitestone in 1933.
(Express & Echo, 29 November 1933)

Preface

For more than eighty years the history of fascism in Devon has remained unwritten and in that time it has become all but forgotten. Both historians working on Devon[1] as well as those writing with a wider perspective have ignored it.[2] The lack of questioning of this aspect of the past has let an extraordinary history go untold. The possible reasons are intriguing. Perhaps it has been supposed fascism was inconsequential or possibly some find it hard to believe that a county best known as a picturesque holiday destination also had an active Fascist history. Plymouth, most popularly associated with Sir Francis Drake, was in the 1930s home to more than a thousand Fascists and hundreds of farmers in the rolling countryside of Tarka the Otter were followers of Sir Oswald Mosley. The latter should not be surprising. Tarka was created by Henry Williamson, an enthusiastic supporter of fascism. Tarka may not have been a Fascist but Williamson decidedly was and spoke warmly of Mosley, and of Adolph Hitler, from his home in North Devon. Another local fascist wrote a fascist interpretation of Drake playing bowls on the Hoe and imagined he was an anti-Semite[3] while another writer envisioned Uncle Tom Cobley as a Blackshirt recruit. In the 1930s Devon had a strong Fascist element which permeated local society. All counties have secretive, shadowy or dark aspects of history but this particular one is black; it is a history of black shirts.

It is not just historians who have ignored local fascism. Hundreds of people have recorded memories of Devon in the 1930s and

1940s but have lacked enthusiasm for discussing fascism. This changed in 2004 when a handful of former young boys recalled skirmishes with Blackshirts in Exeter.[4] Most recently, attempts have been made to record specific memories of two leading Devon fascists who were ostracised in Branscombe when war broke out and of three others who lived quiet lives in the small village of Silverton. One woman recalled Rafe Temple Cotton looked, in his black uniform, 'a very handsome man' and was 'a very nice fellow'. He reportedly claimed to have dated a Mitford sister. Another woman recalled attending a hunt ball in Silverton where Cotton asked her for a date. Shortly afterwards she happened across him speaking for the Blackshirts in Exeter and thought 'there was no way that I could meet him now that I saw what he was, as my mother would kill me!' Her mother was one of the crowd of local people who protested against the Fascists. Another remembered meetings in Sidmouth where the audience 'was mainly against him. They hissed and booed at his meetings. After one they picked him up and threw him in the river but he swam to safety.' Of his mother Lucy memories are less complimentary: 'a hard woman – more like a man really', 'looked like a German. She had a frightening look about her, a very strong character, who walked along besides the procession carrying a banner. She was a tall, well-built woman that always had a fierce expression on her face' and 'a hard woman – she would get whatever she wanted'). Their openness contrasts with others who have said this is a subject best left alone. Requests for information in small villages and towns across Devon, including Colyton, Ilfracombe, Lydford and Paignton, and sometimes in the county's two cities have been met with stony silence. Some denied friends and neighbours were Fascists. Yet these were individuals who were not merely open about their political beliefs but were fervent in spreading their message.

Perhaps it is understandable that not one descendant of a Devon Fascist has helped and only two Fascists agreed to an interview. It is more surprising that others with no connections to fascism have hinted it is too dark and controversial as a subject to discuss and regard it as a shameful aspect of local history. Some have protested they do not want their villages 'sullied by the smear of fascism'. For many the purpose of local history is to provide entertainment or reassurance. But research of any locality and of the lives of those who resided there is, by its very nature, as unpredictable and potentially upsetting as the course of modern lives. It is a moot point as to where a historian's responsibility lies when revealing unexpected or shocking aspects of the lives of loved ones to unsuspecting friends and relatives. Yet, to ignore such an important subject on these grounds, particularly given the current rise of extreme politics, is irresponsible for a historian.

Some reticence can be attributed to the post-war revelations of the horrors of the Holocaust which generally turned whatever ambivalence or support there might have been for fascism into general antagonism and repulsion. For some of those involved in it, or those near to them, there is apprehension and shame. Whatever merits pre-war British Fascism professed or had, the movement became singularly identified with the barbarous excesses of the Nazis. This general viewpoint, although understandable, is curious when considered alongside the atrocities committed by the Soviets. In spite of these other millions of unwarranted murders, there is a general perception that fascism, and those that followed it, is reprehensible and depraved, if not evil, while followers of communism were merely misguided.

In this study I have attempted to record the main events in as much detail as is possible and warranted. Even so, there are bound to be omissions with a book which opens up a new subject. I have tried to explain what drew Devon men and women to fascism in the 1930s. I have been hampered by the lack of Fascists' own accounts. Devon is one of the largest counties in England and it is a major endeavour to try to understand a movement which meant very different things from one community to another: supporters in the north in rural Buckland Brewer, for instance, had little in common with those in the genteel resort of Sidmouth or with those who lived in the slums of Plymouth. Their reasons for being Fascists were very different as well. In consequence, this book relies upon other evidence to understand what type of people the Fascists were and what interested them in a party which they themselves regarded as revolutionary.

Even so, this is an elusive area to research and it did not easily give up its secrets. Local memories have helped but it was the recent

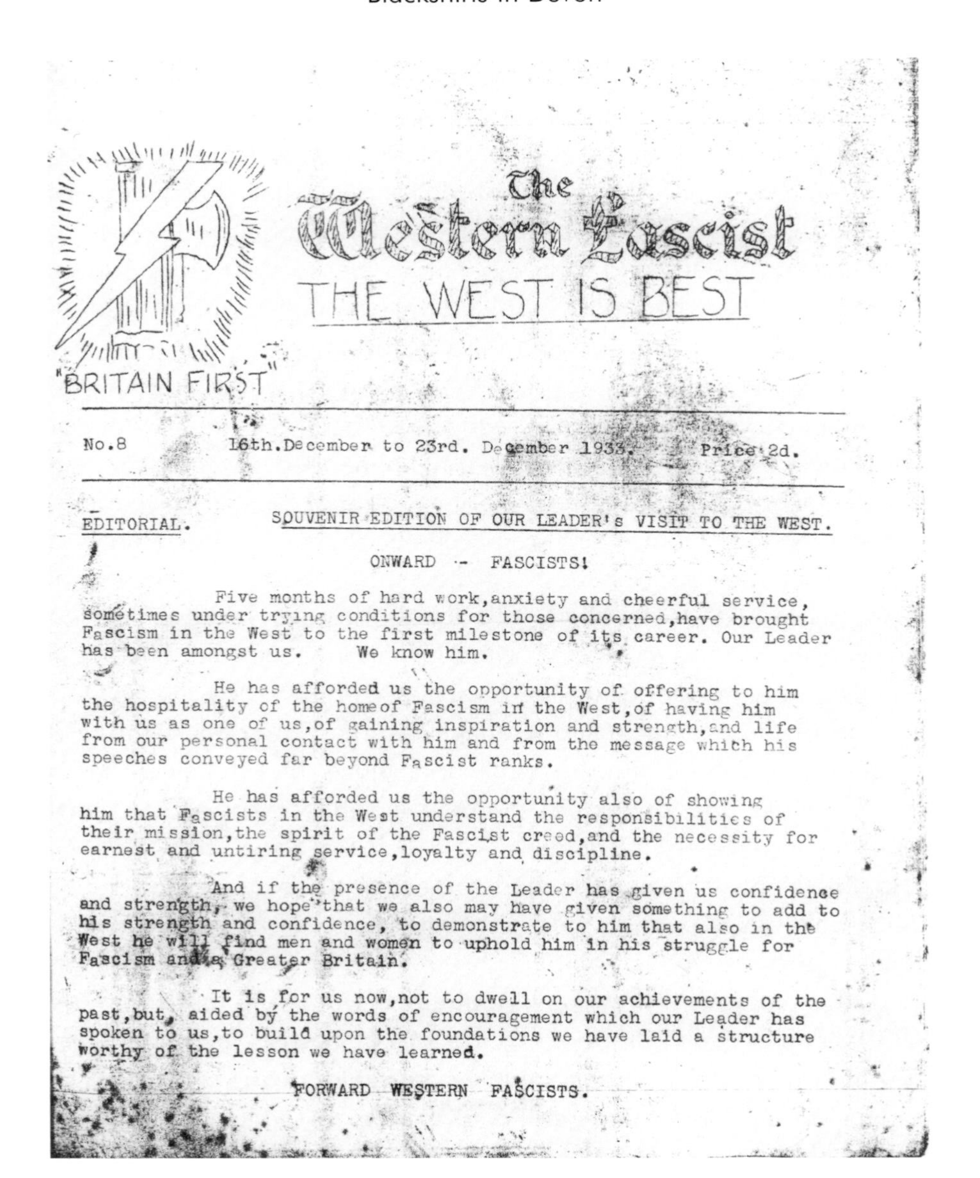
"BRITAIN FIRST"

The Western Fascist
THE WEST IS BEST

No.8 16th.December to 23rd. December 1933. Price 2d.

EDITORIAL. SOUVENIR EDITION OF OUR LEADER's VISIT TO THE WEST.

ONWARD -- FASCISTS!

Five months of hard work,anxiety and cheerful service, sometimes under trying conditions for those concerned,have brought Fascism in the West to the first milestone of its career. Our Leader has been amongst us. We know him.

He has afforded us the opportunity of offering to him the hospitality of the homeof Fascism in the West,of having him with us as one of us,of gaining inspiration and strength,and life from our personal contact with him and from the message which his speeches conveyed far beyond Fascist ranks.

He has afforded us the opportunity also of showing him that Fascists in the West understand the responsibilities of their mission,the spirit of the Fascist creed,and the necessity for earnest and untiring service,loyalty and discipline.

And if the presence of the Leader has given us confidence and strength, we hope that we also may have given something to add to his strength and confidence, to demonstrate to him that also in the West he will find men and women to uphold him in his struggle for Fascism and a Greater Britain.

It is for us now,not to dwell on our achievements of the past,but, aided by the words of encouragement which our Leader has spoken to us,to build upon the foundations we have laid a structure worthy of the lesson we have learned.

FORWARD WESTERN FASCISTS.

Title page of an issue of The Western Fascist, the in-house circular for Western Area members of the British Union of Fascists.

discovery by a builder of a collection of Fascist newspapers, hidden for more than sixty-five years under the floorboards of the home of Devon's leading Blackshirt in the late 1930s, that began revealing some of this forgotten history. A framework was constructed from visits to read some three dozen newspapers[5] held in more than twenty libraries, archives and museums across the South West and in London. This was followed by time spent in the Midlands to research the correspondence of a Dorset Fascist active in Devon and to the National Archives to read the Home Office and MI5 files on local Fascists. Another great source are the four remaining copies of *The Western Fascist* found in a Plymouth attic.[6] These offer a unique and personal view of the local scene which has proved incredibly useful. The British Library's copies of Fascist newspapers and journals were also illuminating as were ancillary documents seen in the three Devon record offices at Barnstaple, Exeter and Plymouth.

Many aspects remain unknown including the identities of the financial supporters in Plymouth and why there was a concentration

An aerial photograph of Knowstone Manor with the shape of the building almost visible, 1939 (courtesy of Devon County Council).

of Fascists in Bovey Tracey. There are other elements I have not been able to explain. For instance, for many years stories have circulated about Knowstone Manor, a small country house in north-east Devon; it has been said that the owner, Leo Alexander, built it in the shape of a swastika in the mid-1930s. The building was destroyed by fire in about 1970 but one aerial photograph shows it had an extraordinary layout. I have not been able to confirm he was a Fascist nor offer any other explanation given for the shape of the house.[7]

Active Fascist supporters lived in every corner of Devon. Branches were formed throughout the county and many thousands of local people were drawn to meetings. An extraordinary range of individuals was involved although some were active for short but intense periods. Devon also had two leading national figures in A. K. Chesterton and Henry Williamson. The latter is better known for his writing but Chesterton went on to found the National Front. Each of them was committed to the Fascist cause. It quickly became apparent there were some major themes in Devon: in 1933 and 1934 great political meetings and counter demonstrations resulted in violent disorder involving many thousands of people in Plymouth where the party was regionally organised and then it suddenly collapsed, a resurgence of fascism took place in the new capital of local fascism at Exeter in 1937 and 1938, hundreds of meetings, parades, marches and rallies were held in villages and nearly every town, farmers worked closely with Fascists in a war on tithes, and the county became a refuge for dozens of Fascists who had fled their own homes in the second world war.

Even so, what follows is only a portion of this history of fascism. No single collection of documents for a local Fascist has been found and the deliberate destruction of the central papers of the British Union of Fascists and National Socialists in 1940 means much will remain unknown. A Devon man later claimed to have helped burn those papers and, I suspect, was instrumental in the loss of local papers. Also, a list of local members was taken in London in 1940 and sent to Torquay where the police confiscated it. This appears to have been lost. Yet, in spite of the gaps, what can be revealed is surprising and to some will be shocking. It is impossible to understand the second world war without knowing of the rise and fall of fascism in the 1930s. The movement was centred in London but here in Devon there were many enthusiastic followers dedicated to fascism.

The book is broadly arranged chronologically because the sudden rise, intermittent spurts and final collapse of fascism occurred over less than seven years. In that time some individuals and places became highly prominent only to suddenly disappear. Few key players lasted more than a year and while some could be derided as eccentrics or even cranks there was a great range of people of varying backgrounds, qualities and abilities. No place had a consistent history: for some eighteen months Plymouth was the centre and then became irrelevant while other towns developed similar erratic histories. This is a story of extraordinary activity, of short bursts by unusual personalities in disconnected parts of the county and then sudden change. No six months was like any other and for this reason the book begins with the antecedents to Mosley's Blackshirts in 1932 and ends with the ragbag of his local followers, many of whom had been arrested and interned, attempting to revive fascism in Devon in 1946.

Todd Gray
Exeter

Notes

1 The only exception is Gerald Wasley, *Devon At War* (Tiverton, 1994), 8, which has a short paragraph.
2 Niegl Copsey, *Anti-Fascism in Britain* (Basingstoke, 2000), 24, has two sentences on Plymouth.
3 See *Blackshirt*, No. 142, 10 January 1936.
4 Todd Gray, *Exeter Remembers The War* (Exeter, 2005), 112-114.
5 Local newspapers include *Bideford and North Devon Weekly Gazette, Crediton Chronicle and South Molton Gazette, Dartmouth & Western Guardian, Dartmouth and South Hams Chronicle, Dawlish Gazette, Devon & Exeter Gazette, Devon & Somerset News, Exmouth Chronicle, Exmouth Journal, Express & Echo, Kingsbridge Gazette, Mid-Devon Advertiser and Torbay News, Naval & Military Record and Royal*

Dockyards' Gazette, North Devon Gazette, North Devon Herald and General Advertiser for Devonshire, East Cornwall and West Somerset, North Devon Journal, Okehampton Post & Weekly News, Paignton and Newton Directory, Pulman's Weekly News Advertiser for Somerset, Dorset and Devon, Saltash Gazette, Sidmouth Herald and Directory, Sidmouth Observer, South Molton Gazette and West of England Advertiser, Teignmouth Gazette, Tiverton Gazette and East Devon Herald, Torquay Directory, Torquay Times, Totnes Times, Western Evening Herald and Western Evening News, Western Independent, Western Morning News and *Western Weekly.* I have also searched *The Police Gazette, Action, Blackshirt, British Lion, British Union Quarterly, Fascist Week* and *The Fascist.*

6 Plymouth Central Library, 329/950.

7 Anthony James Philip Brewer Alexander had been resident in Knowstone since about 1934. He was reportedly interested in local affairs, notably in farming. He was a former member of the London County Council Public Assistance Committee and Vice Chairman of Mile End Hospital. He was unsuccessful in 1938 in his attempts to win a seat on Devon County Council: *Western Morning News*, 1 September 1939.

Acknowledgements

A great many people have been helpful in many different ways. I would like to thank Priscilla Bandy, Brian Brasset, Tony Burgess, Peter Child, Dr Jo Cox, Lady Violet De Vere, Prudence De Villiers, Malcolm Darch, Jill Drysdale, John W. Edwards, Barbara Farquharson, Dennis Forward, Arthur French, Frank Gent, Dr Tom Greeves, John Hesketh, Professor Colin Holmes, Michael Howarth, L. J. Irving, Bob Letcher, John Lewis, Peggy Moore, Ivor Mosley, Pam Nason, Dr Lawrence Normand, Mary Osborne, Graham Parnell, Margaret Reed, Marion Roberts, Margaret Rogers, Tony Stevens, Professor Andrew Thorpe, Sylvia Tree, Maureen Turner, Malcolm Upham, Andy & Sheila Wilcocks and Jeffrey Wallder. I owe a special thanks to Sidney Jacobs. I apologise to anyone whom I have neglected to mention.

I have benefited from the helpfulness and kindness of the staffs of the British Library, Cookworthy Museum, Cornish Studies Library, Devon & Cornwall Constabulary Museum, Devon & Exeter Institution, Devon Record Office, Dorchester Record Office, Exeter Central Library, Exmouth Public Library, Friends of Oswald Mosley, Honiton Museum, Morrab Library, National Archives, National Museum of Labour History, Newton Abbot Public Library, North Devon Athenaeum, North Devon Record Office, Plymouth & West Devon Record Office, Plymouth Central Library, Salcombe Library, Sidmouth Museum, Sidmouth Public Library, Somerset Record Office, Taunton Museum, Tiverton Museum, Torquay Public Library,

University of Exeter's Special Collections, University of Sheffield's Special Collections, University of Warwick's Modern Record Unit and the Westcountry Studies Library. I am very grateful to them for giving their time and access to the material which they hold. I apologise for not naming each archivist, librarian and curator. I would also like to thank the Friends of Oswald Mosley and also Special Collections of Sheffield University for permission to quote from collections they hold.

For Tim

Introduction

The First Fascists, 1923 to 1932

The first Blackshirt to be seen in Devon was almost certainly in a street in Plymouth, possibly on the Hoe, in July 1933. This was nine months after the party started in London. Devon was not in the forefront of the Fascist movement but once it arrived there was a frantic level of activity.

Sir Oswald Mosley began his new party, the British Union of Fascists, in the autumn of 1932 with 30 followers in London. By then the public had been reading news reports of other Fascist groups in local and national newspapers for over a decade. Fascism had been introduced to Britain in 1923 following the success of Benito Mussolini in Italy the year before. At first Italian fascism was the only one known to the British. Mussolini filled columns of English newspapers and much of it was favourable. Italy was often presented as a dynamic country, a former ally of the first world war which had successfully reinvented itself in the face of the Communist threat.

Anti-Communism was one of the main appeals of fascism in Britain. Russia had experienced its Bolshevik revolution only a few years before, in 1917, and many became concerned it would spread into western Europe. Some in Britain perceived the rise of trade unionism and the Labour Party movement as part of the new

Communist peril. Italy's embrace of fascism became a role model in how to save society. 'Better fascism than communism' was often said. In this line of thinking, Mussolini was not a threat. He was a hero.

Even so fascism had various meanings to different people. When it arrived in Britain it appealed to ardent patriots partly because of its strong support for the monarchy as well as the flag waving and the singing of revered anthems which enhanced a sense of nationalism. It was also emphatic in supporting the Empire which then still comprised an extraordinary number and size of territories across the globe including large parts of Africa, the Middle East and the Caribbean and India, Hong Kong, Australia and Canada. Hundreds of years of colonialism were a cause of deep pride to Fascists.

Other policies had less appeal. The overt militarism frightened many. Uniforms, drilling, public marches, military titles and the violence which followed were not uniformly admired. Some voters were strongly attracted to it but others were repelled. Many questioned the need, wondered why a private army was being created and were disquieted at the thought of an armed coup against the elected government. The Fascist view of democracy convinced many the movement had to be resisted. Under Fascism democracy would be eliminated and all political opposition eradicated. Parliament, and party politics, would disappear because private interests had been promoted at the expense of the nation. A strong leader would rule the country and direct the people in their own best interests. Democracy merely muddled thinking and wasted resources. Some aristocratic supporters were attracted by an imagined return to the days of their ancestors when a ruling elite managed British life.

Fascism envisioned resources would be used for the common good and those who put other loyalties first would not be tolerated. This argument was used against the Jews. They were presented as placing their religious or financial loyalties before those of their country and the tag of 'international finance' was applied. As Mosley once stated, it was not the Jew he disliked, it was what he did. Anti-Semitism featured in many far right groups but it was not a defining feature of Mosley's early policies. In the seven and a half years in which his party existed there were considerable policy changes. The degree of anti-Semitism in British fascism was partly determined by the changing world of international politics.

Benito Mussolini dominated Fascist theory in the 1920s and very early 1930s. The apparent success and stability of a resurgent Italy inspired other nationals to emulate Mussolini's example. The sudden rise of Adolph Hitler and his National Socialist party in 1932 created a rival and the two versions of fascism strove to influence the development of international fascism. Whereas there had been considerable positive media publicity for Mussolini, particularly in the early years, the German Fascists largely received negative news reports. Anti-German feeling was strong in Britain after what was still a very short time period from the first world war. British newspapers reported the violence and brutality of the Nazi regime and many readers were influenced by this in their opinion of British Fascists. German fascism was more racially orientated and in Britain it attracted some followers who were already anti-Semitic.

It was this association of Mosley's party with continental antecedents that caused him considerable trouble. Although the startling German successes in the mid 1930s were headline capturing, and coincidentally made Mosley more newsworthy himself, it created deep anxieties amongst the British. Many questioned to what degree the overt Nazi militarism was pro-German in the short term and anti-British in the longer. This coupling of British fascism with German interests caused many to see it as foreign. Some intensely patriotic people, who would otherwise have been drawn to Fascist policies, deeply distrusted a movement they perceived as being un-British. The very name of the first of the Fascist parties, the *Fascisti,* created a gulf which for some was never crossed.

One of Mosley's greatest difficulties in 1932, when he launched his new party, was how to overcome the past. He had two problems. One was of his own making. He entered politics as a Conservative Member of Parliament in 1918 and left that party to become an Independent Labour M. P. only four years later. Two years later he joined the Labour Party. Just as many voters distrusted Winston Churchill for his changes of political alliances, so many regarded Mosley. He was presented as an unreliable opportunist and viewed with suspicion by many of his former followers and colleagues. This was already the case when he left the Labour Party but then he founded his own party in 1931. A year later he began yet another new party, the British Union of Fascists. His second major problem was how to redefine fascism in Britain and dominate it after others had been active for nine years. Mosley was a newcomer. He was fortunate that existing Fascist parties had not been great successes but they had muddied the waters. It would have been easier to have had a clean slate. Instead he had to negotiate through a crowded Fascist, and far-right, political landscape.

It has long been claimed that British fascism originated in the West Country at a dairy farm in Somerset. Miss Rotha Lintorn-Orman, the granddaughter of Field Marshal Sir John Lintorn Arabin Simmons, concluded whilst digging that Britain, like her garden, was overrun with weeds. She regarded the country's aliens, comprising anarchists, communists, Freemasons, Jews and socialists, as contributing towards Britain 'going to the dogs'. Subsequently, on 6 May 1923, she formed the British Fascisti. Lintorn-Orman was then 28 years old, unmarried and subsequently became known as the 'Man-woman' possibly because she dressed in men's clothes. Interestingly, she had also established her own troop of the Girl Guides in Bournemouth. This activity is given some added symbolism by the British Fascisti's President in 1924 having famously said he regarded it as an adult offshoot of the Boy Scout movement; he remarked 'both uphold the same lofty ideals of brotherhood, service and duty'.[1]

There is no evidence Devon was important in these early years except one Member of Parliament took a lead in this first Fascist group. Lieut. Colonel Sir Charles Burn, later Sir Charles Forbes-Leith, the Conservative M.P. for Torquay from 1910 to 1923, was one of the nine members of the Grand Council of the British Fascisti. He died a few years later and thus did not live to see the subsequent impact Fascism had in Torquay or across Devon a decade later. Given the proximity of her home to Devon it could reliably be assumed that Lintorn-Orman knew the county fairly well. At the least, shortly after she started her Fascist party Lintorn-Orman went to Devon for a visit. A Metropolitan Police officer then described her as 'a crank'.[2]

In neighbouring Cornwall there were two members. One was probably fairly minor: the Reverend K. L. Kempthorne of Falmouth was a party officer. Surprisingly he was not the only Fascist cleric in the South West: a few years later, in 1930, the Reverend Ellis Roberts moved to Devon. Little is known of Kempthorne's activities but the other early Cornish Fascist was highly visible both locally and nationally.

Paymaster Rear Admiral W. E. R. Martin was a Devonian who retired in the early 1920s to Saltash, the town situated on the border with Devon on the Tamar River. Martin was the chief Fascisti organiser for Cornwall. He was been born at Devonport in 1867, educated in Plymouth and spent part of his holidays on Dartmoor at Poundsgate, the small remote village in which curiously another Fascist later found refuge during the second world war.

Martin was a prolific writer on fascism in local newspapers such as the *Saltash Gazette*, the *Western Independent* and the *Western Morning News*, and in the national Fascist press including *Action* and *The British Lion*.[3] The letters gave him a prominence few other local Fascists enjoyed.

Martin was committed to the cause. He attended an Anglo-Italian symposium on fascism and his paper was published in a collection by the National Institute of Fascist Culture at Pavia. In 1923 he tried to personally present his autobiography, *The Adventures of a Naval Paymaster*, to Mussolini in Rome but only managed to see an official. Martin was later thanked by the Italian leader for trying to guide the British media in providing positive reports of his government. He retired a year before the British Fascisti was formed and wrote he felt the country was then like a piano out of tune. In 1928 he gave a speech at Saltash to promote fascism in which he praised Mussolini. There were Cornish branches of the British Fascisti in Penzance and Porthleven.[4]

Martin was not a member of Mosley's party although he co-operated with it. He referred to himself as a 'British Fascist' and disagreed with Mosley having established a political party. This came to the fore in September 1933 in criticism of him at a Yelverton meeting of the British Legion. Martin had suggested it should work 'hand in hand' with British fascism. The chairman stated 'we have I believe good Liberals, good Tories and good Socialists and we may even have good Fascists but when we meet together as British Legionnaires we do so for the work of ex-servicemen, leaving our politics outside' and a resolution was passed expressing disapproval of the Saltash branch for allowing its meeting to be used for political purposes.[5] Earlier in the year, at Callington, Martin made similar remarks when he opened the Legion's annual fair. However, subsequent criticism resulted in his leaving but not before claiming fascism was apolitical. Martin believed fascism would come to power via means other than the ballot box and that it would replace party politics. In contrast, Mosley was willing to work the political process and win a parliamentary majority. Martin considered this a betrayal of Fascist ideals and wrote 'I have no faith whatever' in 'Fascists of the Mosley type'. The two men later met in Plymouth.[6] In spite of Martin's protests about not being a Mosleyite, in 1933 and 1934 he cooperated with the party and organised their meetings in Saltash.

After a year the first Fascist party, the British Fascisti, was renamed British Fascists Ltd. It was a para-militiary group created to save the country from socialism and was a more radical version of the many other anti-labour organisations formed after the first world war. It adopted a blue shirt as part of its uniform. Within a few years the British Fascists fragmented into various groups including the British Loyalists and the Imperial Fascist League. The latter became one of the largest Fascist groups but the closest branch to Devon appears to have been Bristol.[7] One Devon member was Violet Francis who lived in Manaton. In 1933 she saw her party as standing 'for King and State and the upholding of all the fine old traditions of the British Empire'. It also, perhaps most importantly, fought communism and socialism. Francis did not approve of the British Union of Fascists and thought its members were not true Fascists. No doubt there were other Devon members who have yet to be identified.[8]

Also at Bristol for a short while was the most famous, or infamous, recruit of another party, the National Fascisti. Valerie Arkell-Smith had worked at a remount depot for horses in the city during the first world war and after she joined the party she

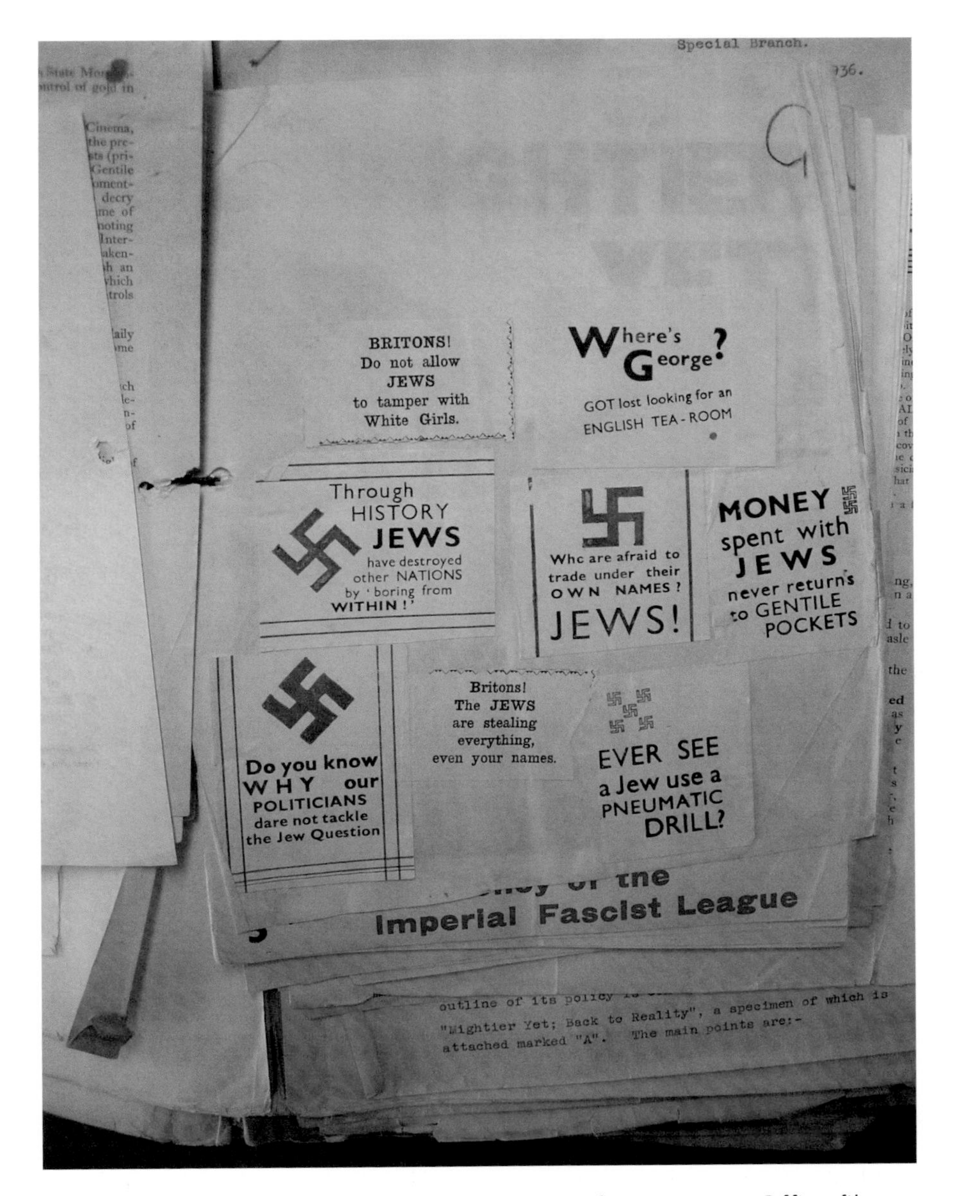

Propaganda of the Imperial Fascist League from a Home Office file (National Archives, HO45/22454).

lived at National Headquarters as Captain Barker, dressed as a man, where she taught young recruits how to box and fence. She also encouraged them to avoid the company of women. The thirty-seven year old transvestite was exposed several years later for having married, as a man, one woman and for living with two other women. Extensive newspaper coverage subjected the Fascists to public ridicule. It was widely reported the prosecutor had said she 'profaned the house of God . . . outraged the decencies of nature, and broken the laws of man'.

The official newspaper of the British Fascisti, *The Fascist Bulletin,* later renamed *The British Lion*, has few references to Devon. The county had little activity unlike Dorset where a carnival was organised in July 1926 or Somerset where a dance was held at the Assembly Rooms in Weston-Super-Mare in March 1926. Until about 1926 Rear Admiral Martin's official position in the British Fascists was County Commander for Cornwall. Who served in this capacity for Devon is uncertain. Martin also funded a competition in the newspaper for children on the best essay on British Fascism. One prominent party member was Charles Edward Pole-Carew of Parkhill in Littlehempston near Totnes. He was possibly a member of the family of that name from Shute near Colyton in East Devon. Pole-Carew contributed towards the party's national fund in the summer of 1925. Two other active members were the aforementioned Reverend Ellis Roberts and his daughter Winifred. In 1930 they moved from Alberbury to Ipplepen in Devon. In December 1926 Miss Roberts wrote from her father's Shropshire vicarage asking for a pen pal; in the newspaper she placed in the classified ads 'solitary Fascist would be glad to correspond with another'. Reverend Roberts joined Mosley's Fascists in 1935.[9]

Other similar groups formed about this time included the Britons, English Mistery, the Nordic League, the Liberty League, the White Knights and the Order of the Red Rose which were in outlook fervently patriotic and racist. Many were anti-Semitic.[10] In Devon there was little activity by any of them nor does the county appear to have created its own Fascist group unlike Yorkshire. There were some prominent members with Devon connections of the British Empire Union, a movement which grew from the Anti-German Union in 1915 and which aimed to counter Communist propaganda. The notable Devonians were the Duke of Somerset, the Earl of Plymouth and Viscount Astor. The Union is a good example of the complicated politics of the 1930s in that it co-operated with the Fascists but had been opposed to them. Another group with similar links, which was active in Devon, was the

National Citizens' Union. One of its leading members was Sir Charles Burn, the aforementioned Torquay M. P. and one of the country's first Fascists.[11]

These movements arose out of the extraordinary economic and politic climate following the first world war. A number of factors threatened the established order: the return of more than a million disabled servicemen (as well as the loss of nearly a million lives during the war), the uncertain implications of the formation in 1920 of the Communist Party of Great Britain after the Soviet Revolution of 1917, the rise of the Labour Party and trade union activity, a faltering economy with high inflation and the loss of exports to the more vibrant American and Japanese economies and giving the right to vote to women (some of them at least).

It was Mussolini's success which initiated Lintorn-Orman's movement in Britain in 1923, only five years after the ending of the first world war, and shortly afterwards the British Fascisti was challenged by the General Strike which took place in May 1926. It began to collapse shortly afterwards. In Devon the strike crippled the transport system and the police drew their batons against rioters but disorder was not as serious as elsewhere.[12] The effect it had on any Devon Fascists is unknown.

The early Fascist parties appear to have made little impact on Devon. The defining moment for local fascism was when on 1 October 1932 Sir Oswald Mosley, just short of reaching his thirty-sixth birthday, formed the British Union of Fascists. His party came to dominate the British Fascist movement but at the time of the launch Devon's newspapers made little or no mention of the event. In London Mosley told his followers they would 'face abuse, bitter animosity and possibly the ferocity of struggle and danger'. The party would continually modify its uniform but stuck with a black shirt. The initial design was inspired by Mosley's own fencing tunic.[13] Uniforms, and a military air, were defining features of the party and it owed its initial character to Mussolini's movement.

Mosley's policies would change over the next eight years but his main thrust was to introduce what he called The Corporate State. Central planning would oversee capitalism and democracy would be replaced by a body of representatives chosen from particular walks of life which would help run government under the overall control of Mosley. Party politics was, according to Mosley, divisive and ineffective in a modern society. The empire was a central feature of British Fascist policy: its purpose was to maximise wealth and power for Great Britain. Mosley promised a 'Britain First' policy but advantages would be given to the 'white commonwealth' countries of Canada, Australia, New Zealand and South Africa.[14] Racial policy, particularly that relating to the Jews, evolved and become increasingly extreme. Within weeks followers in London had chanted 'to hell with the Jews' but Mosley responded to criticisms by ordering Jew-baiting to stop. Subsequent changes were due partly to the rise of German fascism under Hitler and the waning influence of Mussolini in international affairs. Policy was also influenced by covert funds from Mussolini to the party: at least £200,000 was supplied between 1934 and 1937 but the extent of German money is uncertain.[15]

Mosley was not welcomed by the British Fascist movement and was treated with scepticism and suspicion because of his chequered career of having already belonged to three other parties. In 1932 Fascists remembered Mosley's previous hostility to their movement. At a meeting Mosley held at Cambridge in 1927, while a Labour supporter, hundreds of undergraduates, carrying the Union Flag and Fascist flags, interrupted him and he responded they were no more than 'black-shirted buffoons, making a cheap imitation of ice-cream sellers'.[16] In another instance, in 1930, in a speech to advertising men in which he solicited support for a cross-party solution to the economic crisis, Mosley reassured them they would 'never see in England people walking about in black shirts'.[17] It was not surprising some Fascists were scornful.

The support for Mosley in Devon came from a variety of reasons. Some responded to his patriotic politics and many younger supporters identified with Mosley's message the country needed a fresh youthful direction. In fascism many saw a solution to the threat of communism while others were attracted to his support for empire. The party was created during the Great Depression and Mosley's main contention was the existing political framework was unable to deal with a modern world. He argued the depression, with its mass unemployment, faltering industry and middle-class uncertainty, would create conditions ending in a Communist revolt. This was the British Fascists' *raison d'être*. Equally, it was said, the Fascists also needed such an opportunity. As the movement changed over the decade so too did the type of enthusiast in Devon. Each year, from 1932 to 1940, was radically different and the one consistency was that there was none. Also, membership had a high turnover rate: it is thought that nationally some were attracted to the opportunities of engaging in violence[18] but many were political novices, from the fringes of society, who were incapable of staying within any movement or party.

In 1932 Devon was, like the rest of the country, caught in the midst of the Great Depression, or the 'Slump', caused by the Wall Street Crash of 1929. Plymouth, the largest urban area, was dominated by the navy and dockyard, Exeter had some light industry but was mainly a retail centre although there was great influence exerted by the cathedral authorities, the coastline was largely given over to summer tourism and the countryside was dotted with small family farms engaged in mixed farming with dairy cattle the main interest. The year before unemployment had been high in Devon but it was not nearly as severe as in other parts of the country: Tiverton had 3.5%, Torquay 6.7%, Exeter 8.1%, Barnstaple 8.8% and Plymouth 10.9%. In comparison the industrialised town of Camborne in Cornwall, like others in the rest of the country, had 21.0% unemployment.[19]

Before the war Devon was not highly cosmopolitan. It had only 536 foreign nationals in 1933. Their number increased by only six the following year. Interestingly one of the largest groups was Germans: there were 76 in 1933 and 95 in 1934. The Americans were the largest overall with 96 resident in 1933 and 98 the following year.[20] There were synagogues in Exeter and Plymouth but the number of Jews was not high. There were no mosques and the majority of the population were either Church of England or non-Conformists, particularly Methodists. The vast majority of the population was white with a very small number of residents from other races.

Even though much of the county was remote from major political events there were opportunities to publicly engage in international affairs. For instance, on October 22nd 1932 a talk was given at

Exeter's Royal Albert Memorial Museum by Dr Adolph Wolfers of the Berlin School of Politics on 'German Nationalism and National Socialism' in which he stressed it was not possible for Germany to consider attacking other countries. The principal of the University College of the South West, later the University of Exeter, chaired the meeting and there was talk of reviving the German Club which had been disbanded during the first world war. Interestingly, the college was later criticised by Fascists for its associations with Sir Henry Lopes because he was Jewish.[21]

While 1932 was an insignificant year for Devon fascism less than two months after the formation of the new party another movement began in Devon. In mid November the Devon Tithepayers' Association was formed at Newton Abbot.[22] This body would, over the next few years, become one of the leading promoters of fascism although it continually protested there were no formal links between them.

1932 ended for Mosley with his family at Christmas in a country house in Yarlington in nearby Somerset. He also brought with him Diana Guinness, his mistress and later his wife, whose Devon connection was that as a teenager she had holidayed at Bucks Mill near Clovelly.[22] As yet, neither Mosley nor his own brand of fascism had made a mark in Devon. This would change in a few short months.

Notes

1 A. W. Brian Simpson, *In the Highest Degree Odious; Detention Without Trial In Wartime Britain* (Oxford, 1992), 116; Thomas Lineham, *British Fascism 1918-39; Parties, Ideology and Culture* (Manchester, 2000), 61-3; Martin Pugh, *Hurrah For The Blackshirts; Fascists and Fascism in Britain between the Wars* (2005), 51, 64.

2 National Archives, HO144/4775.

3 See issues No. 8, October 1932, No. 11 January 1933, No. 2 Vol. 2 April 1933, Vol. 3 No. 6 August – September 1934, Vol. 5, No. 1 March–April 1936, Vol. 7 No. 8 October 1938, Vol. 7 No. 9 December 1938, Vol. 8 No. 9 April 1939. In his letter of August 1934

he corrected his criticism of the Western Morning News for not printing a letter and noted 'in 50 years only known courtesy' from the paper.

4 Simpson, *Odious*, 117; Lineham, *British Fascism*, 45, 62, 155; Benewick, *Political Violence*, 33; W. E. R. Martin, *The Adventures of a Naval Paymaster* (1924); W. E. R. Martin, 'The Great Dictator', in Erminio Turcotti (ed.), *Fascist Europe* (Milan, 1939), 67; *The British Lion*, No. 20, July 1924; Robert Earl, 'When right and left clashed in Plymouth', *Plymouth Herald*, 22 February 1978.

5 *Devon & Somerset News*, 28 September 1933.

6 *Western Independent*, 25 June & 1 October 1933.

7 National Archives, HO45/24967, A note by Special Branch of 9 March 1936 noted the IFL began in November 1928 and had a branch in Bristol.

8 *Western Morning News*, 6 November 1933.

9 Kenneth Lunn, 'The ideology and impact of the British Fascists in the 1920s', in Tony Kushner and Kenneth Lunn (eds), *Traditions of Intolerance* (Manchester, 1989), 146; *The Fascist Bulletin*, No. 18, 31 October 1925, No. 7, 25 July 1925, No. 18 31 October 1925; *The British Lion*, No. 11, 20 November 1926, No. 12, 4 December 1926.

10 Lineham, *British Fascism*, 46, 61-79; Pugh, *Hurrah*, 54-5; Gottlieb, *Feminine Fascism*, 281-2. The White Knights were described in a Home Office report as being 'a frank imitation of the notorious American secret society, the Ku Klux Klan.' They were split up into lodges and the chief knight met at a Masonic temple in London. They were considered to be highly anti-Semitic and used the black swastika in their regalia: National Archives, HO144/20154.

11 Benewick, *Political Violence*, 39-41; Lineham, *British Fascism*, 130.

12 *Western Times*, 14 May 1926.

13 Dorril, *Black Shirt*, 217.

14 Dorril, *Black Shirt*, 217-220.

15 Renton, *Fascism*, 13; Dorill, *Black Shirt*, 220-1.

16 Dorril, *Black Shirt*, 109.

17 Dorril, *Black Shirt*, 154.

18 Benewick, *Political Violence*, 108.

19 I am grateful to Professor Andrew Thorpe for these figures which are based on Parliamentary constituencies noted in the 1931 census.

20 *County of Devon Chief Constable's Annual Reports* for 1933 and 1934.

This does not include the cities of Exeter and Plymouth or the town of Tiverton.

21 *Express & Echo*, 24 October 1932.

22 *The Western Times*, 25 November 1932.

23 Dorril, *Black Shirt*, 224; Mary S. Lovell, *The Mitford Girls* (2001), 84-5.

PART ONE

Expansion and Implosion, 1933 to 1934

Developments from 1933 to 1934

Early in 1933 *The Times* commented that the country's precarious political state, with a faltering national government and shaky economy, increased Sir Oswald Mosley's credibility. The *Manchester Guardian* warned he was mimicking Hitler's strategy in inciting violence to gain power.[1] In this uncertain political climate the British Union of Fascists had been born and sought control of the country. Mosley had established a Defence Force with trained uniformed men and admitted they would be used if communists attempted a coup. The I Squad, the elite, even wore jackboots. Violence was first used against hecklers in Manchester in March and this was repeated through the history of the party including in Devon. Some questioned whether there was an unofficial policy to goad opponents into violent resistance in order to create the very chaos Mosley needed to gain power.[2] Hitler's rise to power in 1933 and aggressive rule of government was regularly reported in local newspapers and all manner of news stories and features on Germany were regularly printed, among them the visit to Plymouth of the *Deutschland*, a 'Nazi yacht'. One paper reported it was crewed by storm troopers and on a propaganda mission, with films onboard, to inform Germans abroad of the Nazi state.[3] Germany's prominence made Mosley's party more newsworthy but complicated efforts to present his party as being singularly loyal to Britain.

In this atmosphere, in midsummer, the British Union of Fascists began to organise in Devon. Three themes dominated 1933. One was the great effort made to publicise the party throughout the South West such as in Exmouth, Torbay and Okehampton where one writer to *The Okehampton Post* noticed in September 1933 and again in early December two Blackshirts distributing party literature.[4] The party was keen to increase membership which, according to a Home Office report of the time, then comprised marginal people from all social and economic classes.[5] Another priority in 1933 was the national 'tithe war' which in 1933 finally came to Devon and the British Union of Fascists was prominent in it.

However, the main concern was setting up the party in Plymouth. National Headquarters supervised this. Among the senior officers was Ian Hope Dundas, Mosley's aide-de-camp, who had been educated in Dartmouth at the Royal Naval College. Dundas helped launder money from European Fascists, notably Italian, into bank accounts of the British Union of Fascists.[6] He was later a key figure in the development of the regional headquarters. Devon was organised from the start with tremendous enthusiasm and energy. The region was defined in administrative terms as 'The Western Area' and Plymouth became its centre. Branches were formed at Plymouth, Exeter, Exmouth and Torquay and possibly at Honiton and South Molton.

The organisation of Devon began with the arrival of Richard Plathen in the summer of 1933. By mid-December they were claiming they had 'five months of hard work, anxiety and cheerful service, sometimes under trying conditions for those concerned'.[7] Mixed news reports appeared locally while Devon's Fascists laboured to represent their movement as being British in character and stance while supporting the cause of international fascism.

A great factor in Devon's development, as elsewhere outside London, was the variable nature of national finances: wild fluctuations in funding resulted in periods of exuberant expansion as well as drastic cuts. In August, when Devon's branches were being organised, the party was flush with money and moved into grand offices in Chelsea in the 'Black House'. Within this building a para-military existence was created and this atmosphere set the tone for provincial branches.[8] One of the Black House's near neighbours was A. K. Chesterton, the Torquay newspaper editor who had just moved to London and who would shortly become a leading Fascist.

Detailed insights into the first months of the Devon operation can be gleaned by the fortunate survival of copies of an internal circular written for members: in 1995 four of the sixteen issues of *The Western Fascist* were found in the attic of the former Fascist headquarters in Plymouth. This weekly newssheet was on a spirit-duplicating machine in Plymouth between 28 October 1933 and 18 February 1934.[9] It was sold to party members for a penny and gives valuable insights during these crucial weeks. It has been described as being 'filled with tediously sycophantic praise for 'The Leader' and exhortations to hard work'[10] but it could also be seen as typical of political party literature of the period. Mosley's appearances at Plymouth and Exeter in 1933 caused great excitement amongst the members.

The first full year of the party in Devon, that of 1934, held great promise for the British Union of Fascists. Nationally it began with a move to increase influence among the wealthy and powerful: the party formed the January Club, a group of some 200 prominent men and women who met in London at the Savoy or the Hotel Splendide to support fascism. Among them was Lord Iddesleigh of Newton St Cyres near Exeter.[11] Interestingly, Iddesleigh admired Hitler but in July 1933 had warned him publicly that his treatment of the Jews 'would nullify all the good which he had brought and might end in the collapse of his regime'.[12] The British Union of Fascists increased its national prominence and popularity through to early summer and then had a sudden setback in June with a loss of prestige and influence that stopped cold the extraordinary momentum.

In 1934 the Home Office closely monitored the party's activities with regular reports from constabularies in every county and from informants within the organisation. Special Branch and MI5 also filed reports. Many were marked Secret. One from late summer noted:

> *Superficially at any rate the British Union of Fascists follow Nazi methods very closely. There is the same massing of banners, the same spotlight on the Leader, the same defence force, the same facile promises of relief from economic stress, the same kind of excessive simplification of thought wholly at variance with the complexities of life and the infinite variety of scientific facts. There can be no doubt that, logically, they lead up to the same conclusion – the capture of power at a general election, followed by the suppression of all opinion opposed to the policy of the Fascist Government.*[13]

In 1934 the party in Devon began with branches in Exeter, Exmouth and Torquay.[14] It was a key year with extensive canvassing and extraordinary coverage in many local newspapers. The party built support in two ways. First, it targeted the general population through meetings and setting up of branches. Plymouth remained the centre and had a hectic level of activity but meetings were increasingly disorderly and violent. By June it was claimed there were more than a thousand members in the port but then, as nationally, support peaked including in Exeter, Honiton and Exmouth. In the spring meetings were held in such places as Lifton and Lynton followed by a summer campaign targeting South Devon. In the autumn the first meeting was held at Braunton. The Fascists' second strategy was to build support amongst farmers. The 'Tithe War' rumbled through rural Devon but it too faltered by early summer 1934.

National headquarters sent prominent figures to help campaign: Richard Plathen, John Beckett and Tommy Moran spoke throughout the region. Moreover, Sir Oswald Mosley came and his appearances reflected the party's strategies. He spoke at Plymouth and Barnstaple in October 1934. His visit to Plymouth proved disastrous in terms of public relations while the audience at Barnstaple was more attentive and it was relatively well received.

The West Country

Branches were started throughout the South West notably in Cornwall. By October 1933 Henry Christopher Trengrove of Penryn had been appointed Deputy Area Officer for Falmouth. He had joined by May 1933, possibly as early as 1932.[15] In 1934 Cornwall had considerable activity. The Falmouth headquarters was at Commercial Chambers in Arwennack Street. Trengrove tried to place Fascist books in the town's public library but the librarian refused them. There were plans to open branches in Truro, Bodmin and St Austell. Plathen spoke in Victoria Square in Truro in February to a crowd of some 300 people including a 'sprinkling of the pink element'. Shortly afterwards the Fascists promoted the British Union of Farmers in the city. By mid March it appears Truro and Falmouth were one branch. Unit Leader Woolhouse was promoted to Officer in Charge. In April house-to-house canvassing took place in Falmouth, led by Fascists Kenchington and Tooley, and anti-Fascist meetings had also taken place. District Branch Officer Trengrove countered their claims.[16] There was a meeting in February in Helston. The Honorary Secretary was Mr Johns.[17] In early June Fascist Moore had organised meetings in the North Cornish village of Bude: one event attracted some 200 people.[18]

In 1934 national speakers roamed the county giving speeches such as that in January by Richard Plathen at Stratton[19] and in April John Beckett was in Launceston. He had previously promoted the Independent Labour Party in the town.[20] Beckett was a recent convert to fascism and kept his Jewish ancestry secret even from his own son.[21] In June he spoke outdoors at Redruth and Camborne to 'fairly large crowds'.[22]

The state of Cornish fascism in June 1934 was indicated by a Bodmin Division report to the Labour Party national headquarters. It was the only Cornish report and noted considerable activity: large public demonstrations had been held in Bodmin, Liskeard and Saltash, a local branch had been started in Bodmin but there were no details of membership, outdoor meetings were held often but none of them indoors, Fascist literature was on sale and it was reported the Cornish press did not report fascism unlike *The*

Western Morning News. The division also claimed the Fascists were organising Cornish youth.[23]

A contradictory view of Cornish fascism was recorded in a Home Office report at this time. It was uncertain of the overall number of members but reported confidently 'efforts have been made to form branches without success, except at Falmouth, where only a few local youths have joined; they have no local influence and no importance can be attached to the movement in the county'.[24]

Saltash was active because of its proximity to Plymouth. Meetings were held in Alexandra Square and organised by Rear Admiral Martin. Two meetings were held on Friday evenings in June 1934 with Tommy Moran as the speaker.[25] At one event Moran and Fascist Rogers spoke to a small audience. The *Saltash Gazette* gave a full report and noted 'Admiral Martin, in thanking Mr Moran for his speech, said in Saltash they were proud of their heritage and venerated their ancestors. He had met Sir Oswald Mosley who had assured him that he did not want a dictatorship but was out to help all classes. Sir Oswald was courageous and full of knowledge, he knew what had made many a man a communist'.[26] Another long article a fortnight later noted the same two speakers attracted an audience which 'listened with much attention to the Blackshirts who came from Plymouth.'[27]

On the last day of August there was another meeting but shortly afterwards the party suffered a setback: in early September an open-air meeting had moderate interruptions from the audience but then the town clerk asked the Fascist speaker, Deputy Branch Officer Mason, to lower his voice because town councillors were in the midst of their own meeting. Mason proceeded to lambast local politicians and perhaps not surprisingly the council decided further meetings had to have permission. The move prompted disquiet with one councillor noting local people considered the square 'where meetings of all creeds and persuasions could be held'. He cautioned his fellow councillors 'be very wary indeed before you curtail the right of the public because of a little inconvenience to ourselves. There is the possibility of avoiding the nuisance in some other way than such a drastic manner'. However, another councillor spoke of the 'many ugly scenes' he had witnessed and the motion passed.[28]

Martin was furious. He had advertised a Fascists' meeting and was waiting for them to arrive on the Plymouth train when a letter from the town clerk informed him the meeting could not be held. Martin later explained in length to *The Western Morning News* he had permission from Saltash's mayor for the first meeting in the summer of 1933. He was then told 'why not? The Square is a public place'. Martin claimed Fascist meetings were no noisier than those of other parties or of church groups such as the Salvation Army. It would appear other sensibilities took precedence.[29]

In the rest of the South West there was a varying degree of activity. In Dorset there was a branch at Weymouth by January 1934, headed by G. T. Wiltshire, and another was at Minehead in Somerset. The local organiser was R. Bullivant of The Antique Shop in The Parks.[30]

The Labour Party reports show a mixed state of the party by June. The division for Dorset North reported branches at Blandford and Shaftesbury and there were two recent public meetings ('practically washouts') but little or nothing else. In contrast, Bournemouth was very active. Three Labour surveys were returned from Somerset. Frome's report noted occasional meetings were organised from Bristol but there was no other activity of any kind. Yeovil was slightly more active. Its report showed only a week before there had been a meeting held to form a branch, membership was small ('one or two joined the Fascists but I do not know actual membership'), there were no regular meetings, Fascists had previously been selling literature in the town but not recently and there was little or no press coverage. A meeting was subsequently held in mid August at the town hall; S. H. Holly and W. Barry spoke to a large audience. The county town of Taunton was the exception to the other reports. About twelve months before a branch had been started although membership stood at 12 or less a year later. There were regular outdoor meetings, literature was on sale on Saturday evenings but press coverage was non-existent. It would appear, by the middle in the year, the most active place in Somerset was Taunton but even there the party struggled.[31] A higher level of activity is supported by a news report in early February that Taunton had temporary headquarters donated by a sympathiser. Meetings were then regular and propaganda sales increased.[32]

There were changes in Somerset in the second part of 1934. In June fascists in Weston-super-Mare recruited members to form a branch. By November they had succeeded and there were regular Saturday meetings. Fascist Stabbins of the town was one speaker.[33] Fascism had taken a sometimes active but often irregular course.

However, the key to the region was Plymouth, the regional headquarters for the party and Fascist capital of Devon.

Plymouth and the Western Area

Plymouth was the obvious place to establish fascism. From there it was easiest to organise the region. The population of some 208,000 people in the 1930s was the largest[34] and more diverse than anywhere else in Devon. The navy with its great dockyard dominated the economy and the grand buildings were owed to a long naval and trade history.

A national official, Richard Plathen, was sent to open the headquarters and coordinate the West Country. He recruited members from all corners of Devon. Plathen arrived in July and on the 22nd was interviewed by a *Western Independent* journalist who had in the previous week noticed young men wearing the 'Mosley black shirt'. Every morning a group of them met in an unidentified café to discuss politics. This news report has details not recorded elsewhere: the new branch had thirty

Photograph entitled 'BLACKSHIRT, Mr R. A. Plathen, the national political officer of the British Fascisti, who addressed a gethering in Market Place, Plymouth last evening, August 1934' (Western Evening Herald, 4 August 1934).

Richard Plathen and two other Fascists selling literature in Plymouth, c.1933–4 (Friends of Oswald Mosley).

members and a secretary whose identity was being kept secret. Plathen said there was 'a fair sprinkling of Devon members'. Initially they were young but more ex-Servicemen were joining. Plathen was, in the journalist's opinion, a striking figure with black shirt, breeches and leggings with the badge and officer's insignia on his chest. Members, Plathen said, were not required to wear a uniform. When asked 'do you use any rough stuff' he replied 'no, we only use force to meet force'.[35]

An enthusiastic profile also appeared in *The Western Fascist*:

> *We are very fortunate in the West in having with us Staff Officer R. A. Plathen. Those of us who have come in contact*

with Staff Officer Plathen have met a man of striking personality; one is immediately impressed by the power his whole being exudes. Not only are we fortunate in the West Country but the whole movement must be. He possesses everything that is necessary for this great work; personality, strength, courage and untiring energy. Further, his heart and soul are in the work, his knowledge second to none. With such men as this we are bound to succeed. Staff Officer Plathen is an excellent pattern for all members.

Richard Adolph Plathen was instrumental in these first months and he was then a young man; a Home Office report noted he was born in 1901. His father was Austrian and his mother German but he was born in Leith.[36] For a short while, from July 1933 through into the winter of 1934, he was the public face of fascism in Plymouth.

The Western Area Headquarters

The headquarters were initially located in the Empire Services Club in Millbay Road[37] but moved in November 1933 to a grand building in Lockyer Street. The opening coincided with the first issue of a Fascist newspaper. Bill posters were up in Plymouth, as in some other parts of the country, showing a Fascist giving a salute with the date 'November '10th'. Their appearance caused alarm and speculation there would be a stunt immediately before Armistice Day. One local newspaper was reassured it was a publicity act and informed readers 'there is no need for alarm'.[38]

The Western Fascist noted the South West was the 'youngest area in the country' and shows how the Plymouth office promoted the party to its members with articles on empire, India, women, housing and religion. Many were intended to boost morale. In a Christmas message the writer implored Fascists 'keep a stiff upper lip and be proud of the movement. Never let the movement down by forgetting its principles. We are the type to save the nation as we did in 1914–18. A crisis may arise from the failure of the old parties to meet the present'.

Each issue reflected Mosley's personality cult. His 'initial qualities', and those of the cause, were given as:

Manliness	Faith
Organisation	Ardour
Service	Service
Liberty	Chivalry
Enterprise	Intrepid
Youth	Sincerity
	Triumphant

Mosley visited Plymouth and Exeter in December and a report appeared in *The Western Fascist*. 'An Enthusiast' gushed:

> *Fascists, the Great Day has come and passed. In actual terms, it has gone but in our minds we live over and over again the Day of Our Leader's visit to Plymouth. What man who was in H.Q. at the time will forget the undercurrent of tension and excited anticipation which became prevalent as 3 pm approached on Friday? Who will ever forget those magic words – 'He's arrived! He's here!' when Mosley reached the gate.*
>
> *Outwardly calm, but inwardly seething with excitement we waited for his entry. With bated breath we waited as he strode past the Guard and came into the building; as he entered the Common Room where a number of Fascists off duty sprang to attention and gave the full salute as one man.*
>
> *And then his words . . . 'Splendid! This is splendid!' Though it would be an error for us to over-estimate our abilities and smartness, may it be said that*
>
> *PRAISE FROM THE LEADER IS PRAISE INDEED.*
>
> *We had lived for the time when Sir Oswald would visit Plymouth, and now that he has come and gone, I ask you, are we satisfied? Are we appeased? And I presume to answer for you with a very definite NO. We want to see him again and again. However, I suppose we must reluctantly relinquish him, for there is the rest of Britain waiting to hear him speak.*

> *Sir Oswald is one of the few orators alive today. For a public speaker is not necessarily an orator, far from it. At the Guildhall, he held the audience to a man. In the Civic Hall, Exeter, those who came merely to see what it was all about, found themselves clapping vigorously, applauding enthusiastically every moment Sir Oswald paused to let his words sink in.*
>
> *At the end, many formerly apathetic men and women were seen to be joining in with the Fascists in cheering the Leader. What a smack in the eye for those who said 'Fascism will not come to England'. It's here and now there is no stopping it!*

The writer compared the Fascists' work in propaganda to that of a marksman loading his rifle. He thought the bullet 'of fascism is speeding straight to the mark. Right into the hearts and minds of the people'.

Several articles admitted the movement was imperfect but improving. Others were critical. In the second issue a new member's rebuke appeared under the headline 'Black Thursday'.

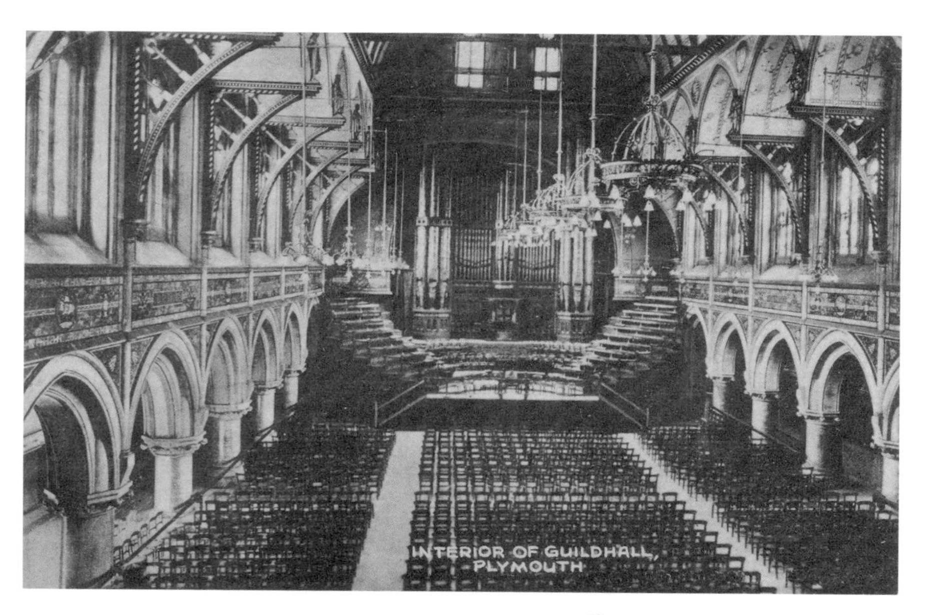

The interior of Plymouth's Guildhall, where Sir Oswald Mosley spoke in 1933 (private collection).

> *I had just left Mr Mason, feeling convinced of the necessity and benefits of organisation of discipline. Imagine my surprise on meeting within ten yards of the gate a large crowd of uniformed Blackshirts surrounding three other members engaged in a common street brawl. Immediately my mind flashed one of my questions to Mr Mason: 'is it true that some of your members go around looking for trouble', and also Mr Mason's reply: 'I can assure you that ours is a disciplined movement and we are too concerned with political affairs to find time for brawls'. The foregoing are the thoughts which passed through a Fascist-minded person. What then must be the thoughts of the general public?. . .*

The tag of thuggery was applied to the Blackshirts from their earliest days and this new member castigated members not upholding the party's principles.

'Tramp, tramp, tramp'. This was the sound the *Western Independent* reported would soon be heard in Lockyer Street. Number 6 was leased and the greenhouse replaced by concrete for drill exercises which each active member was required to do three hours a week. The building's facilities were extensive. A sentry guarded the door and saluted every visitor. Of the four floors, there was accommodation for fifty men, a gymnasium, a common room for active members, an educational room, a canteen for meals, a licensed bar and lounge. The Quartermaster's Department was in the basement. Membership had apparently doubled since the club opened but the organiser insisted prospective members learned about fascism before joining. Women were not allowed and it was expected they would have their own premises. One woman was employed at the headquarters as a typist because men were considered too slow in their typing.[39] *The Western Fascist* reported on the 11th of November decorating work was still in progress; 'Many willing workers can be seen daily at Headquarters, either painting, polishing floors etc – it will not be long before we are ship-shape!' It reported:

> *Already members have made use of the facilities afforded by this acquisition. This club has its value apart from*

finances, it is a means of social intercourse amongst members and will bring about a better understanding amongst them, which will strengthen our unity of purpose. BROTHERHOOD in a gigantic Movement for the betterment of the Community.

The editor, Propaganda Officer Arthur Cyril Cann, tried to instil an easy camaraderie. He described a jocular evening at the headquarters.

6 pm – the active members arrive – the bar is open. The Propaganda Officer was looking very fat around his darby Kelly and we found that he always wore three or four Charlie Prescotts under his dicky-dirt. He commenced the evening in his usual manner by rattling some bees and honey in his sky-rockets, but he also kept his German bands in them and as no one asked him to have one, he scarpered back to his den. A little while after (the bird-lime was now 7 pm) he came back again with his great friend, the Transport Officer, who was also rattling some bees and honey in his sky-rocket. They entered into a long argument as to whose turn it was to pester, but eventually the transport Officer proved to the Propaganda Officer that he had bought him a skimish 3 weeks before, and that this was the last time either of them had pestered for a skimish out of their own sky-rocket. The Propaganda Officer's deuce and ace dropped, but after giving his ginger moustache a twirl, he said 'I'll pay. The Transport Officer said he had a bad cold in his I suppose, and that a double dad and mum would do it good.' After the Propaganda Officer had recovered from his heart attack he said he felt too sorry and sad to think of pestering for a double dad and mum then, so, as usual ¼d went up on the slate.

The headquarters offered social events such as dances and a variety of services including hairdressing and repairing shoes and boots. The editor noted 'we will put up with your long hair and lack of shampoo for a while longer, as our saloon is not quite ready. When it is, form your queue and support headquarters' trade'.

Fitness was stressed: 'all active members are expected to take part, as fitness of body is just as essential as fitness of mind under Fascist ideals'. The gym was supervised by Fascist Ashley. *The Western Fascist* reported sports teams were formed and hopes Plymouth Branch would compete with others. On December 2nd J. H. Woolhouse reported two football teams were picked and a trial match was played on November 25th. Rugby was problematic in obtaining access to a ground. Plans were ambitious but 'Plymouth are fortunate in having at their disposal the services of members who are expert instructors of boxing, ju-jitsu, physical training, and honest-to-goodness wrestling, and also a masseur. With such guidance, the rest of the country will soon be hearing from us with a vengeance'. There was a dare made to Exeter Branch: 'what about it? You great, big athletic he-men'. A particularly patriotic angle featured in the sport report:

> *I was in North Cornwall recently and became very interested in lusty Cornishmen who were wrestling in the good old clean style which has always been associated with England's furthest West Country. I was most struck by the sporting way in which they took occasional hard knocks with a laugh. I think that it is right to say that wrestling is very close to the average Britisher's heart, because of its sporting appeal, and it would not surprise me in the least if there was a revival in Cornish wrestling throughout the West, especially if Fascist branches take an active interest in it.*

Even so, the headquarters sold cigarettes, albeit the party's own brand.[40] A later report noted they had:

> *The services of men who are, or have been, very prominent in sport circles. For instance, some of you may have heard of Lewis[41] who was a well-known three-quarter for Plymouth Albion a couple of years ago. He is a member of the British Union of Fascists now and has taken over the organisation of the rugby section, so that we may rest assured that it is in*

good hands. Offers of fixtures are beginning to come in now and the first match is expected to take place in the second or third week of January.

There was a 'Dry Canteen' in addition to the 'Wet Canteen' where members were exhorted to 'buy your beer, more beer and more from us – support home industry'. The Dry Canteen was run by Mr Terrell, a branch member, who was 'undoubtedly the smallest in stature of Fascists but a wonder with the culinary art. He is not often seen but his presence is realised in every meal. We have certainly a find in this member. His smile is as delightful as his various confections'. *The Western Fascist* printed the canteen's rules.

Please make your purchases or have your snack and then: 'Depart in Peace'
The Dry Canteen will not be used for the following:
The Playing of Games,
A Lounge,
A Boxing Booth,
A Doss House,
A Lovers' trysting place, etc.

It is also forbidden to use the Canteen carpet for 'All in Wrestling' or as a 'Pocket Handkerchief', and please remember that the fender is not a boot scraper, or the fireplace a spittoon for 'whosoever will may come'. And please to note also the bars of the chairs are not 'foot warmers' or 'height increasing appliances', anyone who cannot reach the bar counter can have the loan of a pair of steps which are to be found at the rear of the premises (perhaps).

Grumbling Strictly prohibited.

Extra note. Seeing that the tablecloths are new, will patrons kindly refrain from 'tattooing' floral designs upon them with the table forks.

On November 24 the first meeting of the Women's Section of the Western Area was held. Their headquarters was at 10 Carlisle

Terrace on the Hoe. Mrs R. M. Down, the Women's Organiser, addressed them on the party's policies and *The Western Fascist* noted 'there was good attendance and great enthusiasm was shown, each member offered her services to the movement whole-heartedly'. A few weeks later 'Fascism in relation to women' appeared:

> *It has been said repeatedly that women should keep out of politics. Baldwin when he brought in the young women's vote soon discovered the value of women. We all know what happened to him! In Fascism, women will have a very real place for it touches them nearly [sic].*
>
> *Over in Germany, physical culture is given the prominence it deserves. Under Fascism, England will train its men and women to be strong and vital, for from them will spring a stronger and even more purposeful nation. Women, who are mothers, will teach their sons and daughters the true spirit of Fascism in their immaturity, so that, when they become of age, they can be called upon with certainty.*
>
> *They are in the majority in this country, and it is very much according to the way they vote as to the fate of parties. Also women do not lack courage, which they proved during the war, whether they went out as nurses or stayed at home to keep things going. Women are as equally well able to fight for the cause of Fascism. And if it seems, at times, to be up-hill and wearisome, they are to carry on in the same spirit as the men who struggled so bravely in the beginning, and proved their metal.*

At this time it was suggested 'the ladies' section are hopeful of inaugurating P. T. classes but the trouble is to find an instructor. Are there any volunteers? Come early and avoid the crush'.

The newssheet's 'erbs' indicate how male-dominated the Western Area was and how women were viewed including such lines as 'Is it true that the Senior Unit Leader bribed the D/A/O of the Ladies' Section to let him take over the Ladies' Gym Classes? And did he get it', 'Who is the fair charmer who made so many conquests at a recent rally?', 'What did the elderly married man say to her to make the Unit Leader blush? And did a senior Officer disapprove or was he satisfied with his share of the feminine company?', 'Who is Ivy? And does she cling to a certain Unit Leader?'

Classes were held because 'it is essential that every one of us must know something of Fascism and to gain this knowledge attendance at the Propaganda Classes should be the duty of all of us so please make a point of attending the next class'. They were held on Tuesday and Friday evenings.

From Plymouth the tithe agitation was coordinated; local Fascists were sent to farms in Cornwall and Devon. They were prompted by the threat of the seizure of goods by bailiffs and this issue had an odd echo in Plymouth. The Fascists did not have a local issue in the city although many speakers spoke of unemployment and slums. However, on November 21st three Blackshirts intervened on behalf of an unemployed Plymouth sailor threatened by bailiffs. These three men visited his home and stayed until the landlord agreed to withdraw the distraint order. There 'was no fuss'[42] but it must be wondered whether there was any intimidation or threat of violence. There would have been far-reaching consequences had this become standard practice for the party in Plymouth or elsewhere.

Plymouth Branch in 1933

Richard Plathen's arrival was immediately followed by outdoor meetings. The *Western Independent* reported an event that week in the market. At the end communists sang the Red Flag, 'rushed' the speaker, there was a skirmish and the police intervened. They brought the Fascists under escort to the police station from which they left via the rear entrance.[43]

It was with this first report that the *Western Independent* began hostile reporting. Its tone and subject matter differed greatly from its two Plymouth rivals, *The Western Herald* and *The Western Morning News*. The latter two were sympathetic if not active supporters: the headline in the *Western Morning News* was 'Communists vs Fascists' and the report made it clear Communists caused trouble. The reporter noted at the end of Plathen's speech a Communist cried 'Let me have it' and the police had to intervene to stop disorder.[44]

In contrast, the *Western Independent*, which more often supported the Labour Party, made its views clear with an editorial entitled 'Black Shirts and Red Flags':

> *The Red Flaggers at Plymouth utterly spoiled the comedy of the Black Shirt incursion into Plymouth. Extremists always spoil everything.*
>
> *What could have been more entertaining than the spectacle of a valiant army of Six Blackshirts taking possession of the Market Place at Plymouth, and standing solemnly at attention in front of the soap box whence their leader solemnly proclaimed the necessity for overthrowing the British Constitution and putting Sir Oswald Mosley in its place? A large crowd of spectators were quite eager to enjoy the comedy. But the Communists insisted on breaking up the meeting and driving the army into the hands of the police who escorted them to Catherine Street and let them out by the back door.*
>
> *There is no sportsmanship in this. It is sheer brute force against moral outrage. Whatever may be charged against the Fascists they do not lack courage. For it is a very brave man who will wear a comic uniform like the Black Shirt in an English street, and gravely salute his superiors by holding up his hand like a policeman controlling the traffic. Even more valiant than the public confession of the pathetic belief that England is dying for a dictator.*
>
> *England has always had a short way with would-be dictators. On one occasion only it was a violent way. For the rest it either voted them down or pushed them across the Channel or laughed them to extinction. Public laughter is the most deadly weapon known to England. And the Black Shirts are a scream.*[45]

A week later the editor kept up his criticisms. He noted Continental countries were trying on black, brown, red, white, blue and green shirts and disparaging democracy. He commented with great sarcasm in a leading article heavy with warnings that:

> *In the streets of Plymouth those fine upstanding young fellows, in black shirts, earnest and persuasive, who well earn their bread by their courage, would teach us. They thrill with the thought that their great leader, whose portrait may yet adorn one of the windows in the guildhall, and whose very presence may honour the presence of a reformed City Council. He handing the care of the city to his worshipful steward. An occasional hold-up of suspected members of the Council would be useful as a warning.*[46]

Another public meeting took place on August 3rd. The *Western Evening Herald* reported 400 people gathered mostly 'to see what would happen'. The journalist described the British Union of Fascists as 'British Fascisti'. He reported a substantial police presence, a good-humoured crowd and a considerable number of questions. The journalist noted one questioner had a foreign accent, implying he was not a Plymothian.[47] In contrast, the *Western Independent* report had a mocking tone; it was entitled 'A Back-of-the-Market Comedy'. The reporter thought the crowd was there for a 'rumpus' and was patient in spite of the hot temperature. Plathen had borrowed a box from a public house and was heckled by the communists but they let him speak. The Fascists were, he wrote, 'excessively young' by which he meant under the age of twenty and only some wore a black shirt, mostly under their ordinary clothes. Their distinguishing feature was they were hatless and had 'well-greased hair'.

The journalist's tone was not respectful: he noted topics included Mussolini, Hitler, castor oil and rubber truncheons but also reported quips from the audience. When Plathen said 'those who believe in our ideology cannot afford to stay outside the movement' he was told 'I'd rather be inside the cemetery'. When he explained Parliament would be replaced by another group of people Plathen was told 'and when you get them there they would stay there'. Commenting on his black uniform someone shouted 'How much would you give me for Napoleon's hat' and another said, apropos of nothing in particular, 'Lend me your black shirt and I will go in mourning'. A plane happened to pass over the market during a question about German bombing and prompted someone to shout 'here comes Hitler'. The crowd roared with laughter. At the conclusion the Fascists intended a public march but failed and ended up walking to the Hoe where, the journalist noted, they had a cooling lemonade at a café.[48] Two weeks after their arrival, the Fascists had two newspapers supporting them and the other writing with ridicule.

A fortnight later another meeting in the Market Place was marked by continual interruptions. Once again a number of young men dressed in black shirts and grey trousers supported Plathen and one held a Union Flag. The *Herald* noted Plathen appealed to local youth to join them.[49] A week later another meeting's audience was large but contained a vocal opposition which heckled and sang popular songs to interrupt the speaker. The six Blackshirts marched at the conclusion but there was no attempt to 'molest' them.[50] Up to this point the *Herald*'s reports were objective but a week later an editorial on dictatorship made it clear the editor was against fascism. Its reports became less regular although many letters were published regarding fascism.[51] The Fascists now had two hostile papers and only one which was sympathetic.

Plymouth's police sent a report to the Home Office of a meeting held on August 31. A policeman noted:

> *About one hundred persons were present including thirteen members of the party in black shirts and six in plain clothes. The members of the party were, with two exceptions, youths under twenty. The only speaker was Plathen, the organiser of the movement in Plymouth.*

Plathen spoke of the failure of democracy, protection of trade and of Jews. He urged the audience to study the Fascist programme and support the movement.[52]

On the 22nd of September the *Herald* reported a meeting at the market had continual heckling and the Communists sang the Red Flag. The crowd, it was stated, called out 'Put your head on the block first' and 'We don't want Hitler here'.[53]

On the following day, the 23rd of September, there was an interview in the paper with Plathen who was 'drinking coffee and smoking a cigarette in a quiet corner of a Plymouth café'. This may have been Risdon's Restaurant in George Street, a venue the Fascists then met at. While the reporter quizzed the National Political Officer 'a little stream of young men, some in black shirts, others merely with the insignia of fascism in the form of a little badge on the reverse of their coat, passed to and from the table at which their leader was seated. There was an air of quiet but purposeful energy in the demeanour of these determined young men'. Plathen would not comment on a rumour of a Fascist headquarters being established in the city but spoke of the Tithe War in neighbouring Cornwall.[54]

The *Western Independent* also interviewed the party. Under the headline 'The Mosley Fascists' Propaganda in the West Country' the journalist reported growing Blackshirt confidence, that they were looking for premises and had arranged for a visit by Mosley. He noted the prominence of Blackshirts in the streets and interviewed Cyril W. R. Cann, Area Administration Officer. Cann lived at 4 Vapron Road in Mutley. He was probably related to the other senior officer at the branch, Alfred C. Cann, who was Propaganda Officer. Cyril Cann would not disclose numbers but said membership had surprised national headquarters and they were recruiting ten to fourteen members a day. 'It is like a snowball' he claimed and stated Truro was another part of the region recruiting well. Cann also disclosed he hoped to lease the Empire Services Club as the new headquarters. The projected office would contain administrative offices, gymnasium, canteens and a room for 'courts of enquiry, court-martials and proceedings of a disciplinary nature'. Cann admitted Plymouth members had already been court-martialled for breaking rules and he hoped to have a 'sentry' at the door. He also disclosed the Fascists had been drilling in Marsh Mills and they hoped to obtain a motor van for use as a 'Defence Car'. Lawrence Mason was unveiled as the local secretary.[55]

Several of the disciplined members had already made their feelings known. Two suspended Fascists approached a Blackshirt selling literature outside Plymouth's main post office. Curiously, Communists accompanied them. The party had been forewarned and mobilised six or seven members as a bodyguard. Words were spoken but there was no violence. Until the headquarters opened the Fascists conducted discipline in the open streets. Outside the same post office one member was publicly suspended and had his black shirt held for three months.[56]

The headquarters opened in the first week of November and on the 6th a letter was written to the *Western Evening Herald* from 'Uncle Alfred', presumably Propaganda Officer Alfred Cann who gave an upbeat report on British Union's progress. He responded to another writer who asked 'why is the Hitler salute being used so widely in Plymouth?' Cann wrote 'there is actually a branch of the British Union of Fascists with a real headquarters in Plymouth and there are hundreds of real enthusiasts in the movement. Perhaps he has seen these men saluting. They do.'[57]

In the November municipal elections Labour made gains. Alderman Dunstan was one politician who lost votes. In the election he had described himself as 'a little Hitler' and, in an indication of popular feeling about fascism in Plymouth, the voters had turned against him. Three weeks later he resigned as Chairman of the Drake Division of the Conservatives and Unionist Association.[58]

The year ended for Plymouth's Fascists on a high note. On the 15th of December Mosley spoke at a public meeting at the Guildhall. It was this event which *The Western Fascist* gushed about. This was not his first visit. Mosley had campaigned in the city for Lady Astor in a Parliamentary by-election in November 1919 and spoke at meetings in local schools and at Lockyer Hall. Another canvasser was Lady Cynthia Curzon. They were both guests of the Astors at their house in Elliot Terrace overlooking the Hoe, off Lockyer Street. They married six months later in the Chapel Royal at St James' Palace with King George and Queen Mary present. She died thirteen years later[59] and only seven months afterwards Mosley, as a widower, returned to Plymouth. He visited the Regional Headquarters yards from where he had first wooed his wife.

How Lady Astor viewed Mosley's return to Plymouth is unknown. Within a few years she would be called a Nazi sympathiser but appears to have had weak associations with British fascism. Mosley himself later stated Astor had no interest in the movement.[60] Yet, it is curious she does not appear to have criticised the excessive disorder which was to mark fascism's first two years in Plymouth. She was fully aware of the violence: her scrapbook of Plymouth newspapers cuttings included the Fascist meetings.[61] The only occasion I have found when she was publicly confronted with local fascism was on October 16th 1934 when attending a meeting of the Plymouth Parliamentary Debating Society at Goodbody's Café where seven Fascists, including two women, were introduced.[62]

According to the *Western Independent* Mosley's audience on December 15th was partly of the converted, partly of the hostile but mostly of the curious. The latter were citizens of Plymouth who had observed men walking in the streets in their black shirts and were intrigued by the novelty while others were hoping for a 'row'. There were prominent people from all parties, including a former mayor and a political agent. The journalist noted the hostile element at the back of the hall and that tempers never rose above 'mild turbulence'. Order was kept by the Defence Corps and by the police who were outside. The reporter observed nervousness of the local Fascists in performing military duties in front of Mosley and the audience: their precision was, he wrote, ragged. So too were the young female Fascists, the dozen young women wearing black berets who paraded and timidly took their places. The journalist added they were not in full uniform because these had yet to arrive from London, so recent was their membership and the branch.

Mosley arrived from the back of the hall, flanked by eight Blackshirts who positioned themselves below the dais. They wore Fascist badges and belt buckles, stripes and chevrons, Union Flags and medals. Only Mosley, dressed in a black pullover, black trousers and plain black belt, stood on the platform. The journalist thought he looked like a private amongst generals, rather than the general amongst his privates. Mosley began without an introduction and spoke without notes for an hour and a half. He told them 'the opening of a Fascist meeting is as different from the opening of an ordinary political meeting as fascism is different from the ordinary political parties.' Hecklers occasionally interrupted him and the journalist noted bursts of applause notably when Mosley said fascism would come to the country's aid with force if the communists attempted a coup.[63]

The journalist doubted whether many were convinced but the meeting was orderly. The editor's view, after five months of local Fascist activity, was clear. He could discern the voice of Hitler behind Mosley's words ('fascism was not so much a dictatorship as a leadership of the people with their glad consent') and noted in the two Fascist countries in Europe, Italy and Germany, dissent was dealt with by violence followed by exile, gaol or concentration camps. The *Western Independent* was certain it did not want this for England.[64]

Mosley visited the region's headquarters and among those who greeted him was Hamilton Peters, newly-appointed District Branch Officer of Plympton. The guard had a new winter uniform. It was a dark grey greatcoat 'in the Guards style, with black buttons, black shoulder straps, and black tips to the collar. On the shoulder straps the insignia of rank is worn, and on the black tips of the collar the Fascist badge in gilt. The uniform caps are black peaked, with the Fascist badges worn in front. The customary black shirt and trousers are worn beneath the greatcoat.'[65]

On the 30th of December a confident interview with Propaganda Officer Cann appeared in the *Western Morning News*. He outlined the region's election campaign for 1934 from a room with constituency maps placed on the walls. Cann expected every other branch in the West Country would adopt Plymouth's strategy. He claimed every division in the two counties would be contested if the party continued to make the strong gains already achieved. Red flags on the maps indicated success with farmers over tithes but his more startling claim was that former Conservative members of Plymouth City Council would stand as Fascist candidates. The campaign, with 'the most perfect electoral system yet devised', would begin on the first of January.[66]

1933 had been a surprising, successful and frenetic year but there was trouble in the Fascist paradise. The year's final issue of the Devon Fascists' own newsletter included a curious, and puzzling, piece entitled 'Lost Sheep' that hints at deep dissatisfaction within the ranks. The editor wrote:

> *It is not often that our financial magnates or experts come down to earth to explore the simple mysteries (to them) of the countryside. When it happens that they do leave their City fastnesses and enter the more easily accessible fields of rural England, their actions astound the world and acquire real news value. Photographs are published in Society papers,*

> *long paragraphs are written for the 'Gossip Columns' and the weeklies that provide humour for the nation dare not ignore such incidents of national importance.*
>
> *We, ourselves, have now seen such a financial juggler in action.*
>
> *We found him on all fours, 'Ma – a – a – a' ing in the corner of a field. We saw him chasing four harmless sheep with his high-powered car as he might chase an equally harmless pedest[rian] in the city of London. We knew that he aimed at catching four sheep; we know that his experience of figures made him think that three he did catch were equal to the four he set out to catch. We know also that his mastery of figures applies only to such as can be put down on paper, to be judged with under the guise of 'accountancy'.*
>
> *One sheep has been lost and in consequence we now find one black sheep temporarily in the ranks of Western Tithe Warriors. National Headquarters has been disgraced by one of its representatives; what is N.H.Q. going to do about it?*[67]

Who this relates to is uncertain. Within the same issue was another short piece reporting the visit of four other officers from the national headquarters who came with Mosley to Plymouth. The report was positive and carried no hint of any dissatisfaction with the actions of the, presumably, other official. In January 1935 one leading local Fascist would claim Mosley in December 1933 had been deeply impressed with Plymouth Branch. Cann even stated this on the 30 of December to the *Western Morning News*.

On Christmas Day the men lodging at the Lockyer Street building were treated to a Christmas lunch of soup, fish, turkey, roast pork, Christmas pudding, sweets, nuts, wine and cigars. In the afternoon they had a sing-song and then further entertainments in the evening.[68] The branch was flushed with great success in 1933 but the challenges of 1934 would be much greater.

Opposition to the British Union of Fascists

In 1934 fascism's success in Devon was accompanied by a marked increase in other political parties warning voters of the dangers of fascism. One concerned the political significance of wearing coloured shirts. Black or brown could signify fascism, grey was both Fascist and anti-Fascist, red denoted International Labour Party, khaki was for Young Communists, white was the Jewish anti-Fascist group the Blue and White League, green stood for Social Credit and blue for British Fascisti, Jewish United Defence Association or Irish nationalists.[69] Lady Astor made light of it when talking to students. On March 6th she said Parliament was at risk:

> *if you young people go over to Blackshirts and Redshirts and all the other coloured shirts. I do therefore implore you to beware of shirts. I don't think there is any real danger in these coloured shirts, for the people of this country don't like dressing up, and if they did begin to do so they would merely die with laughter at each other.*[70]

Apparently the only other 'shirts' yet to solicit support in Devon, besides the Communists, were the Green Shirts. Mrs Chapman tried to rally support in Paignton for the Green Shirts, the followers of the Douglas Social Credit Scheme. There were great similarities between the Green Shirts and Blackshirts but they were also rivals, particularly in Liverpool where the Green Shirts' headquarters was ransacked by Blackshirts.[71]

One consistent critic of fascism was Charles Curzon, Bishop of Exeter, who warned the public against both Mussolini and Hitler. In 1933 he visited Germany and wrote deploring the Nazi's war attitude and their attacks on Jews.[72] At least one local fascist also felt the Dean of Exeter was unsupportive: Captain Hammond regarded him as being anti-Nazi and pro-Communist.[73]

A curious speech was made by Miss Athill of Willand, Secretary of the Cullompton Women's Unionist Association, at their meeting in June. She asked 'Is Cullompton Going Fascist?' and asserted grumblers in the party were turning to the Fascist party although she confessed she did not know whether this was happening locally. In her opinion most Fascists were former Conservatives.[74] Viscount Hinchingbrooke, Honourable Treasurer of the Junior Imperial League (the youth group of the Conservative party) denied at Braunton in North Devon there were large defections from the League to the Fascists. He said 'I have made very careful inquiry and I am unable to find any but isolated instances of people who have left us to join the Fascists, and they are mostly people we do not want to have in the League anyway.' He may not have been familiar with the situation in Plymouth.[75] In March Cedric Drewe, M.P., warned the Junior Imperial League at Sidmouth:

> *I think the Fascist movement in this country is a dangerous movement. When you listen to speeches by the Fascists you will find they give expression to ideals which we hold in the main in the Conservative Party. You find they make speeches which are patriotic and you wonder if they could not equally well have been made by Conservatives. But the trouble in my opinion is that they have methods which would prove thoroughly dangerous if they tried to put their ideals into practice. I don't believe anyone in this country wants to see individual liberty done away with. If we had fascism in this country we should have no more individual liberty, we should have no free press and we should have no parliamentary government. It is for these reasons that I want to warn you against these dangers of the Fascist movement.*[76]

Another, M.P., Lieut. Col. G. Acland Troyte, declared in Tiverton that in the tithe dispute the 'Blackshirts were now butting in but they were not wanted'.[77]

Plymouth's organised opposition was more akin to other parts of the country than the rest of Devon and reflected the movement's importance in the port. Some local politicians were vocal opponents such as Alderman Churchward, a Labourite, who said in October 'fascism is based upon violence and murder. We know what happened in Germany, Austria, Italy and what is happening today in Spain. You have a clear indication that their power is based on brutal violence, and that freedom of thought and speech is brutally thrashed out of those who try to use it.' He also said 'If I had my way there would be no political uniforms in this country . . . I know their danger. I know their attraction to youth. It is the negation of everything that the Labour movement stands for. We don't want the herd mind. We don't want flag waving and goose steps. We want men. We want absolute freedom of speech.'[78]

In addition to local men and women there were considerable numbers of supporters brought to Plymouth from elsewhere. For example, the New World Fellowship coincided their meetings with Mosley's visit in October. Two of its chief men came to Plymouth; Isaac Morris was the General Secretary and Nathan Birch was Director of Propaganda. Birch was also reportedly intending on standing against Mosley in whichever Parliamentary seat he vied for. The men brought three loudspeaker vans with them. One meeting was in the morning at North Quay on October 7th. A fortnight later Herr von Schonreth of the Hamburger *Frendenblatt* came down for further meetings.[79]

In the rest of Devon opposition was less organised. It could be argued that up to this date those who were stopping the freedom of expression were the protesters: their barracking, heckling and singing effectively stopped the Fascists being heard. They would argue they had learned from continental experiences, anticipated Mosley's party would adopt similar repressive policies and sought to stop the party before it became a powerful force. There is no indication in Plymouth that the Fascists interrupted other meetings although they were accused of goading the opposition to violence and of having members in plain clothes manipulate audiences.

Politics were a livelier affair in Plymouth than the rest of Devon and it had a wider political spectrum. At the same time as the Fascists were holding open-air meetings there were similar events in Market Square and in Devonport put on by the Anti-Socialist and Anti-Communist Union, a national 'pressure group' which was also on the political right. Their speakers were Captain J. F. Finn, Prospective Conservative Candidate for East Woolwich, and Mr G. Easterbrook. Finn spoke of 'moaning socialists' who were either warning of war or complained of the Great Depression whereas Finn noticed 'thousands of people visiting cinemas, theatres, dog and horse racing tracks, seaside resorts and other places of amusement'. He knew there would be no war and that the poor should be more content with their lives. The national chairman of Finn's organisation also chaired the Link, the virulently anti-Semitic group which had been started to spread propaganda against war with Germany.[80] The Economic League also spoke in May and had another campaign in July with meetings at employment exchanges, the gates of Devonport Dock and Market Square.[81]

Negative comments on fascism were also made by some unconnected with any particular political party. One example is the Headmaster of West Buckland School who warned his students in October of 'the poisonous doctrine of the Fascists'.[82]

Membership of the Fascist party was incompatible with some police duties. A confidential memo was sent by Major L. H. Morris, Chief Constable of Devon, on 23rd February that:

> *Membership of the Fascist organisation is, by its own rules, incompatible with observance of the condition of service in the special constabulary. Superintendents will therefore please inform me if at any time it should be found that any of their Special Constables are, or become, members of the Fascist party.*[83]

Less than two weeks later he publicly announced Fascist party membership conflicted with the duties of a police officer. He expected special constables who had joined to resign from his force.[84]

Plymouth Branch in 1934

Activity across Devon in 1934 was marginal compared to that in Plymouth, the centre for the Western Area. Richard Plathen increased his stay into February when he said he was 'more than satisfied with the progress of their movement in the West and although he first came to Devon and Cornwall for a period of a month the prospects became so good that that visit was extended. Devon and Cornwall were now so strong that they *could stand on their own feet*.'[85] As National Political Officer he remained active in the tithe war in Devon and elsewhere.[86] Fascists across the country read in *Blackshirt* a glowing account of Plymouth Branch in the first issue of 1934. It was claimed the tithe issue had 'almost converted the whole of western England to fascism' and praised the branch for its transport system of lorries, motorcars and motorcycles.' Plathen, D/A Officer Cann and four other Fascists visited national headquarters. They 'created quite a stir' with their smart uniforms, excellent bearing and pride in the movement. It was, according to the writer, 'a revelation to many'.[87] This praise would be bitterly regretted. A week later another group of Plymouth officials visited including Branch Officer Reeves.[88] These trips were, in all likelihood, part of an unfolding investigation launched by national headquarters.

In the midst of all this activity the Western Area's own propaganda newssheet suddenly ceased. On February 18th 1934 the last *Western Fascist*, with its motto 'The West is Best', was published. The editor explained it had not received sufficient support and planned a newssheet to supplement *Blackshirt*. It is doubtful it was printed.[89]

How popular the party was in January 1934 in Plymouth, or across Devon, is difficult to gauge. The audience Plathen addressed on one occasion at Market Square was, it was reported, 'a large meeting' but there was also considerable heckling. The number of supporters or opponents was not specified. A week later the audience stood at some 300 persons but interestingly the event was reported to have been 'one of their most lively meetings'. The speaker was Area Propaganda Officer Cann who addressed the crowd from the party's lorry. There was 'constant interruption and many unpolite and unprintable remarks were flung at him. The feminine sex was quite as rowdy as the male members of the crowd.' They 'made every possible endeavour to drown Mr Cann's voice with their constant jeers.' The opponents were said to be socialists and particularly loud during certain parts of his speech. Cann's themes were intended to resonate locally: he spoke of the mismanagement of agriculture, the need to demolish slums and that those involved in protecting the country and in law & order, that is the military and the police, would not be interfered with. He said 'what this country needs is organisation – past governments have been sadly lacking in this respect and the Fascist movement is an organisation with a thrust-full power behind it which will pull the country through the crisis.' At this point, when he cited the example of Italy under Mussolini, the crowd roared and he was loudly jeered. Nevertheless, even though the meeting closed with what was described as deafening cheering and booing, there were no attacks on Fascists.[90] *Blackshirt* noted Cann appealed to servicemen to join them. It stated the crowd was the largest ever assembled in Plymouth and that they were kept in order only through the skill of the speakers. The newspaper also reported meetings in the market where Sherriff opened 'in his usual brisk manner' and Carroll denounced communism. There followed 'a scrap'. It also noted a meeting at the Octagon when Plathen, Cann and Sherriff spoke on January 30th but it noted the Defence Force Cars had been overhauled and new bodies fitted to the lorries for conveying stewards.[91]

On Sunday the 11th of February the party organised another event. It marched to the Church of St John the Evangelist, Sutton-on-Plym, on Exeter Street. In the morning five or six units, with ten men to a unit, paraded from Lockyer Street. One local paper reported it and noted the cleric met the Fascists. The event was prearranged and the Blackshirts assured of a friendly welcome. The vicar asked what they stood for and they answered 'for God, for King, for country' upon which he agreed to the service. Father Simpson Matthews used their response as the first words of his sermon. At the conclusion of the service the National Anthem was sung and then the men 'as one man' gave the Fascist salute. *The Western Fascist* noted:

> *Five units of Fascists attended and marched through the streets of the city, in full uniform, and with the Union Jack flying at the head. Comments could be heard, from passers-by, on the size and smartness of the contingent. En route to the church, the party passed the Communist headquarters, and remarks such as 'Hitler, Murderers!' were hurled at the Blackshirts . . . after the service, the men marched back to headquarters, by this time there were more people in the streets, so that Plymouth experienced yet another Fascist march.*[92]

The accounts, in the Fascist newssheet and in Rothermere's newspaper, are nearly identical.

In early February Dr Robert Forgan, one of Mosley's inner circle, spent a weekend at Plymouth lecturing and inspecting the branch. *Blackshirt* reported his approval but it is likely he was sent as part of the subsequent big shake-up. Several men were promoted: Terrell to Sub Branch Officer and Pyatt, A. Sherifff, John Pascoe and J. Cartwright to Unit Leaders. There is a hint of discord in the report: Forgan appealed for unity and comradeship.[93] Nearly a year later one local Fascist revealed in February the branch had asked for additional funds and it was this request which made the national headquarters look more closely at Plymouth. A secret Home Office report of early March noted 'It is reliably reported that Sir Oswald Mosley is very perturbed over the conditions in many of the provincial branches. For this reason, and with a view to cutting down expenses, by fifty per cent if possible, a complete reorganisation of the movement is now being undertaken.'[94] This was not the entire picture for Plymouth but he no doubt contributed to what was about to happen.

A Special Branch report of 9 March revealed 'a commission of inquiry has also been set up to investigate the financial position of the Plymouth Branch. It is understood that accounts outstanding amount to nearly £1,000. Mr Thompson the head of the accounts branch, has gone to Plymouth and he is expected to be joined by A. G. Finlay, deputy chief of staff.' A week later a report showed 'Ian Hope Dundas, Chief of Staff, British Union of Fascists, proceeded to Plymouth on 10th March in connection with the financial position of the local branch.' By the end of April the police noted Lionel Aitken was officer of charge of Western Area but it was 'temporarily controlled by national headquarters'. He had at that time, presumably, replaced C. W. R. Cann as Area Administration Officer.[95] The Plymouth Headquarters was imploding in February and March.

Meanwhile activity in the streets was hectic. On February 13th another meeting was held at the Octagon. *The Western Fascist* noted it was 'before a large audience. Unit Leader Sheriff opened and was followed by Fascist Carroll. D/B/O Mason gave the principal speech of the evening and very successfully put our policy over. There was good publicity as a result of this meeting'.[96]

The next public meeting was held on February 15th and was marked by violence. It had been quieter than the meeting of a week before but towards the end Cann was interrupted by 'a burly member of the audience' who 'began addressing the speaker in language which hardly befitted a public meeting'. There was some verbal interaction between the two but when ignored the heckler turned upon the Fascists guarding their lorry. By this time the crowd was asking questions and one man said to the heckler 'why don't you wash your mouth out' and fists were raised, both men turned down Market Place and the crowd attempted to separate the two. Policemen monitored the meeting and they parted the two men. Afterwards the crowd returned to hear Cann.

The main reason for the lack of a hostile crowd was another meeting. John Wilmot, M.P. for East Fulham, was holding an anti-fascism meeting at the Guildhall. Presumably, men and women who heckled previously were there.[97] *Blackshirt's* view was violence was caused by a 'Red' who 'at a previous meeting assaulted a W/F [possibly *Western Fascist*] reporter attempted to break up the meeting but was reprimanded by an onlooker. The Red turned on him and was eventually arrested by the police'.[98]

The violence escalated. On the 22nd one newspaper reported 'persistent booing, shouting and singing' but questions were answered and threatened violence only occurred at the end with 'an ugly rush'. The crowd filled Market Square and the police, once again at the meeting, 'with great promptitude' formed an escort for the Fascists to march back to Lockyer Street. Some 400 people tried to follow them but the only damage was the loss of a couple of caps in the crowd's rush.[99] Plymouth's police also reported the meeting and their account to the Home Office is dramatic with different details. It noted some 1,500 people heard Fascist Adams began speaking but:

> *It was very difficult for this speaker to make himself heard above the din of an almost constant flow of abusive remarks which were directed towards him from the crowd. For minutes on end his voice was rendered inaudible owing to the singing of 'Tell me the old, old story', this refrain being taken up in a wholehearted fashion by most of the audience.*

He was followed by Propaganda Officer Cann:

> *Whose appearance was greeted by a tremendous outcry of catcalls and ironical cheering from the crowd who by this time had become thoroughly worked up into what was as yet a high pitch of good-humoured chaffing.*

The police report also noted that

> *at the close of his speech the Fascist guard, as is customary with them, attempted to fall into two ranks with the flag-bearer at their head, in order to march back to their headquarters. The crowd by this time had grown to huge proportions and the efforts of the Fascist guard to come through the crowd resulted in a great deal of pushing and shoving. Some of the younger members of the crowd composed chiefly of the hooligan type, had by this time worked themselves into a high pitch of excitement and suddenly someone, I could not distinguish who on account of the crush, knocked a hat from the head of one of the Fascist guard. This action served to spur some of the more timid to greater effort and in a few seconds the guard was besieged on all sides and cut off from one another by the crowd. The position then for a few moments assumed a very ugly aspect, and but for prompt action on the part of the uniform and plain clothes police on duty the position might have assumed serious proportions. As it was only the greatest efforts succeeded in collecting the Fascist guard and marshalling them together.*

The police report then detailed a police guard accompanied the Fascists to Lockyer Street. They were followed by some 500 people. The observer added he had not seen any local communists and 'the whole of the trouble ensuing at this meeting can be attributed to young hooligans forming part of the audience, and there was no evidence of any organised effort on the parts of any particular persons to upset the meeting.'[100]

There were also quiet meetings. On the 20th one was held in St

Clement's Hall in Devonport. Cann and Mason spoke and it appears the audience was quiet and attentive.[101]

On March 1st another meeting was marked by turmoil. There were three speakers, Cann, Sheriff and Mason, and more than a dozen police officers watched the crowd. Instead of marching the 20 or so Blackshirts arrived on their lorry and they altered their return journey: the lorry used the back lane at Lockyer Street and the crowd was thwarted in its efforts to harass the Fascists.[102] *Blackshirt* noted an attempt to overturn the lorry but the Defence Force stopped them.[103] The three men planned to speak a week later but the police advised them to change venues a few miles to Ker Street, the principal street in Devonport. A large crowd gathered in Market Street and the change resulted in an unusually quiet meeting until those in Market Street arrived in Devonport. Once again the police intervened as the Fascists attempted to leave.[104]

Union Street, Plymouth (private collection).

Plymouth had been reading weekly accounts of violent meetings but there was a short lull and then on April 6th they had the rowdiest yet. The police suggested moving meetings to the Octagon, the traffic island in Union Street, and these became quieter than in the market. The street had long been the centre of Plymouth's nightlife and the Octagon was only a few hundred yards from Market Square and not much further from Branch Headquarters. At the meeting trouble began when Lawrence Mason finished speaking. Mason had been the first Plymouth man to 'don the Shirt'. Fourteen uniformed Fascists were in a square from within which he addressed the crowd. When he finished the Blackshirts broke formation and the crowd surged. Despite police assistance there was a scuffle, the Fascists dispersed and blows struck. The Blackshirts marched to Lockyer Street carrying Frederick Finch of Rendle Street who was unconscious but a considerable crowd followed. Scuffles continued along Union Street and under the railway arch in Millbay. The Fascists and police threw a cordon of men across the street in order for Finch to be brought to safety. He was afterwards taken to the City Hospital.[105] R. F. Bowden, who had recently become Western Area District Officer, said the Reds had come for a brawl. The *Western Independent* deplored what it called *Rouge et Noir* and suggested, in a rare piece of support for the Fascists, that the Blackshirts were genuine in claiming their Defence Force was intended to be just that but also thought the presence of uniformed young men at meetings, with a 'I'm ready for you' attitude, invited trouble. As an aside the journalist noted young Blackshirts were anticipating spring by wearing their 'summer costume' of black shirt, flannel trousers and no hats. He felt they had never taken to the peak caps and grey-green overcoats partly because members of the public unfamiliar with fascism mistook them for tramway conductors.[106]

Blackshirt viewed the events of April 6 differently. It reported violence and noted Finch had been knocked down and kicked. It was while he was being carried into the headquarters that another attack was launched. The newspaper suggested trouble had been brewing for some time but 'as the Blackshirts gave a good account of themselves the opposition will not be so eager in future to molest them'.[107]

It was at this time a member of Plymouth Branch went missing: Cecil Morris, married, 31 years old and living at Efford Fort, disappeared after signing out at the Lockyer Street headquarters on the night of March 21. Fascism, according to his wife, was his 'hobby'. Morris had been in the navy and had a head injury. He was 'a big man, as strong as a horse and subject to fits of depression.' His wife initially presumed Morris was on another of the Fascist 'stunts' but called for a search by Fascists who could not find him.[108]

On April 16th the police noted a rowdy Communist element at a meeting and ejected one of them from the crowd.[109] Violence escalated on April 26 at a meeting held in the Corn Exchange with John Beckett, the M.P. known for walking out of Parliament carrying the mace. Two local newspapers, one Fascist newspaper, an official police report and a Communist's account show the different ways the night was viewed.

A stampede occurred after trouble started and the majority of the women rushed for the door. The *Western Morning News* reported Fascist stewards, policemen and a caretaker tried to restore order but 'the rowdy element' hurled chairs at them. Police reinforcements calmed the meeting but when the speaker resumed those at the back of the hall caused 'pandemonium'. It was reported 'within a minute there was hardly a chair standing and the Fascists and disorderly elements were again exchanging blows'. Some one hundred men joined in this 'free fight'. Yet more police arrived, the hall was again calmed and the majority chose to leave. Frederick Finch, who had previously been injured, was once again taken to hospital as were a number of others. Some had cuts and bruises from either blows from fists or broken chairs. The speaker, Lionel Aitken, was bleeding from a gash to his right temple but the meeting continued for a further 90 minutes. There was more trouble when the waiting crowd of both sexes tried to attack the Fascists as they carried the Union Flag and marched to Lockyer Street. They had an escort of policemen in plain clothes.[110]

The police recorded it as disorder caused by communists and noted 'Fascist stewards. Fighting took place with chairs as weapons. Police restored order and ejected extremists'. They also reported the disturbance in Lockyer Street with 'some fighting, police cordon dispersed crowd'.[111]

The *Fascist Week* saw it differently. Under the headline 'John Beckett's Campaign in Plymouth' it noted 'Fascist progress in Plymouth has thoroughly alarmed the very considerable Red element, and the local speakers have been facing increasing trouble from organised hooliganism at their meetings'. On the one hand it noted seaports were 'fertile ground' for left wing propaganda but the journalist also blamed trouble on the ninety percent of the opposition which came from 'cosmopolitan elements'. There was, he wrote, little of the 'pleasing West Country accents' in the shouting and heckling of the crowd. The journalist recorded:

> *Mr John Beckett's visit brought matters to a head. At his first meeting at the Octagon (where one of our members had been kicked in the stomach the previous week), a group of about 25 made every effort to prevent a meeting being held. It was only after Mr Beckett and several members of the Defence Corps had dealt with some of the most insulting hecklers that the crowd of several hundred were able to hear Fascist policy.*
>
> *Three days later a further meeting was held in the Market Place. Several thousand people were present but about 100 Reds effectually prevented the speaker from being heard. A large force of police prevented the Defence Corps from obtaining order.*
>
> *The campaign finished with a packed indoor meeting at the Corn Exchange with over 1,000 people present, many of whom had paid for their seats. Immediately the meeting opened a large group of rowdies started to sing the Red Flag. Mr Beckett attempted for about 15 minutes to speak, but organised shouting and singing made it impossible. Finally, two visitors, not connected with the movement, and sitting beside the ringleader of the interrupters, protested and hit him. This led to a brisk fight. Sub Commander Aitken and Section Leader Connolly led about six of the Defence Corps to the assistance of the visitors.*
>
> *The Reds attacked with chairs and Sub Commander Aitken's head was cut open. After arranging for the two thirds of the audience who were not near the area of the struggle to be effectively stewarded, Mr Beckett and another half dozen Fascists went to help restore order.*
>
> *The Hall Attendant then sent for the police, who arrived in*

> *time to escort the Reds from the hall, and to take one to hospital.*
>
> *No serious injuries were incurred on our side, although bruised legs from kicks were fairly general. Not many of the Reds were seriously hurt, as they mostly lay down quietly at the first punch or before.*
>
> *The meeting was then resumed, and the policy explained for an hour and a half to an enthusiastic audience, who joined wholeheartedly in singing the National Anthem at the close.*[112]

Not surprisingly, the communists saw it differently. They denied starting trouble. Mr A. J. Willis claimed Beckett had taunted and provoked them in calling them 'red dogs' and challenging communists to come to the meeting. Willis wrote their policy was to interrupt only by heckling and that a Fascist in plain clothes had started the fighting by attacking another man. It was at this point the Defence Force intervened.[113]

The *Western Independent* viewed the meeting with alarm and suggested the clashes were 'getting beyond a joke'. It reflected local people had indulged them ('adding a little spice to a dull life') but the level of recent violence, with it spilling out into the streets and the police brandishing truncheons for the first time since the General Strike, was potentially dangerous. It warned there could be a death. It also had apprehensions of a Fascist march at May Day. This was, to the relief of many, denied by Lionel Aitken who said 'this is the one day we should not organise anything. We do not believe in inviting breaches of the peace. If it is forced upon us it is another matter'.

The numbers of both sides in Plymouth is difficult to gauge. It was suggested there were only about 30 communists actively agitating at meetings. They were, however, strengthened by other organisations including the Friends of Soviet Russia, the United Front, International Labour Defence and the National Unemployed Workers' Union. Willis suggested it was an alliance of working class men and women. The Fascists did not reveal their membership but it was thought about 30 members appeared in uniform at meetings and overall they numbered up to 200. The total number was unknown.[114]

By early May the police had asked the Fascists to suspend their meetings. *Blackshirt* reported the reason was traffic congestion[115] but it is more likely continual violence was a concern. A change in leadership took place at this time which had great consequences. Western Area Officer in Charge C. W. R. Cann had been replaced by Lionel Aitken, Sub Commandant at the national headquarters. Cann reverted to the status of an ordinary member as did Deputy Propaganda Officer Alfred Cann.[116]

A month later there was a new twist to meetings. On May 29th the venue was once again Plymouth Market but a rival group, the South of England Economic League, also held a meeting. The Fascists were addressed by Thomas Moran, a well-known national figure in the movement particularly in Newcastle-upon-Tyne. Moran was an ex-miner and Royal Navy boxing champion. There was only one point of violence when two men attempted a fight but the police kept them apart. The police recorded it as a night of 'considerable heckling and organised interruption by Communists who endeavoured to address crowd in opposition to Fascists.' Two nights later, on May 31st, Moran and Beckett held another meeting at the Octagon. They had been refused the use of the Guildhall on the 22nd.[117] There was only heckling and the communists tried a new tactic: they had community singing. They sang popular songs which attracted a greater number of the audience. The crowd had grown to as many as 3,000 people.[118] The two men also spoke in Barnstaple. At this time *The Western Morning News* printed a full feature article by Beckett. This positive coverage of fascism had three headlines; 'Meaning of the Blackshirts, New Machine to Meet New Times, Planning a Greater Britain'. The paper had a proviso it did not necessarily agree with the views but extended to the party an opportunity to state its case.[119]

Plymouth Branch made as much of Moran as they could. On the morning of June 1st he gave yet another talk, to some 700 people, outside the Plymouth Employment Exchange. Fourteen policemen watched the heckling from half a dozen communists. At the same time another speech was being given in Moon Street near the Devonport Employment Exchange. It was reported there was no trouble and the two policemen present merely had to keep the pavement clear.[120]

There was a two-week interval while national headquarters

organised the great Olympia Rally on the 7th of June. Presumably local Blackshirts were called to steward. Shortly afterwards the violence was the most serious known in Plymouth yet positive press coverage continued; only in the last few paragraphs of one *Western Morning News* report was there any mention of Fascist involvement. Two anti-Fascists were sentenced to three months' hard labour for assaulting constables on the night of June 13th. One of the two, Jack Berry, a thirty-four year old who lived in Saltash Street, had recently arrived in Plymouth. His real name was Jacob Goldberg but he was also known as Jacob T. Goldberry. The police stated he was well-known to London police, had been convicted of forgery and was 'a most offensive and aggressive man'. The other, Harold Jones, a labourer who lived in Claremont Street, was 'a man of violent disposition and his conduct was very bad'. Policemen were injured during a large anti-Fascist demonstration in Market Street and in a march to Lockyer Street on the 14th. The two men disputed police evidence they enticed and implored the crowd to violence, particularly to 'smash the Fascist headquarters', but no details were given for the demonstration nor of the men's political allegiances. Goldberg was sentenced to three months' imprisonment and released on August 29th.[121]

Under the headline 'The Police, the Blackshirts and the Communists' the *Western Independent* reported it differently. It revealed on the 13th the Fascists had held a meeting and a crowd of some 1,500 people reacted with great hostility. The police then prevented the communists from holding their own meeting after the Fascists had finished on the grounds it would lead to violence. The violence did happen but to the police themselves when the crowd rushed them. John Huddy of 15 King Gardens was arrested. The police managed to keep order, and make the arrest, but only through the timely intervention of a passing naval patrol. Hostile crowds followed them to their station and the patrol to St George's Hall in Stonehouse. Huddy, who had been in the navy, was sentenced to two months' hard labour.

The official police report to the Home Office recorded different details. On the first night 1,000 people attended the Fascist meeting and there was 'considerable heckling and jeering by rowdy Communists. Some missiles thrown. Alien Communist element'. At the communist meeting, which had 1,500 people, the 'crowd became ugly and menacing, but cleared by police (2 p.c.s received rough handling in melee)'. The disorder on the second night was blamed on the communists.[122]

In contrast, Exeter's *Express & Echo* reported it under the headline 'Wild Scenes at Communist Meeting in Plymouth – free speech demand' readers were informed that 1,000 people were addressed by the Fascists at the Octagon and a communist tried to speak after the Blackshirts left. The police ordered the speaker to stop but the crowd demanded he be allowed to speak and surged around him to prevent arrest. Nevertheless the police drew their batons and brought the communist to the police station. A crowd gathered around the building and two Royal Naval patrols, which were on duty in the neighbourhood, helped to keep order. The communist was allowed to leave once the loud demands of the crowd subsided. Several hundred 'comrades' marched off with him.[123]

On the 13th a Fascist meeting was attempted at Prince Rock Tram Terminus where it was reported some two thousand people waited. Moran spoke from a lorry for seven minutes but the din of the crowd convinced the 30 police that the meeting had to be cancelled. The Fascists later claimed they heard there was intended to be trouble and dismissed the Defence Force in order to be less provocative. Meanwhile the communists held their own meetings in the Octagon and in Market Square. It was in the subsequent march on Lockyer Street that the communists found a cordon of fifty police with their batons drawn. Soon afterwards they arrested Goldberg and Jones. The Fascists were inside their headquarters listening to Charles Bradford lecture on trade unionism.[124] The protesters had allegedly threatened to 'smash the building up'.[125]

The meetings continued that week. Two days later Fascist meetings were held outside the labour exchanges in Plymouth and Devonport which were rowdy but not violent. Altogether twelve meetings were held including at Ker Street, Devonport, Prince Rock, Hooe and Camel's Head. That at Friary Green was said to have been the rowdiest. The police had to approve public meetings and a list of meetings in the third week of July comprised Ker Street on Monday, the Octagon on Tuesday, Prince Rock and Millbay Park on Wednesday, Friary Green on Thursday, Saltash, Beacon Park Road and Devonport Labour Exchange on Friday, and Camel's Head on Saturday. The Fascists were also challenged to hold a meeting at Clare Buildings,[126] a working class tenement in Coxside. It was pulled down in the 1960s and the Plymouth & West Devon Record Office now occupies the site. At one Devonport meeting the police removed 'the customary crowd of children' from below the front of the speakers' platform. Juvenile rowdiness was evidently a problem. The anti-Fascists used this tactic in a meeting at Friary Green: the young 'shouted and bawled' until the speakers could not be heard. The increased number of meetings was part of a determined campaign by the new Branch Organiser, William Milligan, to refute the anti-Fascist propaganda.[127]

One disappointing meeting was held in Swilly at North Down Crescent. Three Fascists arrived to an audience of mostly children who had been playing in an adjacent waste ground. The 'shrill voices' and the children clambering onto the van disrupted the meeting. Two women proved problematic by commenting on the young Blackshirt's speech; 'We don't want atheism here', 'Your'e putting Tommy-rot into the children's heads', 'Your'e teaching them murder' and 'You want to do the same as Mussolini and its not coming off'. One heckler turned her attention to a local youth wearing a black shirt and said to him, reportedly in sorrow more than anger, 'You ought to be ashamed of yourself, you ought'. One man asked a question about the Nazis and the Blackshirt asked 'Sir, am I in Germany?' to which he replied 'No, but you ought to be'. After the meeting the Fascists left to 'a chorus of juvenile booing'.[128] At a subsequent meeting the Fascists countered this by calling in the Women's Section. The women organised games and during the intervals talked to the children on King and Country. At this second meeting a 'persistent woman' interrupted Tommy Moran and he invited her onto the platform. It turned out to be Kate Spurrell, prospective Parliamentary Candidate for Camborne.[129]

The *Western Independent* revealed increasing disorder could result in banning potentially violent meetings. It also reported the Fascists claimed membership was increasing because of clashes between the communists and the police. One woman, whose dress was torn in a disturbance, allegedly came into the building the next morning to enrol. A representative also stated an Anti-Fascist

League had been established in Plymouth and communists were petitioning for the removal of the Fascists.[130]

Jacob Goldberg was committed to anti-fascism: immediately after his release he addressed another audience, along with the aforementioned Kate Spurrell, probably a member of Independent Labour,[131] and one Mr Jones, in the market place. Goldberg was again arrested. A week later Detective Sergeant Denley testified he heard Goldberg speak of the June events when the crowd 'could have eaten up the police and smashed the Fascist headquarters'. He reminded them Lockyer Street was being repaired and stones were available for throwing at the Fascist headquarters. Goldberg also spoke of iron bars, pieces of rope and staves. Moreover, he told them:

> *There is no getting away from it; you will have to learn the science of street fighting. You will have to fight the police and what is more, fight them with their own weapons . . . Take it from me, the next time you are mixed up in a fight kick the hell out of the police.*

Goldberg agreed with this account but pleaded not guilty to inciting the crowd and stressed he had had no political activities since. He had promised his wife to give up politics and the court freed him on condition he kept that vow.[132]

The period up to June 1934 had been busy for the local branch as was shown on the 20th by reports from the two Plymouth Divisions of the Labour Party to its London headquarters. The Plymouth borough honorary secretary informed London *Blackshirt* was on sale, there were no regular reports in local newspapers but there were comments on disorder and clashes with communists, letters were published by Fascists and representatives of other parties responded, there were outdoor meetings but permission for council buildings was refused owing to disorder, the largest meeting had been in December 1933 with Mosley and weekly meetings followed. The report also claimed women and the youth were being organised. A final note was added: 'there have been several clashes between Fascists and communists resulting in the communists demonstrating outside the Fascist headquarters. Batons were used by the police and three communists have been sent to prison for periods of three & two months for attacking police. Both Fascists and Communists apparently to blame equally for disorder but having roused the crowd the Fascists succeed in vanishing & leaving the mob in the hands of the police. This seems to be deliberately arranged. The party locally has kept out of any street clashes.'[133]

The Sutton Division details were strikingly different. It noted Mosley's meeting attracted about 1,500 people but it was orderly 'although he endeavoured during the whole of his speech to incite the audience'. There were occasional indoor meetings and those outside were 'twice daily. Outside Labour Exhanges and at street corners. Occasional Sunday Church parades.' It confirmed literature was sold and occasionally Fascists' letters appeared in the press. It noted *The Western Morning News* 'gives full reports of all meetings held. Two leading articles by Mr Beckett (ex-M.P.) have also appeared.' It confirmed there was a Women's Defence Force and that 75% 'of the local Fascists are young men and women of independent means (sons and daughters of the military)'. Interestingly, it noted 'no prominent local politicians or personalities are associated with the Fascists. The majority of their members are entirely new to politics.'

Most extraordinary are other details on Plymouth Branch. It reported 'a house-to-house canvass has now been commenced by both the men and women members of their movement. I have private information from the Town Clerk who is the R[ecording] O[fficer] to the effect that at least one candidate will be forthcoming at the next General Election.' In respect to the number of Plymouth members, the report added 'I have no accurate knowledge of membership but I believe it is in excess of 1,000'.[134] The Fascists themselves announced their canvassing strategy. They had devoted one room in their headquarters with a card index of all the wards and their electors. They intended to canvas each elector every week and 'if he is thrown out on his ear he will come back in a week's time ready to talk just the same'.[135]

At this time, a report was sent to the Home Office, probably from the Plymouth police. It was unsure of the membership but noted 'it is stated that 150 Fascists in Blackshirt uniform are available and that

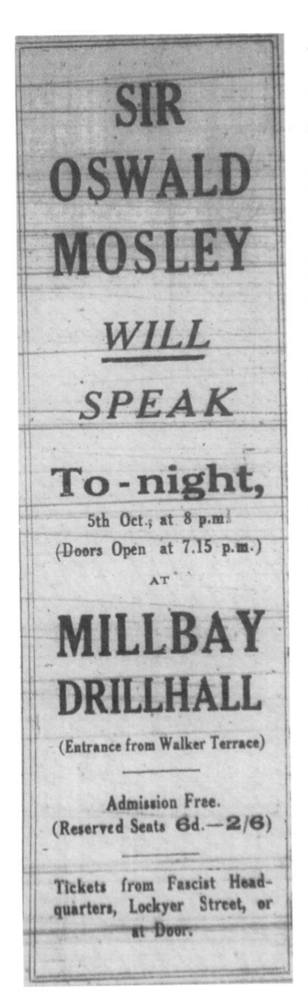

Advertisement for Mosley's meeting at Plymouth (Western Evening Herald, October 1934).

they only represent a small part of the membership. The movement has attracted several men and youths of a somewhat shady character. Several minor disturbances have occurred at Fascist meetings. The movement is growing.'[136] It would appear administration problems had not yet affected the movement. Yet in June it was claimed their neighbours in Lockyer Street had turned against the Fascists. Complaints were made of disturbances and one resident said 'we wish they would pack up and get out'.[137]

On June 7th Mosley held his great Olympia Rally with some 12,000 people including many invited VIPs. The counter-demonstrations by anti-Fascists and the staggering level of violence within the hall was not the break-through Mosley had anticipated. Instead political enemies used it to demonstrate fascism had to be stopped. Many middle-class supporters left and not long afterwards, in the middle of July, Rothermere withdrew his support. Membership fell from some 40,000 to about 5,000. The fall of the party was also due to one particular foreign event: three weeks after the Olympia Rally Hitler disposed of a number of his political rivals in the 'Night of the Long Knives'. The general public, shocked and repulsed by the violence, questioned British and German fascism and the prospect of Mosley in power.

By June fascism in Plymouth was tainted by disorder but there was a lull during Plymouth's Summer Season, possibly through police pressure in not allowing meetings in particular streets. This finished at the end of September when political meetings and agitation resumed. The tempo quickened with an appearance by Mosley on October 5th at the Drill Hall of the 5th Devon Regiment. The period immediately up to the meeting was fraught. At the end of September a thousand people gathered in the Octagon for a

Photograph entitled 'Sir Oswald Mosley arrives by air. The Fascist leader, Sir Oswald Mosley, wearing leather coat, photographed on arrival by airliner at Plymouth Aerodrome yesterday. He spoke last night at the Drillhall and today visits Barnstaple'. From left is Eric Piercy and then the pilot Peter Symes of whom Mosley is said to have remarked 'I only flew with Symes once to Plymouth. That was enough, he was mad as a Jack Rabbit. Nobody ever went up in a plane with Symes twice.' The third figure may be an airport official and Mosley is in the centre. To his right are Richard Plathen, Geoffrey Dorman, who wrote for Action, and Lionel Aitken (Western Morning News, 6 October 1934).

Fascist meeting. *Blackshirt* reported the opposition only numbered fifty but the meeting was rowdy.[138] The Fascists held a meeting at Prince Rock but the speaker only had three stewards. They proved unable to withstand the crowd. Their opposition stood behind rows of children and the speaker managed to endure 15 minutes of a hail of turf, stones and sticks. The police then removed the children and the disorder ceased.[139]

On Saturday, the 29th of September, there were demonstrations in Union Street against Mosley. Five days earlier Plymouth City Council refused permission to use the Guildhall but the Fascists were certain they would have it and printed tickets.[140] They were forced to change to the Millbay Rinkeries on Millbay Road but on the 1st of October it too was withdrawn. This was not unusual as many local authorities had banned the party from renting civic halls or imposed restrictions.[141] Richard Plathen pointed out a previous Guildhall meeting had been peaceful and successful in terms of 'being representative of a real Plymouth type of respectability, drawn from all sections of the community'. He suggested local politicians were intimidated by 'rowdy' elements but said the meeting would be larger and more successful than before.[142] The Rinkeries was privately owned. Political motives for cancelling are indicated by its use that night as a fundraiser for the Distressed Miners' Fund. One patron was Leslie Hore-Belisha, the Plymouth M.P. who was Jewish.[143]

The refusal of the Rinkeries was surprising. Allegedly, John Brock, the owner, had already agreed with the Fascists. There was also a rumour, denied by Mr Cohen, the president of the local synagogue, that Jews had influenced the decision.[144] Brock was Jewish, had emigrated to Britain and had changed his name from Jacob Nathan.[145] There might have been another connection. A curious public spat involved Mr E. Brock in May 1933 at a meeting of the Plymouth Public Assistance Committee. Mr J. W. A. Campbell, another committee member, was irritated at being interrupted by Brock and said to him 'Sit down. You ought to be in Germany.' Brock responded 'Perhaps you will be there too and we will be handcuffed together . . .' Campbell then asked the chairman 'Are you going to allow an alien to dominate the meeting?' to which Brock asked 'How long have you been here?' Campbell responded 'I never came from Palestine.' Brock replied 'You cad. You bounder.' The Chairman then insisted the comment on being an alien was withdrawn.

The following night, the 2nd of October, a crowd of between two and three thousand people gathered in the Octagon for a Fascist meeting. Constant shouting, jeering and loud community singing made the speaker inaudible. The number of people increased so no car or tram could pass along Union Street. The police then closed the meeting and the evening passed without further incident once the Fascists marched back to their headquarters.[146]

The week culminated with Mosley's appearance three nights later. The night was a public relations disaster and possibly the defining moment in Plymouth's Fascist movement. It pitted the Blackshirts against the might of the *Western Morning News*.

Mosley had flown into Plymouth Aerodrome on the 5th and had speaking engagements in the nearby Cornish town of Bodmin and further afield in North Devon at Barnstaple. There was a contingent of stewards sent from London: Eric Hamilton Piercy, who was later arrested over events that night, commanded the Fascist Defence Force and arranged for 22 Fascists to travel by train and in two vans to Plymouth. Altogether 50 stewards watched a crowd estimated as being between 3,500 and 4,000 people.[147]

Piercy, then in his early thirties, was at this time under a cloud at national headquarters. His full title was Officer Commanding National Defence Force Control. Piercy was having an affair with Mrs William Joyce. William Joyce later become infamous as Lord Haw Haw but at this time was a senior member of the party. Piercy had been a salesman and also special constable inspector until he was forced out because he was a Fascist. Special Branch noted 'it has been apparent for some time . . . that E. H. Piercey and Mrs Joyce have been on more than ordinarily friendly terms. The matter has been brought to a head owing to the fact that Mrs Joyce is about to be confined and it is freely alleged that Piercey is responsible for her condition. In order to avoid further trouble Piercey has been appointed chief inspector of branches. This will have the effect of getting him away from headquarters . . .' Piercey was at the end of his career in the party and left six months later. Mrs Joyce divorced her husband and married Piercy. The members of Piercy's Defence Force lived in free lodgings in dormitories in Black House where they had a military existence of reveille, inspection, physical exercise, drill and discipline. They had communal meals at the canteen and numbered somewhere between several dozen and 400 men. Among their duties was accompanying headquarters staff to steward or attend meetings in the provinces.[148]

Blackshirt saw the evening clearly. It was 'in every way a triumph for Fascism in the West Country'. Under the headline 'HUGE PLYMOUTH AUDIENCE CHEERS THE LEADER' with sub-headlines 'Seaport's Enthusiastic Reception Of Blackshirt Policy' and 'Townspeople's Expression Of Admiration' readers learned cheers rang out from the 4,000 people who came to hear Mosley and gave him a 'wonderful reception'. 'You have my admiration and support' was typical of the accolades given him. The great Plymouth crowd, the paper reported, witnessed with open admiration the manner with which the handful of stewards thwarted efforts to disrupt the meeting. Their asinine braying and parrot-like screeching was to no avail when faced with the courage and restraint of the Defence Corps. Mosley commented on the way his followers silenced their opponents' efforts 'if you owe nothing to the Blackshirt Movement you owe the return of free speech'. An attempt to cause disruption at the end of Mosley's speech was handled particularly well by the stewards and although this won the audience's approval it was the manner with which Mosley moved, practically alone, amongst the disturbers to calm the situation. 'There's not one of the old party politicians who would dare have walked into that lot' said one member of the audience. A wave of admiration spread through the hall at his simple dignity and bravery.[149]

All other papers saw the night differently. It was reported in *The Western Herald* as 'Blackshirts' Outrageous Conduct At Plymouth' and coverage in other regional newspapers was also negative. The *Western Evening Herald* and *The Western Morning News* were owned by Lord Rothermere and their version was widely repeated. They reported the meeting was rowdy with a large group of protesters interrupting Sir Oswald partly in singing 'The Red Flag'. Throughout his speech there were attempts to break up the meeting but the Fascist stewards kept order. Towards the end opponents began singing, Mosley turned up his loudspeakers and then 20 men and youths rushed his platform. At that point the lights fused and the hall was plunged into darkness. Fighting between the two sides continued.

The disaster in public relations terms was when the newspaper's photographer, Leo McCormack of 7 Windsor Terrace on The Hoe, as well as his colleague, a reporter by the name of H. J. Swift, were assaulted by up to 20 Blackshirts. The reporter recalled:

> *Immediately I saw the commotion I rushed to the back of the hall. Socialists and Blackshirts were involved in a clash,*

> *chairs were thrown about and forms overturned. One woman I saw was on the point of fainting and was held up by a man. There was a sudden flash, from a press camera, and the next thing I saw was a camera flying through the air. It was only then that I saw my colleague surrounded by Blackshirts. He was thrown to the ground and a blow caught him full in the face, knocking off his spectacles. In a second I was surrounded by the Fascist guard and dragged back with others around me to the centre of the hall. The people around me were not interrupters of the meeting, but apparently all those unfortunate enough to be near the disturbance were manhandled. What happened to my colleague after I did not know. I was dragged along by my collar. Innocent people were grabbed by the guards and forced through the doors.*

Mr McCormack said:

> *Sensing that a skirmish had broken out in the rear of the hall I moved forward to get an elevated position on a bench. From this position I fired a flash-light to endeavour to get an impression of the turmoil. I was the only photographer present at that end of the hall. Quickly reloading my camera and recharging my lamp, I moved forward to the outskirts of what appeared to be an even more serious disturbance, waiting several seconds as the police entered the hall. I had no sooner done this than I was rushed from every quarter by as many Fascists as could get to the spot. I was seized from behind and on all sides, my valuable camera (which we always carry strapped to our hand) was seized, and several of the Blackshirts endeavoured to pull it away. Some dozen Blackshirts had hands on me by this time. Some tried to tear the camera to pieces, some reaching over others' heads and hitting at me, others pulling my clothing, and even some in front kicking and kneeing me. My spectacles had been torn from my face. I felt as if all my clothing was already in shreds and I felt myself being forced to the floor. The camera by this time had been torn completely from my wrist, despite the*

strap adhering to the steel side, and I saw a Fascist deliberately rip the back off, declaring triumphantly that he had the plates.[150]

His camera was destroyed. In the subsequent trial witnesses heard Thomas Wilder say 'I am going to smash this to pieces' and Arthur Sharman said 'this is my revenge for the cuts I got at Olympia'. Order was restored by the police who were forced to enter the hall. Several thousand people, more anti-Fascists, waited outside.

The newspaper interviewed Sir Oswald immediately afterwards and he said 'you fellows think you are God Almighty, and the Press is not going to be God Almighty. What good have the newspapers done us?' The following morning he was again interviewed, at Branch Headquarters, and told the newsman 'You have told the usual pack of lies. You can go to hell out of here!' Mosley spoke of the incident the following day in Barnstaple in response to the widespread headlines 'Another Fascist Outrage in Plymouth'. He dismissed it as a 'cocky young pressman taking photographs to the public danger'. Mosley noted the photographer complained of being beaten up but thought the damage was only to his 'colossal' vanity.

In fact, it was reported there had been no moves to stop photographs at other points, notably of Mosley himself, but the Fascists acted when one was attempted of the clash. None of the

In the execution of their duty a "Western Morning News" photographer and reporter were assaulted by Blackshirts in Plymouth Drillhall last night.

If this is the treatment afforded accredited representatives of a reputable newspaper, it is small wonder that the movement is regarded with suspicion.

Until some adequate explanation and reparation is forthcoming "The Western Morning News" will close its columns to anything associated with a body which cannot control its "stalwarts."

The Western Morning News announces its boycott of Mosley's Fascists (Western Morning News, 6 October 1934).

The unrest at the meeting (Western Morning News, 6 October 1934).

casualties were serious: several women who had brought babies with them were knocked down and one Fascist, Robert Tweedle, of 18 Portland Place in Devonport, was taken to the Prince of Wales Hospital for rib injuries.

Shortly afterwards an editorial entitled 'tooth and claw politics' in *The Western Morning News* deplored the 'un-English and brutal methods employed by Fascists' and the editor referred to them as akin to gangsters and Nazis.[151] A letter in *The Western Evening Herald* the same day was written by 'disabled ex-tommy' who had read Fascist leaflets and went to the meeting to assess the movement. He was disappointed protesters stopped him fully hearing but was shocked by the violence. He wrote 'I was certainly not prepared for the organised brutalities on the part of a gang of pantomime soldiers or hooligans who, following a little innocent heckling, rushed among the audience lashing out with belts, chairs, rubber truncheons and knuckledusters. I narrowly escaped injury from a piece of lead piping. If this is a sample of what we may expect if ever Fascism gets into power (God forbid) then it is the duty of every man and woman to demand from their Members of Parliament that a searching inquiry should be held into the mental condition of its leaders.'[152]

The accounts by the two Rothermere papers were different to the *Western Independent*. Its reporter noted the 'delicious irony' of Mosley thanking the audience for a 'comparatively quiet meeting'.

In the journalist's opinion Plymouth had not seen such political violence since the Reform days of the early 1800s. The journalist sat next to a German visitor, who had stood with an English friend to give the Fascist salute, and he thought the meeting was comparatively quiet. The German was disparaging when he compared it to political meetings when Hitler had sought power. He noted Plymouth Fascists shouted and fought while German Fascists shot their opponents: the German said 'here they only shout, in Germany we used to shoot'. The journalist watched the meeting work up to a climax with a woman's scream, the expulsion of hecklers and the return of the stewards 'breathless but triumphant'. It had started with great enthusiasm on the part of party members at the front of the hall and his supporters even included a woman in a fur coat who blew Mosley a kiss. He taunted his opponents at the back with 'you are not going to like this' but the power of the loudspeakers gave him effective control. When the lights went out Mosley continued to discuss Argentinean beef, Jewish usury and 'alien' finance and when light was restored he quipped 'a little symbol that there is no amount of corruption or jobbery that can put the lights of fascism out for very long'. Then a woman screamed and the back of the hall turned into a 'swaying mass of humanity'. The reporter thought an opponent had started the fracas but fifty stewards in the crowd of some 4,000 managed to control the situation with the exception of one man with a fractured rib. The report noted the fracas over the camera and Mosley's explanation flashes would lead to a stampede.[153] He neglected to mention flashes were allowed at other points in the evening.

On October 11th, six days after the now-infamous meeting, another night of violence further exacerbated the situation. Four Fascists were arrested during fighting at a meeting in Market Square. The *Western Morning News* reported up to ten thousand people, a staggering number, had packed the Square and the approaches to it. There was one injury; for the third time Frederick Finch was hurt and taken to hospital. Uniformed and plain-clothes policemen could not prevent violence. Some twenty party members arrived in a closed van to an already crowded area. One Fascist speaker referred to the previous incident involving the *Western Morning News* and the crowd commented 'You dirty dogs' and 'You

Photograph of Michael Goulding which appeared in Action, 12 February 1938. (Friends of Oswald Mosley).

were afraid to let him [the photographer] print it.' Another speaker, Michael Goulding, annoyed at not being heard, raised his right hand and ordered 'Go on, boys, get stuck into them'. Violence ensued and four Fascists were arrested.

For the first time Plymouth's press was in agreement but the *Western Independent* was more fulsome in its details and scathing in its criticism.

> *When the Fascists arrived in Market Place a trade union meeting under the auspices of the Trades and Labour Council was in progress, and a large crowd was listening to a speaker on the current campaign for the unions. The crowd had listened quietly until shortly after eight o'clock, when a shout was raised and a rush towards the top of Market Avenue took place.*
>
> *A black motor van could be seen rounding the corner, preceded by two Blackshirts in uniform. The van, with a black-shirted driver, drew its nose up within a few yards of the Trade Unionists' Rostrum.*

Upon this the crowd rushed towards the van, with shouts and gesticulations, but the police forced them back. The two Blackshirts who had been occupying the driving seat dismounted and walked, one on either side, to the back of the vehicle and opened the doors at the rear, whence issued a dozen uniformed Blackshirts to be greeted by the crowd with hostile cries. This began a solid ninety minutes of hullabaloo, during which only a few words of any speech could be distinguished. The Trade Union meeting thus rudely disturbed, at once came to an end. It was quite impossible for the speakers to carry on, and they remained quiescent on their rostrum during the whole time.

The Fascists at once began to hold a meeting themselves. The dozen or so in uniform formed a cordon round the van, and outside it was a ring of seven or eight policemen and an inspector. A Fascist jumped on the roof of the van and began to speak. For ten minutes it was simply a 'speech' of gesticulation. The crowd, which by now filled the street from end to end, and must have exceeded the Drillhall throng of the previous Friday evening, was rip-roaring. Angry people shook their fists at the speaker, and it looked for a time as if a rush might be made on the van.

But just at this time a disturbance broke out in one of the doorways at the back of Woolworth's. I saw a man using his fists. Two constables closed in on him but he broke loose from them and aimed another blow at someone in the crowd, before police reinforcements arrived on the scene and he was marched off.

The Fascist speaker continued with his inaudible oration. A voice barked 'What about the Drillhall?' and some paper pellets were thrown at the van. As a variation to the booing the crowd sang the lugubrious strains of the Red Flag. In one corner the crowd began to shout 'left-right-left-right-left' in a rhythm which carried above the general din and the shouting of the speaker, who bawled on and on. For a short time he got a little respite. There were lulls and squalls, and at times I caught the phrases 'Go where Mosley told us to go!' 'The Dirty Rat!' 'Get some Castor oil' and 'Get down you black swine!' The crowd had an extensive repertory of songs 'Tell me the old, old story', 'Daisy Bell', 'They were only playing leap frog' and other community ditties stood them in good stead. In the intervals they chorused 'Hello, hello, hello' or 'Quack, quack, quack, quack, quack!' and fell upon other noise creating expedients.

At 8.45 the first Fascist, having tired the howling to some extent, was replaced by a second speaker, who started off with some reference to 'dirty street corner boys egged on by Jewish and Yiddish . . .' Tumult drowned the rest. 'The best argument for fascism' his voice sprang again above the din 'is simply to take a look at the opposition'. Shortly after, there came a second violent disturbance at some distance from the 'platform'. A man was on the ground. I saw a policeman picking up his helmet. Then two constables marched a man off.

The second speaker, having failed to make himself heard, was at 9.25 relieved by a third, who managed to get in something about 'dictatorship by Red and Jews' before the common fate overtook him. Shaken fists, more 'left-right-lefts', more singing, and then a scurrying in the direction of Cornwall Street, where it appeared another disturbance had broken out and the police were in action.

The crowd except for its unabated din did not molest the speakers. There was no attempt at a 'mix-up' and the black-shirted men round the van were not interfered with. The three fracas which demanded the attention of the police took place at some distance from the van.

Among the quietest spectators were the Trade Union officials who remained on their platform watching the frenzied meeting without comment. Three small boys who shared their vantage point were, however, less unvocal.

When the Fascists had finished their meeting and the van moved off, there was a rush by the crowd which the police had difficulty in staving off. The van could only move forward inch by inch with the police clearing the way. When the Blackshirts had finally vacated the position, the Trade Unionists composedly resumed their speeches.[154]

The newspaper argued the right to freedom of speech was being denied by the holding of the meetings not by their banning.[155] Goulding's use of anti-Semitism appears to have been different from the content of the speeches of local Fascists.

The subsequent trial was of great interest. When the men were charged *The Western Weekly* noted 'hundreds of people gathered outside the court and queued up for over an hour before the proceedings started, despite the rain. When the door was opened there was such a rush for seats that women in the front of the queue were flung to the ground'.[156] Michael Joseph Goulding aged 24, William Rudolf Malabar McIntyre aged 22, George Harrison Clarke aged 24 and Kenneth Francis Davis aged 20 were charged with assault and inciting breaches of the peace. Plymouth's Chief Constable did not object to Goulding being granted bail but did for the others because he felt their particulars were unsatisfactory. He was right to be suspicious. There were also charges of other acts of violence on October 10th.[157] One 72 year old resident of the Octagon testified he was attacked at home that night by three Fascists because he had given lodgings to Mr Isaacs. Isaacs had helped with the anti-Fascist demonstrations but had already returned to London.[158]

There was immediate condemnation. A few days later, on the 14th, a Labour meeting at Plymouth's Cinedrome heard the Chairman, Mr E. V. Watering of the Plymouth National Union of General and Municipal Workers, say 'the best answer to Fascism is not to go into the Market Place and chase people, or repeat their tactics. The best answer is for all of you who believe in democracy to join up in the democratic movements, whether Co-operative, Labour or trade union, and we shall be able to resist any pebble storm of Fascism or Communism.' There were other comments in the region on the violence.[159]

On November 16th and 17th nine Blackshirts pleaded not guilty at Plymouth Police Court to charges arising from the evenings of October 5th, 10th and 11th. Spectators crowded the court.

Goulding, who gave his address as the headquarters in Lockyer Street, was charged with committing damage to *The Western Morning News'* camera on October 5th as were Thomas Wilder, Harry Henry Paice and Arthur Sharman, all of 33 King's Road in

Chelsea (the headquarters of the British Union of Fascists), and Eric Hamilton Piercy and Arthur Ernest Mills who were also both of London. Goulding, also known as Noel Henry Goulding, faced additional charges on the alleged violence of October 11th as did three other men who each had aliases: William Rudolf Malabar McIntyre was otherwise known as Clouston, George Harrison Clarke was also Geoffrey Clark, and Kenneth Francis Davis whose actual name was Marcantonio.

Seven men were convicted: in respect to the destruction of the camera Goulding, Wilder, Mills and Sharman were each fined £3 and ordered to pay £3 special costs or in default one month's imprisonment for doing wilful damage. McIntrye, Clarke and Davis were convicted of assault charges and sent to Exeter Prison. They were imprisoned for six weeks with hard labour. Other charges were dismissed and Paice and Piercy received the benefit of the doubt.[160]

The Western Morning News highlighted their origins: they were 'bullies and thugs from London' and 'unmistakably strangers to this city'. It stated 'it is against the whole spirit of English political life to introduce into a provincial assembly hooligans from London. We know of no such incident that has stained our Westcountry public life'.[161] Goulding became a feature writer for *Action*, the Blackshirts' newspaper, and was later Prospective Parliamentary Candidate for Shoreditch. He most likely immediately returned to London after his Plymouth experiences. When war broke out three years later Goulding returned to southern Ireland.[162] The police reported Goulding had been bound over for an offence three years before his Plymouth arrest. McIntrye, Clarke and Davis had come from London on the previous day specifically in case there was trouble. Each of the three men had criminal records. Clarke had been summoned for using insulting words following a Deptford meeting in October 1933 and was found over to keep the peace for twelve months, Davis was arrested in May 1934 at Newcastle for fighting in the street and for assaulting the police, Sharman had been on probation for two years and in May 1932 was sentenced to six months' imprisonment for living on the immoral earnings of his wife, and Mills had been arrested in May 1934 for disorderly conduct and bound over for twelve months.[163]

Importing these men from London is significant particularly given other details revealed in the proceedings. One assault charge referred to an alleged incident on October 10th. It was claimed McIntyre, Clarke and Davis had gone to an address at the Octagon to seek two political opponents, Morris Isaacs and Nathan Birch of the New World Fellowship. Presumably they were already familiar with them in London. These two men had been holding anti-Fascist meetings in Plymouth and had also come down from London.[164] Mosley must have been briefed on this because the following day he accused a young man at his Barnstaple meeting of being a member of the 'Yiddish' group. The local North Devon newspaper denied this. Little is known of the New World Fellowship but earlier in the year, on April 24th, it had agitated against Mosley at the Royal Albert Hall.[165] Further details of the workings of these two political parties would no doubt reveal how Plymouth in 1934 had become a battleground in the political strategies of national movements important enough to merit importing those with special expertise.

There was another issue which came out of the arrests. The Fascists had their knuckles bound with insulating tape and wore metal body protectors.[166] *The Daily Telegraph*, *The Star* and *The Daily Worker* published the story on October 13th and embellished it to read the men wore knuckle-dusters. It was brought to court at the High Court of Justice four weeks later and charges of contempt of court were dismissed. The action was brought by Goulding and his fellow Fascists.[167] During their trial in Plymouth the men were questioned about taping their hands. McIntyre, for example, had both hands bound with insulating tape and there were also bandages. The length of tape on one hand was nine feet and six inches long. The men claimed it protected their sensitive hands but the police pointed out it increased the force of any blows. Clarke admitted he was a boxer as did Davis.[168]

After these events only a few meetings continued in Plymouth. There was a debate between fascism and socialism at Drake Street in late October. Propaganda Officer Sheville debated with one Captain Brennan.[169] Unusually, there was no indication of violence.

The October events and the subsequent court case were partly responsible for fascism's collapse in Plymouth. There was one positive development: at the end of November: local Fascists enrolled in the Plymouth Parliamentary Debating Society, a group boasting of members from every political persuasion. The group met at Goodbody's Café and had been formed in 1880. Even so, six Blackshirts and two female Fascists had joined earlier and then either changed their political allegiances or moved.[170] At their first meeting the ten Fascists, including two women, debated Fascist policy. Those attending included C.V.S. Hillman, R. J. Rodgers, and Branch Officer William Milligan.[171] The rest of the year brought dire news for the local branch.

On December 1st Lionel Aitken announced 6 Windsor Villas in Lockyer Street would be given up as the headquarters. He denied a rumour the branch was bankrupt in losing the court case over the 6th October meeting and explained the change was due to national reorganisation in moving from social clubs to a more political focus. Many members were interested merely in the social side of fascism and the party was pruning operations.[172] In November the national leadership finally responded to the summer's drastic fall in membership with cuts and focused on revitalising support through concentrating on local issues and adopting a more anti-Semitic line.[173] However, in Devon one consequence of the crisis of the summer of 1934 was it coincided with a complete withdrawal of Fascist support from the only local issue the party had embraced: the party abandoned farmers in their tithe struggle. There was no other local issue to campaign on and anti-Semitism had little real resonance in Devon. After 18 months of being a targeted area, Devon was a marginal area.

The Plymouth office was a very public feature of this change. Aitken reported the club was closed and the employees on the social side left including the cooks and stewards. Some men were retrained and it was planned to bring them back to Plymouth. This left only three paid members. Aitken also projected plans for the future: he expected the party would offer a Parliamentary candidate for the Drake constituency and would open an office in Mutley. He also hoped to have candidates in the municipal elections and planned to hold canvassing classes. Howsoever he presented the rosy future of the local party, events in 1935 would be very different.[174]

Two reports were also made by the Devon Constabulary for the

Home Office in 1934. The report of July, which probably did not include Exeter or Plymouth, noted 'the activities of the British Union of Fascists have been curtailed in recent months; their numbers are dwindling. Last winter the Fascists interfered in several tithe disputes and 'have left a legacy of resistance to the law'. At the end of September the assessment was even less promising. It estimated membership stood at about 100 and 'the movement has been declining recently. It displayed a greater activity in 1933 in connection with tithe disputes'.[175] These two police reports failed to note the greater change: within the first few weeks of 1935 it would become clear that in Plymouth the party was completely dependent on outside help.

The Fascist Organisation in Devon

After the party sent Richard Plathen to Devon from London in midsummer 1933 it quickly spread its activities across the whole of the county.

Exmouth Branch

In early August 1933 the party made its move on Exmouth where presumably there were established contacts. This town at the mouth of the river Exe had only some 15,000 people[176] and although a seaside resort was considerably smaller than Torquay although larger than Dawlish or Teignmouth. Exmouth was also less prosperous than its neighbour Sidmouth. Fascist meetings were held on Chapel Hill, at the centre of the town, on Wednesday evenings. Plathen was often the speaker.

On the 9th Plathen appeared dressed in a high-necked black shirt, grey flannel riding breeches and top boots. *The Exmouth Journal* reported the event positively with the headline 'Thirst for information on Chapel Hill'; the recruiting campaign had 'met with some amount of success in Exmouth'. Plathen informed the journalist 'We had been told that it would be very hard work propagating our policy in Devon and Cornwall, but the response we have met has greatly exceeded our expectations'. He had with him local members.[177] Two weeks later another report indicated meetings were being continuously held but Plathen was 'again the target of a running fire of questions at the close of his speech'. The *Exmouth Journal* gave a full, if not enthusiastic, account of the party's policies.[178] On September 13th another meeting was held but the atmosphere was aggressive. The *Exmouth Journal* reported a disagreement between two young socialists, who frequently jeered and interrupted Plathen, and an older socialist who rebuked them; he said 'this gentleman is answering my question, not yours, and he is entitled to order, and not what he is getting from you'. The questions and answers following Plathen's speech were also reported in great length.[179]

The meeting on September 20th was according to The *Exmouth Journal* marred by 'an unfortunate incident' with one man taken to hospital. Some 200 people gathered to hear Mr W. Barry but two or three members of the audience, thought by the newspaper to be strangers, caused some him difficulty through their questions and tactics. One shouted 'Pull him down!' and Barry responded 'if you think you can pull him down you had better come and try'. After another remark the questioner rushed towards Barry, the uniformed stewards tried to protect him and one Blackshirt was struck. Two local constables restored order and the Blackshirt, Reginald Seymour, who lived at 31 Exeter Road in Exmouth with his parents, was taken to a nearby café and brought to Exmouth Hospital.[180]

The Exmouth Journal noted 'there was little in the incident which might have been avoided by the exercise of a little tact on the part of the speaker'. Once again the paper reported the event positively and gave considerable space to Fascist policies.[181] A week later, on the 27th, the audience had grown to 500 and Plathen was again the speaker. *The Exmouth Journal* thought it very good humoured and reported Plathen stated party members were being victimised. He said 'employers and business men, although they believe with us that changes are necessary, are not only victimising our members but are preventing others from joining our movement for fear of losing their livelihood'. A week later he repeated the claim and added 'in the same way property owners refuse to let us have premises which we might use as headquarters in this district. Nevertheless, our ranks are swelling from day to day, especially in Plymouth'.

Plathen also attacked the vitality of the Conservative party: he asserted a recent meeting at Exeter of the Junior Imperial League, the young Conservatives' group, mainly comprised people between the ages of 50 and 60.[182] His comments had damaging consequences on coverage in the other Exmouth paper, *The Exmouth Chronicle*. The editor was E. R. Delderfield who had just returned from a holiday in Germany. Delderfield was a leading Conservative in the seaside town and until Plathen's attack on his party the reports were fairly objective. For example, on the 26th of August it had reported the Fascists' meeting with policy details and repeated this a month later. It was this meeting which ended in violence and the paper, under the headline 'Street Fight on Chapel Hill – Fight between Socialists and "Blackshirts" at Meeting' reported it as a clash between ten uniformed Blackshirts and 'a group of Socialists and Communists wearing the hammer and sickle badge'. The antagonists, according to the paper, were not Fascists. *The Exmouth Chronicle* noted concern knuckledusters were used against the Blackshirts although the police denied this. The paper ran another story that day which also viewed the Fascists as victims: under the headlines 'Three Fascists Challenged' and 'Blackshirts Seized by Socialists' it was reported three local Fascists were accosted on the corner of The Parade and Chapel Street by six Socialists late one evening. The meeting a week later also had a favourable report in the newspaper and a month later it even published a photograph of Adolph Hitler as 'Germany's Man of the Moment'.[183]

On November 1st the Blackshirts held another meeting which was in the Branch report for *The Western Fascist*. It noted:

> *Staff Officer Plathen, newly arrived from London, addressed a meeting on Chapel Hill. Nearly one thousand 'five-pointers' advertising the time and place of the meeting had been distributed from door to door in the town the previous day by Unit Leader Devereaux and Fascist Woodgate, but whether*

> *the cold weather or the apathy of the Exmouth folk was responsible, only a small crowd assembled. Staff Officer Plathen gave an inspiring address urging the need for self-analysis by everyone, and the necessity for those who were in sympathy with Fascist ideology to come forward and join us – in other words, to have the courage of their convictions.*

Plathen repeated claims of victimisation and that landlords refused to rent premises. He added 'on December 16th, when Our Leader speaks in Exeter, those of you who are still in doubt, and still imagine we are a small handful, will find it worth their while to attend that meeting, and see something of Fascist organisation and hear something of Fascist speech.' Plathen noted John Devereux made his Exmouth maiden speech and along with 'Fascist Street' had made his debut in Topsham a week before. The report noted 'the echoes of the meeting have been heard as far afield as Exeter.'

It was at this point, in early November, that the spat between the Fascists and the local Conservatives developed. The Secretary of Exmouth's Junior Imperial League publicly rebuked Plathen for his earlier comments. Plathen challenged him to attend a meeting the following week on Chapel Hill where he intended to repeat his views.[184] At this point coverage in *The Exmouth Chronicle* ceased. Perhaps Delderfield countenanced using the Fascists in attacking left-wing opponents but not when they attacked his own right-wing party.

However, reports in *The Exmouth Journal* continued with a news story on November 18th demonstrating the Fascist presence had moved up a notch. Fifty uniformed members 'comprising specially picked units from Exmouth, Exeter and Plymouth' marched through the streets to mark the opening of their headquarters in Victoria Road. Significantly, they held their parade on a Saturday evening, the week's busiest night. At an open air meeting that night Plathen repeated his comments about Conservatives and created more controversy: he claimed young Conservatives were forbidden to attend Fascist meetings. The meeting was also addressed by A. S. Devereaux, Propaganda Officer for Exmouth Branch.[185] There was also a fuller, and more enthusiastic, report in *The Western Fascist* which also recorded the journey from Plymouth and the show in Exmouth:

> *Large crowds congregated in the vicinity of the B. U. F. Headquarters in Plymouth to see one motor cycle, a car and two vans, bearing placards which advertised the B. U. F. Policy, and manned by about 30 or more Fascists, start for Exmouth to steward a public meeting. On their arrival at the Exeter Headquarters they were entertained by the local Fascists, whose catering abilities were much appreciated. A 'Blackshirt' drive was conducted through the streets of Exeter and good sales were made. The Exonians were decidedly impressed by the size and smartness of the Fascist contingent. From Exeter the convoy proceeded to Exmouth, halting on the outskirts of the town. Men of Exeter and Exmouth raised the total strength of the party to about fifty strong. Through the streets of Exmouth they marched, looking neither to right or left, heeding neither insults or cat-calls, keeping in step and successfully holding up the traditions of Fascism. In the Square the Company was halted and six picked men were chosen to stand around the Speaker; the remainder stood by. District Acting Organiser Ellis opened the meeting with a lucid and forceful speech, which was made before a large and attentive audience.*
>
> *Staff Officer Plathen taking the platform, quickly obtained the interest of the crowd and gained their attention by issuing a challenge to the Junior Imperial League which had made certain allegations against Fascism. The meeting continued without heckling and by question time the listeners had received something to think about. At the close of the meeting the Fascist formed up and marched off smartly to the Exmouth Headquarters. The Drill Unit Leader must have made some impression on the bystanders, as well as on his own men, for it is possible that more than one baby was disturbed in its sleep that night by the voice of the Unit Leader. But where, oh where were those pugnacious Communists about whom we have heard so much? Possibly they*

thought that discretion was the better part of valour. Who knows? Who cares?

It would appear they had overcome the reluctance, suggested in September by Plathen, of local landlords to rent property. However, three weeks later it was reported, again only in *The Exmouth Journal*, that the Fascist headquarters relocated to 2 Manchester Street. The main thrust of the news report was the opposition within the town's churches. A Fascist spokesman claimed 'of late there have been references made in local churches as to the menace of Fascism'. The newspaper quoted, at length, the party's policy towards religion with the conclusion 'Fascism does not create its own God, neither will it interfere with the religious views of any-one'.[186] The newspaper's editor was W. G. Gorfin, who had held that position since 1909 when he was twenty-one years old. He did not retire until 1964. What his particular politics were is unclear. But he had helped the Fascist movement rise from obscurity in only a few months. The party finished 1933 as a highly visible part of Exmouth's politics. Hundreds of local people had, over three months, heard policies on national and local issues. At one meeting the Fascists were asked whether the council or the local aristocrat, Lord Clinton, was the better landlord for the seafront.[187]

The location of the new headquarters is in itself interesting. Number Two Manchester Street was the home of Frederick Essery who a few years later moved to Paignton where he opened a bed and breakfast establishment which catered, particularly, for Fascists.

In mid March 1934 Unit Leader Devereaux became Deputy Branch Officer and Officer in Charge. J. Collins became Assistant Propaganda Officer.[188] The first notice of the Blackshirts in the anti-Fascist *Exmouth Chronicle* was a report on March 3rd of Richard Plathen's arrest for tithe activities in Sussex. It noted Plathen was active in Exmouth in 1933 in public speaking and in distribut-ing literature. In contrast, *The Exmouth Journal* printed a letter from S. F. Hockaday, another Assistant Propaganda Officer for Exmouth, who criticised a local conservative for comments on fascism but noted her claim 'watch these Blackshirts for it is our vote they are most likely to catch'. Three weeks later another prominent conserva-tive warned the public about fascism and Hockaday again wrote ridiculing the 'timorous outcry' from the established parties against fascism.

Despite this continued public profile the party collapsed only a month later in mid-April. *The Exmouth Journal* noted, under the headline 'Our Fascists', that 'fascism appears to have faded from Exmouth. The headquarters of the British Union of Fascists, which have been established for some time in a house in Manchester Street, have been closed, and the members have departed, leaving no address.'[189] How active the remaining Fascists were without an office is uncertain. At least one continued: J. H. Allen of 38 Morton Road wrote to the *Western Morning News* praising the aims of the party[190] but less is known of other local members who were active in 1933. Like a comet the party came apparently out of nowhere, burned brightly and then quickly disappeared.

Torquay Branch

Another Fascist target was Torquay, the heart of the English Riviera. The seaside town was very different in all respects to the headquarters of Plymouth. Whereas Plymouth had been industrial for hundreds of years Torquay had been a holiday resort since the late 1700s. The population stood at some 46,000 people[191] and was, with its continual influx of visitors, one of the most cosmopolitan places in Devon to be targeted by the Fascists.

It is curious the Fascists focused on Torquay in 1933 because of the presence there of Arthur Kenneth Chesterton. He had come to Torquay in 1929 to edit *The Torquay Times* and *The Torquay Directory*. While there he was active in The Torquay Citizens' Defence League and a campaigner against replacing trams with trolley buses. His first piece of journalism in the town was partly about the trams. At some point early in 1933 he left for London and that year became a leading figure in the British Union of Fascists. In the late 1960s he helped to found the National Front and when he died his former newspaper described him as a 'campaigning ex-editor' and 'a colourful character' but neglected to mention his political activities.[192]

It is Chesterton's key role in British fascism that makes its arrival in 1933 so interesting. Chesterton's first impressions of Torquay four years earlier was that he would never go back to London because 'at last I have found a place where one may live and not merely earn a living'.[193] He resided at 'Seaton' in Braddons Road West with a woman described in the Voters' Lists as his wife Maie but Chesterton did not marry until four years later. When he did it was not his 'wife' Maie. In the 1920s he had fallen in love with a married woman while working at Stratford and the two lived together in London before his appointment in Torquay. It was this woman who lived as Maie Chesterton. Their relationship must have finished by 1933 for shortly after leaving Torquay that year for London he married Doris Terry. She later noted her husband had been a Labour supporter when she knew him in Torquay but sometime in about 1931 his politics changed.[194] There is little in the newspaper to suggest he leaned towards fascism. His newspaper failed to mention Sir Oswald Mosley had started a new party in 1932 and was mainly concerned with news in and about Torbay. The first recorded Fascist activity in the resort coincided with Chesterton leaving for London. In May 1933 a letter appeared suggesting the resort could use a Mussolini and then several reports, and even a cartoon, appeared of local Fascist meetings. The motto of the private newspaper was 'independent, non-political, non-sectarian'. This was perhaps not compatible with Chesterton's emerging political views. It may be only a curious coincidence that the sudden arrival of fascism to Torbay coincided with the equally swift removal to London of a man who shortly afterwards would be so prominent in fascism.

The British Union of Fascists' propaganda campaign began in May. In the first week 'Old Resident' wrote to the *Torquay Times* that the town needed a local Mussolini to tackle the inefficiency of local government. The timing is curious, if not suspicious, for that same week it was reported 'The Fascist Movement has come to Torquay': the first meeting of the new South Devon Branch was held in St James' Hotel. The chairman was Captain Spalding who lived at The Birks in Lower Warberry Road and Mr W. Lloyd of Exeter addressed the meeting. The *Torquay Times,* and its sister paper the *Torquay Directory,* covered the event but its competitor the *Herald Express* did not. The *Torquay Times* noted branch membership stood at thirty members with twelve joining at the meeting, four of them women. The local organiser, who was not present, was A. S. Grose of Paignton. The newspaper recorded some questions and the report was favourable.[195]

Cartoon from the Torquay Times, entitled 'we announced last week that the Fascist movement has established a local branch. Here we see Torquay's Iron Division marching past Signor Edward Henry Adolf Benito Sermon', May 1933 (Torquay Times, 19 May 1933).

A month later, on June 14th, there was a public meeting in Castle Chambers and Plathen came to talk. Few details were reported except for discussion about the party's policies. Again, the meeting had no other coverage in the resort. No further stories appeared in the *Torquay Times* until the end of August and this was the last the paper had. This may have been due to Chesterton having left for London.[196]

The August report is curious because of the writing. Chesterton had brought a style widely accepted as being witty and imaginative, many have put it down to his years as a theatre critic. The tone of the August article is good-natured, playful and less serious than the news stories surrounding it. The writer, who also worked for the sister paper the *Torquay Directory*, obviously had some knowledge of fascism but by this date Chesterton was being married in London. Under the banner 'Fascism comes to Torquay – A Blackshirt Talks It Over With a Crowd at the Fish Quay' the writer noted:

> *They didn't throw him into Torquay harbour after all.*
>
> *He was rather an upstanding man, as he stood on the wooden box, clad in the black shirt and grey riding breeches that proclaimed his creed.*
>
> *The scene was set on the slipway by Torquay fish quay. The Blackshirt had been talking of British Fascism.*
>
> *But they didn't throw him into the harbour. He talked with confidence, and his face lit with a smile when a shout came from a man at the back of the crowd: 'Chuck him into the harbour'.*
>
> *It made the Blackshirt feel at home perhaps. He is used to fighting for a minority. They tried to throw him into the Docks at Bristol once.*
>
> *On Saturday night at Torquay Staff Officer R. A. Plathen, a headquarters' representative of British Fascism, answered the challenge.*
>
> *'It has been suggested that I should be thrown into the harbour', he said. 'Will the gentleman who suggested that kindly step forward.'*
>
> *But the gentleman who made the suggestion had, strangely enough, disappeared.*
>
> *It was not the only interruption.*
>
> *A patient crowd listened to an address which set forth the ideals of British Fascism. But it was when Mr Plathen asked for questions that things began to liven up.*
>
> *Cockney voices and Brummagen voices; North Country voices and South Devon voices, with here and there the plaintive cry of a visitor from Wigan, assailed him with questions from every side.*

And while the questions were going on, women in charge of the stalls nearby, selling natives from Whitstable Bay and other succulent shell-fish, told Mr Plathen just what they thought of him.

'Go on home and let us earn an honest shilling while we can,' they shouted (expurgated version).

'You've got your Sunday dinner, haven't you?'

'You've been here an hour already,' said one.

'You've been here an hour and a half already,' declared another.

'You've been here two hours. WHY DON'T YOU GO HOME?' added a third.

'MIXED GRILL'

The crowd that pressed the Fascist with their questions was a mixed grill of opposing personalities.

There was the fierce little man who thought things were going fairly well as they are. Though he was not, he said, 'satisfied'.

There were the two young men in khaki shorts, with soft voices, who tried in vain to bring decorum of the uplifting debating society into the meeting.

There was the benevolent man in a brown cap, who was full of good humour and scrupulously fair to the speaker. If only people would use their vote, he thought the present system of government might be made to bring things around.

There was the trade unionist with the North Country drawl, who was opposed to a revolution and with autocracy – both of which evils, he felt sure, would follow attendant on the heels of fascism.

They all had their Saturday night fun on the Fish-quay.

When the Fascist declared the Government did not know their own mind – 'Sir Oswald Mosley knows his, doesn't he?' said one of the crowd.

'Three years ago he stood on the same platform as you and spoke for the Independent Labour Party.'

A ripple of laughter spread through the crowd as the

speaker added an afterthought – 'A better platform than yours, it was. You've only got a box.'

Someone who was probably a resident brought Torquay into the picture.

'What are we to do,' he asked, 'if at the next election we have to choose between a Liberal, a Conservative and a National candidate?'

'We hope,' came the reply, 'that by the time the next election comes along you will not have to make that choice. We hope that Torquay will have a Fascist candidate, and then you will vote for him.'

'You want to carry things further than that. You must bring Fascism into your town life – into your Council as well.'

He was questioned closely about the movements of Sir Oswald Mosley, the leader of British Fascism. He was pressed with queries about the Fascist attitude towards the Jews.

'There is no anti-Jewish movement in British Fascism,' he declared. 'Members are expressly forbidden to have anything to do with anti-Jewish movements. If they do so they are very severely dealt with.'

VISIT TO HITLER?

'Then,' said another questioner triumphantly, 'why has Sir Oswald just returned from a visit to Germany and Hitler?'

The questioner's triumph was short-lived.

'I have yet to learn that Sir Oswald Mosley has been in Germany for months,' was the reply. 'I have yet to learn that he has any dealings with Hitler.'

'Has he just returned from Rome?' was another query. 'What is the difference between his going to Rome and Mr Ramsay Macdonald [the Prime Minister] going there? In your speech you ridiculed Mr Macdonald for going away to other countries.'

'Mr Macdonald is the Prime Minister,' taunted the Blackshirt. 'There was a time when other Powers sent their delegates to us. Now Britain – third-rate Power – has to send delegates to the other countries.'

'Britain did not send the Prime Minister', cried a voice, amid laughter.

'Are you an Italian?' asked another member of the crowd.

In spite of the denial, there were members of the crowd whose argumentative qualities induced them to cry 'Italian!' at odd intervals during the evening.

'We are revolutionary,' declared Mr Plathen, 'but we do not want a bloodbath. If steps are taken in time there will be no need for a bloodbath.'

After two of the stall women had pushed their way into the crowd, interrogating the speaker, not very pertinently on the subject of Sunday's dinner, he called for three more questions, and, having answered them, closed the meeting.

But Torquay's blood was up. They tried to get him to answer other questions.

'I never depart from my word,' he said.

When I left, writes a Directory representative, there were three meetings in progress, though the British Fascists had gone. One of the meetings at least had forgotten all about Fascism.

I listened. It was the old, old argument about private enterprise as opposed to Labour's principles![197]

Fascism had arrived in Torbay but how effective it was in 1933 is uncertain from the lack of subsequent reports. It would have attracted members from other parts of the South Hams too distant from another branch. One such individual may have been Charles E. Simmards of Oakbank, Shaldon Road, in Newton Abbot. He was a correspondent to *The British Lion*, the 'official organ of the Unity Band, associated with the Legion of Loyalists and other patriotic organisations', and a Fascist sympathiser if not a party member.[198]

A meeting was held in the South Devon port of Brixham in the middle of March 1934. More than 8,000 people lived in this fishing port in the 1930s.[199] It was held in the Magistrates Room but the room was only half full and 'the attendance did not enthuse for fascism'. An account of the unidentified Chairman and Plymouth member's speech was printed in *The Totnes Times* and it would appear the main point was to introduce the party to Brixham. It was claimed members 'wore black shirts because they were not afraid of their convictions and because everybody submitted to a voluntary discipline. They had many things thrown at them such as rotten eggs, chairs, cabbage stalks and other missiles but that did not deter them in their work to establish Britain as a Fascist country.'[200] *Blackshirt* reported a sales drive was also held 'in the main streets of the town and considering its size the results were excellent'.[201] The unknown chairman may have been the fascist composer of letters to the *Western Morning News* who wrote under the pseudonym of Demosthenes.[202]

A lack of any subsequent newspaper reports might indicate Fascists were not active in Brixham but on April 27th there was an accident on the road from Totnes to Paignton. Nine party members, dressed in black shirts, top-coats and peak caps, were in a lorry when 'it skidded, swerved to its wrong side, struck the bank, careered back to its correct side, mounted a bank four feet high and remained perched on the top of the bank with an eight foot drop into a ploughed field below'. The seven in the back of the lorry, sitting on mattresses, were flung into the road. One of them said 'I don't know what happened. I felt a bump and then I saw stars!' The driver, John Pascoe of Plymouth, and his passenger were unhurt but another member, Mr Wilce of Roseberry Avenue in Plymouth, was taken to hospital for a minor injury possibly a broken nose. The men were on their way to a meeting in Brixham.

Six weeks later two Fascists appeared in court to answer charges the vehicle was not insured. Lionel Aitken, in charge of the Western Area, and John Pascoe were both found guilty and fined. H. O. Stidston Broadbent, a Plymouth Fascist, represented them.[203] Broadbent's expressed his views in many letters to newspapers including one in which he compared men living close to the equator with monkeys.[204]

In April 1934 Aitken had a meeting at Callard's Café for members and then a public meeting. *Blackshirt* enthused 'the branch membership is rapidly increasing and fascism is rapidly becoming a force in this western town'.[205] This contrasts starkly with a report of the Torquay division of the Labour Party that it was dwindling. In 1933 newspaper coverage indicated a growing branch but the Labour Party report stated that by June 1934 there was no longer a branch but 'only a representative, a Captain Spalding', that 'they worked this constituency from Plymouth' and that there were no indoor meetings and only an occasional one outside. Newspaper coverage, according to the report, was meagre; it was stated the local press did not report local activities and that 'about twice' had the Fascists used the correspondence columns but no notice was taken nor had they been answered.[206]

Exeter Branch

The cathedral city was then, as now, the county capital in terms of local government but not in size: its population stood at some 66,000 people, less than a third of Plymouth.[207] Exeter Branch was located at 85 South Street and was run by Mr W. Lloyd and Mr W. Rowe but mainly by Albert James Ellis who was also active in Exmouth late in 1933. There is little in *The Western Fascist* about the branch although one report appeared on December 2nd 1933. It stated 'this branch continues to progress. A good stimulus was given locally by the splendid *Blackshirt* sales drive on Saturday, Nov. 18th. Thanks to the assistance of the Plymouth members we had quite a large number of men out causing a sensation in High Street.' It also reported a meeting with farmers at Whitestone.

The year's highlight was undoubtedly Mosley at the Civic Hall in December 1933. The *Express & Echo* reported, under the headline 'Exeter guard for Fascist chief: Sir Oswald Mosley's sentinels at civic hall', that he spoke for an hour and a half. Elaborate precautions were taken to ensure the meeting was peaceful: the doors were guarded by uniformed Blackshirts, there were policemen on duty both inside and outside the hall and plain clothes detectives were in the audience. Mosley jumped onto the platform and explained Fascists did not waste time on formalities such as having an introduction. 'A sort of one-man band' someone shouted from the audience. The *Echo*'s report was short with a lack of enthusiasm.[208] The *Western Morning News* was more positive: it thought 'considerable interest' had been shown. The reporter noted booing and hissing when Mosley arrived but regarded the meeting to have been well conducted and thought the audience gave him a fair hearing.[209]

A subsequent letter to the *Echo* from 'S. O. S.' noted 'Mosley has set himself a well-nigh hopeless task, and it is a pity that a man of his abilities, energy and youth cannot use his qualities to better purpose.' The writer claimed to have wondered before the speech whether fascism comprised Mosley and little else. Afterwards the writer noted he was convinced of it.[210]

According to a later police report:

> *Prior to October 1933 there was very little activity in this movement in this city and little evidence of local organisation. About that time a local man named Ellis styled himself the District Administrative Officer and shortly afterwards a local branch office was opened over shop premises at 85 South Street. From that time the movement gained prominence and there were a number of public meetings arranged in local halls and on the usual street pitches, and addresses were delivered by prominent officials of the organisation. Subsequently Ellis left the movement and was succeeded by a man named Oxland who came from Plymouth. Whilst Oxland was in charge of the Exeter branch the organisation took active steps in a tithe dispute at Whitestone, a village three miles distant. This focused public attention on the local branch and public meetings were held at Gervase Avenue (a recognised pitch) once or twice a week. On the 16th December 1933 Sir Oswald Mosley addressed a public meeting of about 700 people at the Civic Hall (which holds an audience of 1,500). He was accompanied by a bodyguard of about 50 Fascists and except for some excitement during question time the meeting was orderly. Following this meeting a decline in local interest was noted . . .*[211]

Exeter Branch dwindled in 1934 although there are odd references to members of whom nothing else is known. F. Ware, for example, wrote to *The Fascist Week* from Exeter on why he joined the party. He claimed 'we have accepted its appeal because it embodies a great adventure and voyage of discovery'.[212]

There were two odd developments at the beginning of the year. During January and February a series of suspicious fires broke out in the city. Among the buildings targeted was the Rougemont Hotel on Queen Street which had at least seven fires. The arsonist appears to have been anti-Fascist. A note warned 'down with Fascists, rulers in Britain'.[213] A second message was delivered to the Exeter headquarters in South Street which warned 'Be prepared. Four hours to go. Who is the maniac? There are other ways besides fires. Fascists beware!' Three policemen guarded the Exeter Branch headquarters through the night and although it was reported an object was thrown at a window there was no attempted arson.[214]

On February 22nd 1934 details of Ellis' activities were revealed in a court case at the Guildhall. It was reported in the *Express & Echo* as 'an amazing and complicated story of domestic life, financial difficulties and Fascist activities and aspirations'.

Albert James Ellis was charged with neglecting to maintain his wife Ada and their two young children. The court was told the couple had met in Egypt where he worked for Lipton's Alexandria branch and where she was living with her family who were Italian citizens. They married in 1927. He had a string of jobs and was apparently incapable of holding steady employment which was the reason for their leaving Egypt for Exeter where they lived with his parents in Alphington. However, Mrs Ellis said that she felt unwelcome in Exeter and returned to Egypt with their newly-born child. She came back in June 1932. At this point Mr Ellis helped run a grocery business with his father in Cowick Street but then gave it up to seek employment with the Blackshirts. The subsequent details raise intriguing questions as to the state of Exeter Branch.

Ellis stated in the courtroom he had been appointed honorary second officer in command of the Fascist movement in Devon and spoke at public meetings. He claimed to be one of the first members in Exeter. Ellis also said 'it was intended when I went into the movement that I might perhaps be able to put up as a candidate for this city as a Fascist.' The *Express & Echo* reported at this point 'this statement caused some merriment among the occupants of the public gallery, and the defendant promptly turned and faced in their direction.' The newspaper suggested he was an eccentric if not comical figure: Ellis continually consulted his overlarge collection of notes and papers and repeatedly introduced unrelated and extraneous matters into the proceedings. When questioned about his financial position he stated he was seeking employment abroad for the then princely annual salary of £450 and Mrs Ellis' counsel responded, with sarcasm 'it sounds just as grand as representing Exeter for the Fascists.'

Ellis had lost his Fascist position, and faced disciplinary action some two months before the trial. He gave details of his former duties. They:

> *Often occupied him from 10 o'clock in the morning until 2 o'clock next morning; he was engaged in operations in various parts of the county. Sometimes for a whole week he did not take off his clothes – when he was engaged in the tithe "war" "guarding the farmers' flocks" in the Barnstaple and Whitestone districts. As an officer in the Blackshirts he was permitted to draw his travelling expenses, and he was paid for petrol and oil, used in his motorcycle, from the petty cash. When he found there was no paid post available for him in the Fascist organisation he came off the active list and tried for a job abroad such as he had been used to.*

He also divulged that a lorry from Plymouth Branch was sent with food supplies for the men camping at these farms.[215] Ellis may have been the young Fascist who was on duty at Hole Farm in Bickington in December 1933.

Interestingly, given the state of Italian politics, there was no suggestion Ellis' Italian wife shared her husband's politics. The couple lived apart: he was with his parents in Alphington and she lived with their children in a rented flat in Polsloe Road. They do not appear to have reconciled. A year later Ellis attempted to overturn the Court's decision. His wife returned to Egypt in March 1933 and he had not paid maintenance money. In early December 1933 Mrs Ellis asked for the order to be enforced and the Bench decided Ellis had to pay five pounds or be imprisoned. Ellis argued her leaving the country negated any legal rights. Unlike the earlier report in the local newspaper, the follow-up story did not mention his political leanings.[216] He remained in Exeter after the war.[217]

Ellis' problems may have been responsible for the dreary state of the local branch. The Exeter Division of the Labour Party, located in Northernhay Place, reported the branch had closed down in February 1934, that there were 'about 20 unorganised members in the division' and that there were no regular meetings nor much coverage in the local paper. Some 25 copies of *Blackshirt* were sold each month through newsagents but there was no targeting of women or youth by the Fascists. The report noted Mosley had spoken in December 1933 and that John Beckett came in May 1934.[218] It appears that in 1934 fascism faltered in Exeter and it is only in mid March 1934 that there is any notice of activity when Fascist Spinks became Unit Leader in the city.[219]

The police report sent to the Home Office reveals some further details. After noting the decline of the party in December 1933:

> *In March 1934 the Exeter office was closed, it is understood without the local members being informed. Prior to the closing of this office, although no definite figures were available, it is thought that local membership was about 100. In October 1934 Ellis addressed a meeting in Gervase Avenue, Exeter, when about 120 people attended. He then stated he had broken away from the British Union of Fascists on account of the dictatorial methods adopted. A man named Langdon was present at the meeting in Fascists' uniform and stated he had been instructed to attend to contradict any untrue statements Ellis might make. Police were present and the meeting was orderly. Little was heard of the Fascist movement here from October 1934 until the latter end of 1936 but during that time occasional street meetings were held.*[220]

As would happen in Plymouth, a former lead Fascist official became disenchanted with the party and denounced it in public. Also like Plymouth, the local party then went into deep decline.

Canvassing across Devon: Branscombe, Lynton, the South Hams, Salcombe, Honiton, Tavistock, Bere Alston, Lifton, South Molton, Newton Abbot, Barnstaple, Bideford and Lundy

By April 1934 it was thought there were some 112 branches throughout the country. The *Daily Mail* reported these stretched on the south coast from Margate to Plymouth[221] although there were also some Cornish ones further west as well. By midsummer Devon's branches were widespread but not necessarily prospering. Who the members were is not known. In April one commentator appraised Mosley's followers and categorised them as 'exiles from Empire outposts, disgruntled Conservative women, hard-faced beribboned ex-servicemen and young toughs from the shops and the banks'.[222] No doubt Devon too had its fair share of these types but no memberships lists have survived. There also is no information on those who funded the local branches but the main leaders, in many cases, can be identified.

From Plymouth efforts were made to spread the word throughout Devon.

Branscombe

Shortly before Exmouth Branch closed an attempt was made to publicise the party in Branscombe, the small coastal village to the east between Sidmouth and Seaton. On February 24th 1934, a Saturday evening, Mr J. E. Fraher, Mr E. E. Devereux and Mr S. F. Hockaday travelled twelve miles to the remote village and spoke in a rear room at the Three Horse Shoes Inn. The audience of some fifty people listened to the three speakers as they stood behind a table draped with the Union Flag but the meeting was interrupted by cries from the audience of 'We don't want any dictators here'. The final speaker was not allowed to finish although he answered questions. The night ended with singing the National Anthem and finally, it was reported, with 'the Fascist salute, which was returned by a few members of the audience'.[223]

The village would hardly have merited a visit, it had a population of just over 500 people in the 1930s,[224] but it was home to Rafe and Lucy Temple Cotton and no doubt it was the two of them who gave the salute. They joined the previous year[225] and would overtake their colleagues to become the most prominent members in Devon.

Shortly before the Branscombe meeting there was a sudden burst of letters to the editor of the *Sidmouth Herald and Directory* regarding fascism. Two local supporters in the seaside town near Branscombe, Arthur G. Dampier-Bennett of Radway House and Col. R. Codrington of Barton Cottage, tried to put across to the public various Fascist policies. Dampier-Bennett, Sidmouth Council's Medical Officer of Health, earlier described himself as a lifelong conservative but he was obviously disenchanted with that party by December 1933. They were joined by Devereux who wrote on several occasions and noted in early March 'the people of East Devon will have plenty of opportunity of listening to the Blackshirt speakers during the coming summer'. If they did visit East Devon villages and towns they were not reported in the *Sidmouth Herald*. The paper also printed several letters from anti-Fascists[226] and each letter would have helped to make East Devon residents aware of meetings.

Lynton

In early February 1934 an outdoor meeting was held on the outskirts of the remote North Devon community of Lynton. Two Fascists, G. & H. Vinecombe, presumably local people, organised the meeting and some two hundred people attended in spite of the cold weather. The speakers were C. Hillman and R. J. Rodgers. Fascist Downer acted as driver and steward for the meeting.[227]

The South Hams & Salcombe

The 'South Hams Campaign' opened on the 29th of June with a meeting along the harbour at Salcombe. Six Blackshirts, including two women, were in attendance. Presumably they travelled from

Plymouth. The local newspaper, the *Kingsbridge Gazette*, described the audience as being a large crowd of residents and visitors. The name of the local organiser was given as Mr W. Rogers of Devon Road. The speakers were Mr P. Attenborough and Lawrence Mason of the Plymouth Branch. The *Gazette* also reported no new members were enrolled. This was the only meeting noted in the newspaper which might indicate that no further events took place in Salcombe. What other places were intended to be targeted in the South Hams Campaign is uncertain.[228] Rogers was probably the Fascist of the same name who lived at nearby Batson and who later advertised for Fascists to holiday in Salcombe.

Honiton

The report issued from the Honiton Division of the Labour Party in June 1934 presented a very inactive picture of fascism. It noted there had not been any large public demonstrations and that the last outdoor meeting was held in the summer of 1933. There were no indoor meetings. Most significantly, it stated the branch had closed down leaving only one member ('one only – Edmond') and that formerly the local youth had been organised but not women. It also claimed that only occasionally the local press reported Fascist meetings but no letters appeared from Fascists in the correspondence columns.[229] Rafe Temple Cotton later claimed to have been the organiser in Honiton but it is uncertain when he was involved in the town.

Tavistock, Bere Alson and Lifton

The West Devon market town of Tavistock was the centre of the Devon estates of the Bedford family. The 12th Duke of Bedford, was one of the most prominent Fascists in the country and in 1939 later formed the British People's Party. However, the Tavistock division of the Labour Party submitted a sparse report on local Fascist activity. It stated there was no local branch nor had there been any meetings except 'just one occasional here and there'.

'Practically no notice taken' by local press of them although *Blackshirt* was on sale in larger centres. Negative responses were given to all remaining questions. It would appear from this that Fascist activity was nonexistent in this small town on the western edge of Dartmoor[230] but John Beckett did speak in mid June in Tavistock Hall.[231] At the end of March the British Union of Fascists announced in *Fascist Week* meetings were held in two communities near Tavistock but closer to the border with Cornwall; the report stated 'new ground is now being broken and the first time meetings have been held' in the small village of Bere Alston, situated to the south towards Plymouth, and at Lifton, another small community to the north.[232] Both places had small populations and it is likely established contacts with Fascists warranted the visits. At Lifton it was Mr and Mrs C. F. W. Sage of the Retreat. Deputy Propaganda Officer Sage was in charge of this new group. His wife was a member of the Women's Section and spoke at the meeting held at the local school. Another couple, Mr and Mrs Hillman also spoke.[233] A Home Office report of 30 April noted a branch at Lifton with women being looked after by Mrs Sage.[234]

South Molton

The report from the South Molton Divisional Labour Party of June 18th comprised a letter from the Honorary Secretary, G. Baskerville, who wrote 'Dear Comrade, in reply to your circular asking for details of Fascist activities, I beg to state that there is no branch of the Fascist party in this division, neither is there any reason to assume that they had any support. Only two meetings have been held to my knowledge both of which were cancelled owing to the fact that no one was present but the usual vanload of organisers'.[235] Yet only six few weeks before there was a meeting of the South Molton branch of the Tithepayers' Association and the speakers were two local leading Fascists, W. A. Down and F. S. Hooper.[236]

Newton Abbot

On June 16th the Honorary Secretary of the Newton Abbot & District Trades & Labour Council submitted his report. He claimed there was neither a branch or regular meetings but noted 'a speaker from the Plymouth Fascist Party held an outdoor meeting in the Market Square, Newton Abbot, two months ago but he drew no crowd and no interest was shown, thus up to the present no further meetings has been attempted'. He also was negative on press coverage and of anti-Fascists he added 'nothing having been done by them locally up to the present, it would be unwise to try and create any interest on the movement'.[237]

The report is curious for its omission of the activities of the Blackshirts in the farming community around Newton Abbot and particularly for their intervention in the market, which generated considerable media attention.

Barnstaple and Bideford

The first Fascist meeting in Barnstaple took place in mid March 1934. Propaganda Officer Cann travelled from Plymouth to speak to what was described as 'a considerable gathering at which many important local people were present.' They included one county J.P. and two members of Barnstaple Town Council. Cann announced premises would be opened in Barnstaple in the near future.[238] There was another meeting in September and two members of Plymouth Branch accompanied by two members of the Women's Section attended Barnstaple Fair. The four sold literature and advertised Mosley's forthcoming appearance. By that date Senior Branch Officer Stanley Ion Murdoch had opened an office in the town.[239]

Cann also spoke nearby at Bideford along with Unit Leader Sherriff. The meeting at the Quay, which had a large audience, had an agricultural theme and one of the main topics was the British Union of Farmers.[240]

The biggest single event, besides the Tithe War incidents, was Mosley's visit to Barnstaple in October 1934. A week before local

MOSLEY
WILL
Speak on FASCISM
at Pannier Market, Barnstaple,
on SATURDAY NEXT, Oct. 6th, at 7.30 p.m.

Doors open 6.30 p.m.

All Entrances in Butchers' Row. Tickets may be obtained at the doors.
Prices **6d., 1/-, 2/-, & 3/-**. No admittance after start of meeting.

WARNING.—The Public are warned to ignore all rumours to the effect that this meeting will not take place.

Reserved seats and other information from :
BRITISH UNION OF FASCISTS,
Tel. 529. Victoria Chambers, Barnstaple.

4166

Advertisements for Mosley's meeting at Barnstaple, 1934 (North Devon Herald, 27 September and 4 October 1934).

opposition began to be organised which was markedly different to that in Plymouth. Barnstaple's Liberals were rallied by Richard Dyke Acland, their Prospective Parliamentary Candidate, at the headquarters in Cross Street. Over the next few months he was the most vocal opponent and gathered together a coalition of various groups. By the time Mosley arrived there was already a counter meeting planned; the Liberal and Labour parties arranged a public meeting for the 20th. As Acland explained, 'their views on the matter were the same and they saw no reason why the speakers of both parties should not be on the same platform together.'[241] The Conservatives were not involved.

On October 6th Mosley arrived at the Pannier Market to a large crowd. Nearly 2,000 people reportedly sat patiently through a speech which lasted for more than two hours. Many had pre-reserved seats but there is no information regarding a guest list or who they would have been. The audience of men, women and children was said to have been 'characteristically tolerant and even indulgent'. It was the main political event of the year and Barnstaple had never seen anything like it.

The two Barnstaple newspapers treated the occasion very differently. *The North Devon Herald and General Advertiser for Devonshire, East Cornwall and West Somerset* reporting was either neutral or positive. The Mosley appearance was given a long article which was concerned with policies and questions from the audience. Three weeks later it proclaimed Hitler and Mussolini had come to power because of the threat from communism and berated socialists for 'abusing' Fascists without acknowledging the dictatorship of the left. This was a public swipe at the very visible crusade led by Acland. *The North Devon Herald* appears to have been a strong supporter of the Conservatives. Earlier in the year the editor warned 'an attempt to establish despotism in this country would meet with the sternest resistance. Dictatorships are tolerable only when they are delivering from something worse, and it is probable that only socialism would reconcile this country to fascism. Those who do not want the one should, therefore, be careful not to attempt the other'.[242]

In stark comparison, *The North Devon Journal* was in the Liberal Party camp. It reported the event in great detail but Mr Manaton, the editor, was clearly opposed to fascism. He suggested during Mosley's speech local people:

> *Appeared to enjoy the novel nature of this political show almost as much as it would enjoy, say, the "pictures". It listened to a wonderfully long tirade against everybody in the state except the small and variegated number at present garbed in the Black Shirt which Sir Oswald assured us was not a symbol of tyranny-to-be but of simple faith enshrined in the glowing hearts of their wearers.*

They not only heard a well-known charismatic national figure, which was a rarity in Barnstaple, but there was on offer theatrical showmanship unlike anything in any other party. The editor reported:

> *I was not prepared for the circus-like staging. I use the term 'without offence' as we say in the West, and purely to convey my idea – of what proved to be an entirely one-man act. When I saw the draped platform, illumined by powerful spot-light, and the beflagged pedestal in the centre, I could not resist, the comic and quite unwarranted feeling that that when the radio music had ceased we should see the drapings parted and the appearance of, say, our friend the performing seal. Instead, from one of the wings there stepped into the light the immaculate figure of a man whom I can best describe as the Douglas Fairbanks of the political platform.*

Mosley spoke of the misinformation spread by the Devon newspapers against his party, gave his version of the events of the previous evening in Plymouth, explained why democracy no longer worked in Britain, discussed the possibility of war and need for stronger defence, and probably most pertinently of all to the North Devon audience, discussed the problems of agriculture and tithes.

Some of Mosley's opponents were there too. Acland raised a question from the floor regarding British Fascism and Mussolini but the most curious comment Mosley made was to a young man who defined himself as a Liberal Party member. Mosley answered 'I think you do not represent the Liberal Party but you possibly represent the

New World Fellowship, a lively little Yiddish concern that yelps about us outside but never before has had the courage to come to our meetings'. He might have been one of the men who had been in Plymouth organising anti-Fascist meetings but the editor of *The North Devon Journal* later denied this. The quiet atmosphere in Barnstaple differed from Plymouth: there were no violent protesters and no sign people were imported to oppose the Fascists.

In fact, the opposition to Mosley and his movement appears to have been organised from within North Devon. In *The North Devon Journal* R. J. Baker of Braunton, a local justice's son who had just returned from Germany, wrote an accompanying article which described the dangers of fascism.[243] Two weeks after Mosley's appearance the North Devon Committee Against Fascism and War held their meeting in the Pannier Market. The event attracted a much smaller audience; only some 700 were there compared to the 2,000 or so of a fortnight before. Acland spoke as did Jack Gaster who came down from London for the Independent Labour Party. A resolution was passed that the meeting 'determines to do all in its power to prevent the destruction of liberty by Fascism or reaction, and the destruction of life by war and pledges itself to try to induce all North Devon organisations to associate themselves with the committee that organised this meeting.'

The vote was not unanimous; there were three dissenters including at least one Fascist. Curiously, the North Devon organiser does not seem to have been in attendance. Instead fascism was defended by a young man with the surname of Martin but news reports did not indicate whether he was local. He was described as a 'young Blackshirt', who was 'pertinacious but rather unwise', who 'despite repeated verbal defeats, went on doggedly with a string of somewhat ineffective questions' and thought Mosley's meeting had attracted 'an awfully nice lot of people of the better class' but thought the follow-up meeting was attended by 'middle and lower class socialists'. It would appear from this there was not yet a large Fascist following in Barnstaple. Martin was clearly an active participant in the general discussions. The *Journal's* editor wrote 'I felt something of sympathy for him, because for all his devotion to his task he only succeeded in providing repeated occasions for amusement on the part of the audience. It was not really an equal contest, for the speakers knew so very much more about the subjects raised than the young Blackshirt. As a consequence, he did his cause no good even if (thanks to his courteous bearing) he did himself personally no harm.' The occasion would have been an ideal opportunity to promote fascism and the lack of an organised opposition indicates north Devon was then dependent upon Plymouth.[244] He was probably Patrick Lionel Martin, a 32 year old member of the party who was a Fascist organiser at Rotherfield in Sussex. He was pulled over by a policeman on Tavistock Road in Plymouth on October 14th for not having a driving licence. Martin was travelling that day to Barnstaple.[245]

The reliance on outside help is borne out by an account of the first Fascist meeting held after Mosley's visit. Forty persons listened at the Drill Hall in Braunton. Murdoch chaired it and spoke of fascism as a crusade; he joined because it was a 'good show'. Curiously, he referred to the recent events in Plymouth as 'a bit of a *schemozzle*'. In Yiddish a 'shlemazel' is a person with bad luck. If this is what he meant then his use of this language is interesting given the party's views on Jews. Murdoch was the proprietor of a boarding house in Trentishoe. The speaker was Captain Hammond of Kennerleigh who was said to have had a quiet hearing and had intensive questioning after giving the Fascist salute. Murdoch closed the meeting with the comment his party would 'brook no interference from the East End or elsewhere. Nor would they stand any damned silly questions'.[246] The following week, on November 1st, a meeting was held at Forrester's Hall in Barnstaple but it was poorly attended. Martin was again in attendance as was a speaker from Plymouth. There was some other local activity in letters from Murdoch to the *North Devon Journal* as well as others from the national headquarters: A. K. Chesterton, who had, only a year before, left South Devon, wrote several letters correcting what he saw as inaccurate press reports.[247]

Lundy

Perhaps the most curious place associated with fascism is Lundy Island. A news item appeared in the *Western Evening Herald*, and other papers, on the 8th of November 1933 entitled 'Lundy Surprise'. It may have been intended to be mischievous. It noted:

> *Curiosity has been aroused in North Devon by the visits of strangers to Lundy Island during the past week. Inquiries have failed to reveal their purpose. Rumour says that the island is to be acquired by the British Union of Fascists, a statement which was neither confirmed or denied by that body last night. Mr C. W. R. Cann (Plymouth Area Organiser) last night said* 'We have nothing to say'.

The newspaper mentioned the island's remoteness and that the owner is 'virtually its sovereign for the island pays no income tax, and has no rates, duties nor closing hours'.[248] This island off the North Devon coast was for sale because the owner, Martin Coles Harman known as the King of Lundy, had been imprisoned for eighteen months in November for fraud. He bought the island in 1925 and had issued his own coinage.[249] It is uncertain whether the newspaper was merely making a mischievous link between Mosley with Harman or if the Fascists were actually interested in Lundy. One possibility is that it was a visit similar to that made to another Bristol Channel Island, Flat Holm, by Clevedon Branch. In the summer of 1934 some twenty Fascists visited the island and met the lighthouse-keepers.[250]

Newspaper politics and Lord Rothermere

The party had a great boost nationally when Harold Harmsworth, first Viscount Rothermere, an admirer of Mussolini, gave his newspapers' support in January 1934 to Mosley and British fascism. *Fascist Week* proclaimed 'We welcome a brave and powerful ally' and Mosley later commented the positive headlines 'came pelting like a thunder-storm'. The most famous was that of January 15th, 'Hurrah For the Blackshirts!'[251] Rothermere's influence was

For the Latest News

From Home Ports
. Garrisons and .
Foreign Stations see

The Western
Morning News
and Mercury

Acknowledged to be the
best-informed Newspaper
for all SERVICE NEWS.

Daily Reports of Warship Movements. | Special Articles on Service Topics.
Official Notifications and Appointments. | Unequalled as an Advertising Medium.

Prepaid Subscription Rates (per post): One Month, 5/6; Three Months, 16/6

Head Office:
9, Frankfort St., Plymouth.

London Office:
114, Fleet St., E.C. 4.

Advert placed in The Naval & Military Record and Royal Dockyards' Gazette for the Western Morning News, with the swastika decoration. The advertisement began on July 19th, with the arrival of Mosley's Fascists in Plymouth, and lasted for five months until December 14th (The Naval & Military Record and Royal Dockyards' Gazette, autumn 1933).

considerable: in addition to the *Daily Mail*, *Sunday Dispatch* and *Evening News* he owned many Devon newspapers including *The Naval & Military Record and Royal Dockyards' Gazette* and from 1919 *The Western Morning News* and *The Western Weekly*, from 1921 *The Plymouth Herald* and from 1926 *The Herald Express*. He later acquired two further titles in Devon: the *Express & Echo* in 1939 and the *North Devon Journal* in 1940.

His support popularised fascism on a national scale not seen before but he then changed his mind in mid July although sympathetic reports lingered until the autumn of 1935. A variety of reasons have been given for Rothermere's decision, including political machinations by him in relation to the Conservative party and pressure from Jews and advertisers. It has also been suggested that in the summer of 1934 the government pressured newspaper editors to deny Mosley publicity. Rothermere's support was important partly because of a ban by the BBC on Mosley which lasted until 1968 although Fascist meetings began to be reported in the summer of 1939.[252] It provided publicity when it was denied Mosley by other sources. The effect of Rothermere's support and subsequent withdrawal of it on Devon's news editors is more complicated.

Rothermere dominated newspapers in Plymouth, Torquay and in rural Devon and his support should have been of great importance yet nothing is known of what instructions, if any, these editors received from their head office. They may have been allowed independence although there is at least one earlier instance in which he dictated policy. When in 1931 Lady Astor's son was imprisoned for importuning guardsmen Rothermere kept the story out of not just his national papers but from his Devon ones. A pre-arranged code was sent to prevent a leak.[253]

It is clear the editorial views of the Rothermere titles in Devon differed. In the English Riviera the *Herald Express* ignored fascism unlike its competitors. In Plymouth *The Western Herald* and *The Western Morning News* were initially supportive before they both became hostile in late 1934. Both papers carried positive stories through to June and blamed socialists or communists for any violence. However, events in October changed editorial policies. After the Fascists' attack on the papers' staff the reporting became aggressively negative and the editor of *The Western Herald* was damning about Mosley and his party. *The Western Morning News* was the most important paper of Rothermere's Devon titles because it was countywide and sold well in rural areas. Perhaps the most striking illustration of the paper's previous favourable treatment was the publication, on May 28th, of a full feature article by John Beckett entitled 'Meaning of the Blackshirt' with sub-headlines 'new machine to meet new times' and 'planning a greater Britain'. The editor included a proviso that 'while not necessarily agreeing with the views expressed in the article below, *The Western Morning News* extends to the British Union of Fascists an opportunity of stating their case'. Also, its' motive in using swastikas as decorative features in earlier advertisements over many months in 1933, which coincided with the Fascists arrival in Plymouth, can only be speculated on.

It was Mosley's own appearance in October at Plymouth when two *Western Morning News'* staff were publicly and violently assaulted by Fascists that caused the papers to withdraw not only any support but all coverage of the party. The headline was 'PRESSMAN ATTACKED BY BLACKSHIRTS'. The editor, James Palmer, wrote in a separate blocked headline:

> *if this is the treatment afforded accredited representatives of a reputable newspaper, it is small wonder that the movement is regarded with suspicion. Until some adequate explanation and reparation is forthcoming The Western Morning News will close its columns to anything associated with a body which cannot control its 'stalwarts'.*[254]

Palmer had been editor since 1921, shortly after Sir Leicester Harmsworth purchased the paper, and continued until 1948.[255]

Mosley refused to apologise the following morning and no subsequent conciliatory gesture was made. The Fascists immediately retaliated, that same day, by limiting facilities to journalists in Barnstaple. The editor of the *North Devon Journal* observed that instead of being given a view of Mosley the journalists were put on a table in an obscure part of the hall from where it was difficult to hear and see the Leader.[256] From that day the *Western Morning News* only printed negative stories. Its sister paper, *The Western Evening Herald* (later the *Plymouth Herald*), was marginally better in its coverage. The party, almost overnight, went from extensive coverage in the Westcountry's largest newspaper, most of it favourable, to a nearly complete ban. Both papers became hostile and this continued through the 1930s: six years later, in the early days of the second world war, the editor of the *Western Morning News* sent to the Home Office, in confidence, a letter written to him by a local Fascist for publication in his paper.

The earlier support of the *Western Morning News* and the *Western Evening Herald* were more evident in Plymouth because of the marked opposition of the other Plymouth paper, *The Western Independent*. In nearly all instances this paper's reporting was more detailed, the stories on Fascists more frequent and the writing more creative and thoughtful than its two rivals. Most important of all, the tone, from the Fascists' arrival in the summer of 1933 through to the closure of the headquarters, was one which ranged from ridicule to clear hostility.

Interestingly, the greater number of press supporters in 1933 and 1934 were not employed by Rothermere but were independent. *The Bideford & North Devon Weekly Gazette* and *The North Devon Herald* were encouraging towards fascism. The latter championed the Conservatives and might have adopted a benign attitude towards fascism because of the hostility expressed by its competitor in Barnstaple. In contrast, *The North Devon Journal* was consistently against fascism in 1933 and 1934. *The Exmouth Journal* was more supportive than *The Exmouth Chronicle* which started off on a positive note but eventually it too became critical of the Fascists. This may have been because the latter supported the Conservatives and it was positive about fascism until they attacked the Conservative party. *The Torquay Times* and *The Torquay Chronicle* appear to have been sympathetic in 1933. *The Crediton Chronicle* carried a positive feature on the first of February 1934 entitled 'Fascism for Britain' by 'a correspondent' but cannot be said to have been generally supportive.

Other independents such as *The Okehampton Post*, *The Totnes Times* and *Pulman's Weekly* were not critical in their reports but merely factual. The Exeter newspaper, *The Express & Echo*, was muted in its reporting. It reported some news stories and not generally in a hostile manner. Most of it concerned fascism outside its readership's area, which might have been due to a lack of activity in Exeter itself, but it is interesting that the report of June 12th on Mosley's famous, or infamous, Olympia meeting was neutral. It was, at best, disinterested in local fascism. When in 1937 there were two near riots in the city the *Echo* did report either event. This is more curious given the ensuing six-month standoff between Exeter's Chief Constable, the Home Office and the national headquarters of the British Union of Fascists. Legal action was threatened and the Chief Constable was called to the Home Office over his ban on Captain Hammond speaking but the *Echo* maintained silence. The two Sidmouth newspapers had scarce interest in politics of any kind and were markedly old-fashioned in general compared to those in the rest of Devon. Their only acknowledging of fascism was each criticised noise from the use of loudspeakers. The politics was immaterial; they were upset at the peacefulness of Sidmouth being disturbed. Across the Cornish border, the *Saltash Gazette* was strikingly enthusiastic in its coverage of early meetings of the Fascists. Several lengthy articles appeared with extensive coverage of Fascist policies and with no criticisms.

In 1935 newspaper coverage would virtually disappear for local Fascists and become largely nonexistent through the late 1930s. This might have been due to the suggested pressure by national government or equally it may be a reflection of the depressed state of the British Union of Fascists in Devon. There were some exceptions in Devon, notably the *Tiverton Gazette's* lengthy report of a meeting at Sampford Peverell and an astoundingly favourable account of William Joyce's visit. These both occurred in 1935. Other local newspapers largely ignored the Fascists and they were forced to use other means to publicize themselves including painting and chalking slogans on buildings and roads.

The Tithe War

The greatest local issue for Devon Fascists was tithes, the agricultural tax collected by the Church of England from farmers. In the mid 1920s an agreement had been reached to change the method of payment from of a portion of produce, whether crops or livestock, to a fixed annual fee. While this may have suited the immediate post-World War One period and modernised a centuries-old tax in which farmers financially supported the Church of England, a changing economic climate rendered the agreement unfair. A sharp fall in agricultural prices resulted in farmers paying a higher proportion of their income to the church. Discontent followed and the Fascists used this to gain support.

The dispute over tithes spread through Devon and Cornwall as the British Union targeted the farming community. It became known as the Tithe War. In 1933 Mosley decided to exploit the issue when in August Fascists supported a farmer in Suffolk who refused to pay her tithe. National Political Officer Richard Plathen organised dozens of Fascists to resist the bailiffs and the police arrested nineteen of them including Plathen.[257] In early December *The Western Fascist* announced a national appeal for funds for 'a great campaign of general and agricultural meetings'. The content of the

The popularity or at least newsworthy nature of the fascists is shown in this photograph of a Bude Carnival tableau entitled 'There Yer Tithes' with Marhamchurch boys (Western Times, 1 December 1933).

Photograph entitled 'agricultural justice, the tithe war in North Devon provided a topical ingeniously contrived tableau seen above which formed an amusing item in Hartland & District's Grand Carnival', October 1933 (Western Times, 20 October 1933).

newssheet reflects its importance: even in its 'herbs' there are reference such as 'Who is the Unit Leader that saw Kangaroos on the way to a Tithe War and did it take him seven hours to discover his mistake?' and 'Are the most handsome members most suited for Tithe War?'

The issue had been building through the year. For example, in the middle of June some 300 farmers stopped the auction of distrained cattle from a farm near St Pinnock in South East Cornwall.[258] Meetings were held throughout the region to organise farmers to resist paying tithes. Many were organised by the Tithepayers' Association, a national organisation recently established with local branches. This won it considerable support within the farming community. In sharp contrast, the National Farmers' Union was criticised for a passive attitude. The Newton Abbot Branch of the Tithepayers' Association appears to have stimulated political activity in Devon. On January 24th one of its officers addressed a meeting in Tiverton but the greatest activity happened at the end of the year. Plathen agitated throughout the South West and tried to politicise farmers: for example, in early October he was in Stratton with 500 farmers and called for the formation of a local branch of the Tithepayers' Association.[259] He was also at a farmers' meeting at Shebbear where he spoke of distraints placed on cattle in Liskeard.[260] Shortly afterwards events publicised the 'Tithe War' more than any public call for meetings and action.

Buckland Brewer, 1933

For six weeks from the middle of September to October 29th the previously unknown farm at Holwell in the parish of Buckland Brewer was the focus of the tithe war. The farm is located in a part of Devon remote from the main centres of population. It lies some four miles from Great Torrington in the north-west corner of the county. Whereas Great Torrington had a population of nearly

Mr Brown of Holwell Farm, Buckland Brewer with R. Bowden, Plymouth Branch Fascist, at the 'Danger Zone!' (Western Times, 20 October 1933).

3,000 people in the 1930s that of Buckland Brewer was barely 500.[261] The population would swell in size.

The farmer, L. W. Brown, had summons served for non-payment of tithes on one rick of hay and two of corn. He had been levied for several years but in 1933 refused to pay. On October 12th one local paper reported 'British Fascists have taken a hand in the affair' and 'villagers had the unique spectacle of seeing six young men in their distinctive uniforms, black shirts and flannel trousers'. They set up camp at the farm and on the following Sunday a further 30 men arrived by car and motorcycle. The newspaper noted 'after a meal, a pow-wow and a pleasant fraternisation' many returned to Plymouth. The remainder stayed to watch the farm day and night. They barricaded the farm entrance, dug trenches and partially cut trees in order to drop them on roads at a moment's notice. Richard Plathen had travelled from Plymouth to take charge of the operation. A bailiff also watched the farm and relations were cordial with the farmer who allowed him to eat with his household.[262] *The Bideford Gazette* enthused about the atmosphere:

> *The inhabitants of Stibb Cross, Langtree, Buckland Brewer and surrounding parishes have not had such excitement for years and young Hitlers and young Mussolinis are bursting for an outlet for their high spirits while their fathers, proud men of the soil who have wrung a living from the soil these thirty years or more, are great sympathisers of Mr Brown.*[263]

Shortly afterwards the atmosphere turned unpleasant. A new bailiff arrived and it transpired that while he was surveying the farm his heavy suitcase and large parcel, in which were his clothes and food, disappeared. They were later returned but in the meanwhile he had to sleep in the nearby village. During his absence the two corn ricks mysteriously disappeared as well as part of the hay rick.

At this time, the 17th of October, the numbers of Blackshirts in the camp increased to eight men. In charge was Mr R. F. Bowden who wore his first world war medal ribbons on his shirt.[264] Senior Unit Leader Bowden was later profiled in *The Western Fascist*. He was:

a man with a personality as fine as his physique. It is due to his fine qualities of leadership that such great headway has been made in the fitting out of headquarters. He deserves great praise for the tactful way he handled the Tithe War in North Devon, for it was due to his leadership that it was brought to a successful conclusion. He has that fine quality of extracting the best out of men in the least offensive way. He has indeed a brilliant future!

Bowden lived in Dorset four years later and offered his assistance to the party but Exeter Branch was told not to have any dealings with him.[265]

A Union Flag flew over the Fascists' tents and they painted in white letters across the road leading to the farm, for nearly a mile, such slogans as 'Unite Against Tithes', 'Abolish Tithes', 'Back The Farmer' and 'The Tithe War: Farmers Will Not Surrender'. A sign near the entrance warned visitors of the Tithe War and a derelict motorcar had been pulled across the road. Nearer the farm the Fascists painted on an old motor van 'The Black Shirts Tank – don't hinder him'.[266]

A second bailiff was sent but neither man was welcomed; they were given no shelter or food during the inclement weather at night. Then the battle suddenly ended on the 29th. A letter arrived from the County Court officer and he withdrew the bailiffs because yet more of the third rick, some two tons of hay, had disappeared. There were no longer sufficient goods at the farm to distrain. Six to eight Blackshirts stayed in residence for a few more days until they were convinced the battle was won. The Fascists then took down their signs and tents, filled in the trenches and returned to Plymouth with their van painted at the front and rear with the slogans 'Tithes – bah' and 'Victory for Buckland Brewer'. Their exit was slightly marred by a collision with a small car but the Fascists had won the battle.[267]

One curious element of the incidents is their reporting by the two local papers. *The North Devon Journal* was hostile from the beginning but the others, including *The North Devon Herald*, differed. In one report, under the headline 'Buckland Brewer Battle Front', it complimented the Fascists on their orderliness: it noted 'the ceremony of changing the Fascisti guard was carried out in strict accordance with military traditions'.[268] A week later, when the Fascists were leaving the farm, the *Bideford Gazette* report was flushed with praise. It noted the minor accident but stated 'none could take offence because the Blackshirts were far too good-humoured'. The reporter also noted the farm was left in a tidy state and that the Fascists 'have left warm hearts too for the Fascists were most pleasant and tactful both to the local inhabitants and to the many visitors. As one inhabitant put it to me *It's been a nine-day wonder enlarged into three whole weeks*. Mr Brown is happy because he has seen his enemies discomfited, Mrs Brown is even happier because she can get on with her household work without being interrupted by bailiffs, farmers, Fascists and newspaper reporters.' The report also recorded a comment by a Fascist that meetings were shortly to be arranged throughout North Devon and that a branch was to be established at Bideford.[269]

Bradworthy, Cheriton Fitzpaine, Holsworthy and Witheridge, 1933

At the end of October Ernest B. Oxland, an officer with the party, spoke at a crowded meeting of farmers in the P. R. H. A. Hotel Room in Bradworthy, the village on the north-west corner of Devon along the Cornish border. He told them 'you have no need, any of you, to pay tithes. We are prepared to help you to fight against it and we are not taking any half measures. We cannot promise to stop the paying of tithes but we are prepared to spend every penny we have to help you to resist paying them.' Oxland was one of the seven Fascists then staying at Holwell Farm. He implored them:

> *I want to tell you how we can help you, if you will let us come on your farm, and you will give us a free hand. And it will not cost you one penny. We take no money from you, therefore you are not responsible for what happens. Do not think we want you to become Fascists, before we help you. Whether you are rich or poor, or to whatever party you belong, we will be with you in your fight against the tithes. I*

may say that we are a political party with a policy, but we are not like the others, waiting to get into power before we do anything. We are starting right away. I want to impress on all present that you should resist tithes. You should all become members of the Tithepayers' Association and the Farmers Union, then as one great body, you will be able to stand out against the burden imposed on you.

His promises to farmers struggling with a faltering agrarian market and falling commodity prices must have been tempting. Mr Down spoke of his experiences.[270]

Protest meetings were held across Devon. On the 10th of November, there was one at Cheriton Fitzpaine where Down and Frederick Samuel Hooper spoke. Five days later there was a similar meeting of farmers at Holsworthy not far from Holwell Farm. The chairman pointed out there was no connection between the Tithe-payers' Association and fascism. Then, a fortnight later, another meeting was held at Witheridge with the same speakers. Local newspapers also, not surprisingly, began to report county courts, in such places as South Molton, Bideford and Great Torrington, had summons being unanswered by local farmers.[271]

Whitestone, 1933

The dispute then spread to the edge of Exeter. In late October the Tithepayers' Association met at Whitestone. It was reported 'feeling is running high at Whitestone and nearly every tithe payer is a member of the association'. The speakers were, once again, Dunning of Newton Abbot and Hooper of Tiverton.[272] Four weeks later violence broke out in this small rural parish. Exeter Branch held a meeting in the parish on November 20th and the tithe issue was a major topic of conversation. A branch report recorded:

A very good meeting was held on Monday evening at Whitestone by special request from the inhabitants. When the Exeter party arrived they found quite a crowd waiting. Unit Leader Devereux wasted no time in opening up, followed by

Photograph of the tithe dispute at Whitestone with one Fascist from Exeter Branch looking at the camera, November 1933 (Express & Echo, 29 November 1933)

District Acting Officer Ellis who explained the Fascist Policy with its application to agriculture. Few questions were asked but after the meeting many stayed behind and the Tithe question was discussed. The party went back having created a favourable impression on the local farming folk. A most satisfactory meeting.

Shortly afterwards, at the end of November, a dispute began with summons served on Mr W. Brimmacombe of Stiles Farm and of Mr G. H. Heard of Hayne Barton. Bailiffs arrived early on the morning of November 30 and a cow was removed and taken into a lorry. The bailiffs then travelled to Hayne Barton where they seized two bullocks. Unfortunately they were unable to leave the farm because a gate was padlocked. Mr Heard's daughter rang Exeter Branch for help and a small contingent of Fascists arrived. By this time neighbouring farmers were also in attendance and a standoff developed. Eventually the cattle were removed but the lorry remained in what was called 'no man's land'. A further group of Blackshirts arrived from Plymouth and outside the gate a trench was dug. The lorry was left behind and the short battle was won by the farmers and the Fascists.[273] Albert James Ellis was probably one of the Exeter Blackshirts. His political activities became well known two months later through the local press.

St Mawgan-in-Pydar, Cornwall, 1933

At this time Plymouth Fascists became involved in a dispute at St Mawgan-in-Pydar in North Cornwall. On November 21st three Fascists camped at Trevarrian, the farm belonging to William Lobb. Once again R. F. Bowden was in charge, He arrived in a large saloon car belonging to a Plymouth member who had only offered

Photograph entitled 'Battle of the tithe – a Plymouth fascist resplendent in his new uniform standing guard yesterday outside Mr W. J. Lobb's farm at Trevarrian which is enclosed in barbed wire'. (Western Morning News, 5 January 1934)

Trevarrian, Mawgan, North Cornwall.
(Western Morning News, 5 January 1934)

his services 30 minutes before the telephone call was made to the Plymouth Headquarters asking for help. Along the way they collected the chairman of the Cornish Tithepayers' Association and Lobb shortly afterwards presided at the first meeting of the St Columb branch of the association. The Fascists pitched a tent at the farm, converted a washroom into a sitting room and cooked on an oil stove. Bowden told a reporter he and his fellow Fascists kept kits packed in order for them to leave in a hurry. Party members also visited Margate Farm near Bodmin where they and the farmer, Fred Riddle, kept watch in the event of distraint action. The Fascists left Trevarrian only to return shortly afterwards to once again defend the farm.[274]

Stoney Cross at Alverdiscott, 1933

North Devon's 'second tithe war' also began at the end of November. Frederick Chipman, of the North Devon Tithepayers' Association, was issued with a court summons for non-payment of his tithe and a bailiff padlocked the gate to his field. The farm is situated near Bideford and the nearby village barely had 200 residents in the 1930s. Unfortunately, several neighbouring families obtained their water from the field and the court official had to return to unlock the gate. In the meanwhile a sign appeared 'Tithe War Number 2, land seized, what next?' The Fascists offered help but Mr Chipman declined until his Association met. He told *The Western Times* the Blackshirts were 'staying in the district ready for any emergency'. These men were involved at Buckland Brewer.[275] North Devon did not have to wait too long for the next instalment of the war at Alverdiscott.

Abbotskerswell, Bickington and Newton Abbot, 1933

The Tithe War finally spread to Newton Abbot at the end of the year. It is curious it took so long. The first branch of the Tithepayers' Association in Devon or Cornwall had started in Newton Abbot two years previously and subsequently spread through the South West. Other parts of Devon subsequently agitated against tithes but it was only in December 1933 that Newton Abbot became the county's focus. The local Tithepayers' Association branch had a membership of 70 farmers[276] and only a few weeks before there was a meeting in Market Square. The principal speaker came from Kent and the second was Down of Tiverton, District Officer for the Fascists.[277]

The 'war' began with a damp squid in the small village of Abbotskerswell, only a few miles from Newton Abbot. On the afternoon of Sunday, the first of December, three Blackshirts arrived at Ruby Farm to help with what they thought was a tithe dispute. They were given a cup of tea by the tenants, Mr & Mrs D. J. Pengilly, and then returned to Plymouth. They had read of the dispute through the letters to the *Western Herald*. The disagreement centred around who was liable: Pengilly claimed he was not liable as a tenant. The Blackshirts offered to protect the two heifers which had been marked for sale. According to Pengilly 'the Blackshirts seemed disappointed to find the bailiffs were not still on the premises and that their services seemed hardly necessary'. He refused their offer of a body of ten men to camp at the farm and guard the livestock because he had received a letter from the High Bailiff apologising for the mistake.[278]

Six days later five sheep were seized and put up for auction at Newton Abbot Market. They, along with four bullocks, had been distrained for non-payment of tithes by Mr J. Easterbrook of Hole Farm in Bickington, a small village between Newton Abbot and Ashburton. The sale became heated and one Blackshirt interrupted the auctioneer with the words 'these sheep are stolen' while another 'black-uniformed man shouted *the distraint was illegal – these sheep were stolen*'. Farmers and Fascists disrupted the action and the animals remained unsold.

That day the livestock were moved to Abbrook Farm in Kingsteignton. It was reported in the local newspaper 'it transpired that the lorry which eventually took the sheep was followed by a number of Fascists to Abbrook Farm at Kingsteignton. Certain people obstructed the Fascist lorries which followed in pursuit of the sheep, and a man was knocked down in the melee that followed. A third Fascist lorry succeeded in getting clear and making the discovery of the sheep's destination.' Percy Chudley, the farmer at Abbrook, said he learned from hostile farmers a week later on the next market day, the 13th of December, that the animals were in a tithe dispute and asked for them to be removed from his care. He later claimed he would have been in danger had he continued to care for them and would rather look after a tiger than one of the animals. The livestock were returned on Saturday, the 17th of December, to Bickington.

Five ewes were sent from Abbrook Farm to Newton Abbot market on the 13th but they too became the subject of considerable controversy. The word 'Tithe' was painted in large black letters on their backs and a crowd of some 150 people, including three Fascists, were hostile to the sale. The animals were not sold and it took an hour to arrange transport for the ewes. It was later claimed the Fascists intimidated transport drivers; the Blackshirts had, allegedly, threatened haulage businesses would suffer if they cooperated with the police and bailiffs. The ewes were eventually returned by lorry to Bickington. The bailiffs and police had managed to keep control but had lost the battles to sell the livestock. All the animals were now at their place of origin and the issue was still unresolved.

At Hole Farm two groups of men then guarded the animals for very different purposes: for several days up to 30 County Council officials and police constables kept surveillance on the cows and sheep as did Blackshirts from Plymouth. On the morning of Tuesday the 20th a large party of law enforcement men arrived, smashed a padlock placed on a gate and loaded the animals onto three lorries. The farmer, Mr Easterbrook, said 'About 7.30 am, whilst I was at breakfast, some 20 men, including about 12 constables in uniform, arrived at my farmhouse and announced their intention of removing the animals.' They were taken for sale outside Devon and were not seen again. It transpired one Blackshirt had been watching the animals from Monday night and was escorted by law enforcers 'at every turn'. He was locked in a barn and released after the animals were taken away. The Fascist attempted to trace their whereabouts but his motorcycle combination became stranded in the narrow lane leading to the farm. This may have been Albert James Ellis, a member of Exeter Branch, who is known to have used a motorcycle while watching farmer's livestock. A lorry-load of Blackshirts arrived at Hole Farm but failed to find the animals.[279]

Fascist Week reported the events as a marked success for the party in that it prevented the sale of the tithe sheep[280] but the Blackshirts were not finished with this incident and several months later it once again made news throughout Devon and beyond. The last word on tithes in 1933 came from Mosley. On December 17 he spoke to an audience, albeit of only fifty people, at the public rooms in Bodmin. His main topic was agriculture and tithes. He stressed the Fascists actions were not illegal but those pursuing the church's interests were.[281]

1934

In 1934 the national 'Tithe War' continued to spread through rural Devon particularly in the north. Devon newspapers reported events extensively and there was some national attention: for example, in mid February there was concern in Parliament about 'recent events' in Cornwall and Devon.[282] Even as the Fascists took a lead role in disseminating unrest the issue, for the local party, came to a sudden and unexpected halt.

The issue divided farmers' loyalties, probably a deliberate Fascist intention. Officers of Devon branches of the Tithepayers' Association publicly and repeatedly criticised the National Farmers' Union for inadequate protests against tithes. In turn, earlier in the year, in January, officers of several Devon branches of the National Farmers' Union criticised their leading rival. It was claimed at the Great Torrington branch that membership had fallen from 140 farmers to 122 and that members had said they could not afford to join both organisations. National Farmers' Union officers perceived a connection between the Tithepayers' Association and the Fascists. At one meeting a speaker warned 'the Blackshirts did not care whether a person paid his tithe or not, it was only a political move and farmers should see what was behind it'. Another claimed the Tithepayers' Association 'was going to get the Blackshirts to help them and it was all very spectacular, but how much further forward were they?' At Bideford it was said 'I know this is a ticklish subject but I think as farmers if we are going to tackle this problem we must do it ourselves. If we accept the help of these Blackshirts we are accepting an obligation, and it is an obligation perhaps one day they will call on us to repay.'[283] In the South Hams in April Mr James of Modbury, who in February had volunteered to be the secretary of the Tithepayers' Association branch, declared he was against demonstrations and law breaking.[284] South Devon's low level of activity may be linked to this meeting.

On May 4th there was a joint meeting of the two groups at Exeter and it ended with the Tithepayers' Association leaving the hall *en bloc*. There was allegedly a misunderstanding over the meeting's purpose and how public it was intended to be. The Tithepayers' Association also seized the initiative by holding a public debate at

Tiverton with the Chairman of Queen Anne's Bounty, responsible for the administering of tithes, before 400 farmers. By April more than 375 farmers in North Devon and around Newton Abbot were refusing to pay tithes.[285] A local battle had ensued between the Tithepayers' Association and the National Farmers' Union.

Another development escalated tensions and must have been seen as a direct challenge to the National Union of Farmers. In the early months of 1934 the party announced it was forming the British Union of Farmers. In January in the nearby Cornish town of Bodmin, Plathen urged the forming of a branch. The organisation, he explained, would only comprise farmers, set out a policy for the benefit of farmers and be non-political but be supported by the Fascist party. He said Fascists would provide the 'necessary spirit and go so that the farmers could get on with the job themselves. Joining the British Union of Farmers carried no obligation to become a Fascist. The subscription was five shillings a year and all legal assistance would be given free'. Most significantly, the man chosen to serve as Hon. Secretary also held similar posts in the National Farmers' Union and in the Cornwall branch of the National Tithepayers' Association.[286] In February the Fascists had a meeting at Liskeard and the *Western Independent* reported, under the headline 'Cornish Farmers Go Fascist', that R. Sanders, former Chairman of the National Farmers Union at Liskeard, and several other farmers had joined the British Union of Farmers.[287] Also that month a meeting was held in Truro where Propaganda Officer Cann spoke. The chairman was H. Dunn of Mevagissey and Mr Johns, Honorary Secretary of the Cornish section of the British Union of Farmers, was also present.[288] There was also a meeting about the new Union at Bideford in February.[289]

In early January 1934 the dispute at Trevarrion Farm in north Cornwall resumed. Bailiffs arrived to seize furniture from a locked room but it had mysteriously disappeared. Mr Lobb, the farmer, telephoned the Fascists in Plymouth for help and two hours later four Blackshirts arrived in 'a fast car'. The bailiffs were however thwarted and left without any property to seize. One Blackshirt was left to guard the farm.[290]

Barnstaple and Alverdiscott, 1934

After an interlude of five weeks the dispute resumed at Stoney Cross in the village of Alverdiscott near Bideford. In early January bailiffs acted on a County Court order and distrained Frederick Chipman's furniture. Shortly afterwards, on the 12th, four Blackshirts arrived from Plymouth early in the morning; *Fascist Week* reported an urgent call had been made for help and members rushed to North Devon. Another large contingent, in their Plymouth lorry, subsequently came to the farm. It was reported 'further excitement was caused in the ordinarily peaceful little village early yesterday by the arrival of members of the British Union of Fascists'. Chipman insisted the furniture belonged to his housekeeper, a relative. Several days later the bailiffs left the house in charge of three men brought in from Bideford Employment Exchange but they left, according to the Fascists who maintained a heavy presence at the farm, when they were told 'of the nature of their task, which they did not relish, being cold, in darkness and not being allowed to smoke'. The court order expired the following morning and the Registrar of the County Court, accompanied by officials, a police superintendent, inspector and sergeant arrived to find furniture valued at £125 and a cow worth £25 had disappeared. The Fascists were housed in an adjoining garage and blocked access to the house with stakes and barbed wire except the rear entrance. The bailiffs gave up their action but the dispute remained unsolved.[291]

At this time a meeting was held of the North Devon branch of the Tithepayers' Association. The branch had grown to 509 members since November 1932. The Barnstaple audience heard Richard Plathen claim Devon's recent tithe disputes were the first the Fascists had taken part in and that 'when they went to Mr Brown's farm at Halwill they had no previous experience in a Tithe War.' After Halwill he revealed party members 'were called to Exeter and to Cornwall. The Blackshirts had a very bad reputation!' Afterwards, he said, the men were involved at Kingsteignton.[292] Plathen's comments indicate the Fascists' skirmish in Devon in September 1933 was the first in the country. However, a few months beforehand, in August, they had already camped at a farm in Suffolk where they also erected defensive barricades.[293]

What also makes the meeting noteworthy was an astounding comment made by Chipman in his role as Honorary Secretary. When referring to Buckland Brewer and Alverdiscott in 1933 he stated:

> *We gratefully recognise the valuable help that has been given us by the British Union of Fascists. Although not invited by the Association they came along and rendered help. We now want a band of men to attend and be ready to help the Blackshirt because a raid may be attempted at any time and we must be prepared.*[294]

Mr Manaton, the editor of *The North Devon Journal,* noted the importance of the comment: Chipman was also a secretary of the Labour Party. Manaton pointed out the Fascists were against democracy and wrote 'perhaps Mr Chipman does not regard these amiable young gentlemen with plenty of time on their hands as being really the advance party of an army on the march . . . it is a shrewd move on the part of the Fascists to champion the tithe payer – but they are doing it in order to propagate fascism.'[295] Chipman immediately wrote 'I am in a burning house, requiring help: the only man willing to give me help wears a black shirt, I suppose I must not accept his offer of help because he has on a black shirt? I ask, what would you do?' Nevertheless, a few months later Chipman resigned from his position in the North West Division of the Labour Party and protested 'he had been called a Fascist but that was no fault of his and he was as strong a Labour man today as ever'. Curiously, he claimed Labour papers were lost in a recent police raid. The newspaper editor also received a visit from the Devon Chairman of the Association, Mr A. Turner, who disclaimed any official relationship between his association and the Blackshirts.[296]

In at least one other part of the country, Suffolk, there were similar suggestions of cooperation. An Association officer denied any ties in February but noted whatever individuals did was their own business. Curiously, in an echo of Chipman's comment, he said 'there is an old saying that a drowning man will clutch at any straw'.[297] Whether farmers were burning or drowning Blackshirts were ready to help. The denial of any official link is interesting. Less than two months previously Turner had explained the situation slightly differently in a meeting at Launceston in North Cornwall held to establish a local branch of the Tithepayers' Association. Turner responded to a question by Plathen that 'since the Blackshirts had come into prominence in this part of the country as a completely new political organisation, and whose activities had coincided with theirs, some people, particularly in North Devon, thought there existed some sort of link between them. We are not linked together but I want to make it clear that we are working for the same end as far as tithes are concerned.'[298]

Two prominent officers of the Devon branches of the Association were also Blackshirts. W. A. Down of Sampford Peverell was Chairman of the Tiverton Tithepayers' Association[299] and Tiverton District Officer of the British Union. He often spoke at farmers' meetings in connection with tithes.[300] Another Fascist, Frederick S. Hooper of Hartnoll Farm near Tiverton, spoke at meetings in South Molton, Chulmleigh and on another occasion sent a message to a meeting at Landkey. Hooper resigned as Chairman of the Conservative Association of Halberton in April and announced he had joined the Fascist movement. Two weeks later he wrote in his local paper there were only two choices in politics; communism or fascism.[301]

The party's level of activity amongst farmers and the acceptance by many of them of the Blackshirts' policy of violent resistance was indicated in comments by the Secretary of the Newton Abbot branch of the Devon Tithepayers' Association on the 12th of February. At a meeting in Modbury he said 'when distraint is made on a farmer in North Devon again he will have a strong body of men behind him and there will be bloodshed, and until there is we shall not get justice.' He also commented that the Suffragettes had had to fight their battles by unconstitutional means and they would have to do the same. He summed up 'the Fascists have chucked a rope to the farmer and we are pulling him out.' The Devon Association then had some 1,000 members.[302]

The intervention of the Fascists at Alverdiscott clearly created waves. The mayor of Barnstaple was a vocal opponent. At the annual meeting of the Devon Closewool Sheep Breeders' Society

Councillor Dart expressed the view 'there was no sincerity whatsoever in their actions, it was no business of theirs. They had no right to associate themselves with it in any shape or form, and he thought the quicker the tithe payers realised that the better.'[303] Yet not long afterwards, in early March, the Fascists held their first meeting in Barnstaple. They met at the Pannier Market and it was reported there was good attendance. The speaker was Alfred Cyril Cann who had come up from Plymouth along with another dozen Fascists from their headquarters. Cann introduced the new party to Barnstaple and explained socialism came from nineteenth-century Germany, liberalism from eighteenth-century France and Conservatism from the Stone Age. After a general discussion, which included questions from two county justices and two members of Barnstaple Town Council, it was announced a branch would shortly be established.[304] Another meeting was held in May addressed by two national speakers, John Beckett and Thomas Moran, again at the Pannier Market. It reportedly attracted a large audience which was quiet and attentive.[305] Apparently there was no organised opposition similar to that at Plymouth. However, letters began to appear in *The North Devon Journal* opposing the Fascists, notably by R. H. Baker of Braunton, and the local organiser, Ion Murdoch of Trentishoe, was one of those who responded.[306] The political ground in North Devon was being prepared for the visit of Sir Oswald Mosley in October.

Kingsteignton and Newton Abbot, 1934

The incident at Bickington in December 1933 had an epilogue. In mid-February the Blackshirts instigated summonses alleging cruelty to animals against Registrar of Newton Abbot County Court Maurice A. Mathew, Police Inspector Francis Coppin of Newton Abbot and two County Court bailiffs.[307] They were heard at Newton Abbot Police Station on the 20th. Two local newspapers covered the case in great detail and noted a crowded courtroom listened 'with rapt interest' for five hours. The information for the summons was given by the Devon Propaganda Officer for the Blackshirts. The prosecutor was under instructions from H. Stidston Broadbent, a Plymouth

Fascist,[308] on behalf of a London firm. Each summons was dismissed.

Alfred Cann claimed the prosecution was a private matter and had nothing to do with the British Union of Fascists. Broadbent's involvement may have raised some eyebrows and the defence lawyer, Mr Laskey, spent considerable time in court suggesting the case was being pursued for political purposes. Laskey stated 'it must be known that these proceedings have been fomented, got up and brought solely by a political organisation and with no desire to alleviate suffering.' Cann refused to disclose his source of funding but Laskey spent considerable time discussing the use of tithe disputes to publicise fascism.

The case revealed odd insights into the local party. Under questioning Cann described himself as a lecturer and stated his activities as Propaganda Officer were merely a part-time hobby. At one point Laskey referred to the senior Blackshirt present during the dispute, Richard Adolf Plathen, as Herr Adolf Plathen and described the Blackshirt movement as an organisation of 'foreign titles, foreign war cries, foreign uniforms and foreign methods of saluting. If such political methods are to be adopted in this country I think we should prefer them to be done in the English way.' Laskey was successful in showing the military aspect of the Fascists; one member, Cornelius Carroll of Edgecombe Place at West Hoo in Plymouth, admitted during the dispute he was under orders from Plathen and as part of a crowd of Blackshirts at the farm he told a policeman 'we won't move; we only take our orders from our officer'.[309] The prosecution failed but the case generated much publicity.

Buckland Brewer, 1934

Stibb Cross, the site of the Fascist victory in Devon's Tithe War in 1933, also resumed in 1934. This little hamlet between Great Torrington and Bideford again became newsworthy.

On May 24th twelve cattle were seized at Holwell Farm. Six days later, on the night of Thursday, the 30th of May, 'an atmosphere of tension' set in with rumours of imminent disorder. It was said the 'usually peaceful little hamlet' had not seen such activity since the Civil War when Cromwell's army had camped nearby. A large number of men and women, many of 'the labouring class', had come by car or bicycle to gather near a field where the cattle had been impounded. The number of protesters reported by local newspapers ranged from 100 to 600. It was estimated by one farmer, a Blackshirt, that nearly 1,000 farmers were at the farm during the dispute. The *Express & Echo* reported some had a genuine protest against tithes and others were there 'just for fun'. Gangs, carrying sticks, paraded the narrow road adjoining the field and shortly after midnight there was a skirmish with a large number of policemen, up to sixty men according to one report, who had been called in from throughout North Devon. Bailiffs and policemen were on duty for six days and a caravan was brought in for use as living quarters and their number was increased that day. Every few yards along the narrow road from Stibb Cross to Clovelly one or more policeman was stationed. Other patrols were on motorcycles in the immediate area. Blows were struck but the police managed to clear the road. The labourers reassembled at the top of the village and the police rushed them to clear the area. The crowd was given five minutes to disperse and by 1 am nearly all had left. There was one further attempt to enter a field but this failed when the police, who had parked their cars facing this direction, switched on the car lights to reveal the intruders. The police were left in peace to watch over the animals for the rest of the night. The following night was calmer but there was still a substantial crowd; some 150 people gathered to parade the main road.

The local paper, *The Bideford Gazette*, commented previously 'the Blackshirts or Fascists were much in evidence but it is noteworthy that up to yesterday none had put in an appearance, at least no black shirts were visible anywhere'.[310] They had a heavy presence in autumn 1933. However, they abandoned the final dispute with the sole exception of Hooper of Tiverton who addressed between 200 and 300 farmers at the farm. Oddly, one man was found by the police 'creeping about' in the road with his face blackened. He had done this, he said 'for a bit of fun'.[311] Thirteen bailiffs and a strong force of police guarded the animals the following day. The dispute ended when the livestock was put in a lorry and sent to London via Torrington Station.[312]

Mr Brown's final costs were high: he paid more than £70 in penalties and must have wondered about the Fascists' earlier triumphal march. Their lack of support was partly due to the arrest of the coordinator, Richard Plathen, in Sussex in March. He had agitated at a farm near Worthing in February and was supported by a contingent of Fascists estimated to be as many as 200 men. The police were more heavy-handed than in Devon and forced many Fascists from the area. However, nineteen party members were charged, Plathen among them, and they pleaded guilty to unlawful conspiracy to erect a public mischief. Plathen duplicated tactics in Devon: they barricaded the farm, dug ditches and pits, and cut down trees to lie across roads.[313] It may have been Plathen, or more likely Mosley, who decided the party could not risk conflict with the police and left the farmers to face them on their own. Mosley was willing to engage in violence but did not want to challenge the law.[314] In November 1933 a Manaton woman raised this same issue. Violet Francis, a member of the Imperial League of Fascists, one of the rival Fascist parties, wrote to *The Western Morning News* in response to another letter questioning why Fascists would involve themselves in public disorder. She stressed her party would never 'mix themselves up with anything like anti-tithe agitations which is entirely outside their province' but was instead formed to maintain law and order.[315] Plathen responded his party maintained law and order in farms by organising 'leaderless mobs' of farmers.[316]

A former official at Plymouth Branch later stated national headquarters ordered the branch to pull out of all tithe agitation.[317] Mosley wanted to save the country from disorder, not be the cause of it. Possibly he regarded the price of supporting the farmers, in placing party members in direct confrontation with the police, was too high. It appears by May 1934 the Fascists gave up on the tithe dispute, at least locally. Three years later Plathen was the organiser for Scotland and retained some interests in agriculture: he addressed a group of farmers at Berwick in 1937 but the meeting was reportedly a fiasco: it attracted an audience of himself, one Fascist and two reporters. The party's appeal to farmers had diminished.[318]

There was also another reason for the Fascists' disappearance. The second Stibb Cross fight coincided with the Olympia Rally and the party's hierarchy were focusing on that national event. They would almost certainly not have had time to support farming in north-west Devon and instead were drafting members from around the country to Olympia.[319]

Brown could have read of these events in *The Bideford Gazette*[320] and realised he was bereft of Fascist help and left to face the bailiffs supported only by fellow farmers. The consequences for the British Union of Fascists was not recorded. It is more than likely farmers felt let down after promises of firm and continual support.

Goodleigh, 1934

The Chairman of the North Devon branch of the Tithepayers' Association also had a court summons served against him. Albert Turner of Dean Farm in Goodleigh saw the bailiffs arrive just as he was leaving to give evidence in London regarding tithes. However, during this short dispute in October there was once again no sign of Fascist support nor that he asked for it.[321]

Notes

1 Stephen Dorril, *Black Shirt; Sir Oswald Mosley and British Fascism* (2006), 224.
2 Dorril, *Black Shirt*, 228-9.
3 *Western Independent*, 3 December 1933.
4 *Okehampton Post*, 23 September & 2 December 1933.
5 Dorril, *Black Shirt*, 247.
6 Dorril, *Black Shirt*, 233, 245.
7 *The Western Fascist*, No. 8, 16–23 December 1933.
8 Dorril, *Black Shirt*, 235, 246.
9 The original copies are at Plymouth Central Library, 329/950. Other copies are at Torquay Library and the Westcountry Studies Library; Westcountry Studies Library, Ian Maxted, A History of the Book in Devon (unpublished manuscript); Ian Maxted, *From Script to print to*

hyper-text: two millennia of Devon's written heritage (2000), 24. The volumes are No. 2, 4–11 November 1933, No. 5, 25 November–2 December 1933, No. 8, 16–23 December 1933 and No. 16, 18 February 1934.

10 Westcountry Studies Library, Maxted, A History of the Book in Devon.

11 Richard Thurlow, *Fascism in Britain; From Oswald Mosley's Blackshirts to the National Front* (2006), 70; National Archives, HO144/20141. On 18 May 1934 the Earl of Iddesleigh was at the January Club.

12 *Royal Dockyard Gazette*, 5 July 1933.

13 National Archives, HO144/20142.

14 The contacts were G. Ellis, 85 South Street, Exeter, D. R. Street, 50 Egremont Road, Exmouth, C. W. R. Cann, Lockyer Street, Plymouth and Captain Spalding, The Birks, Torquay: Blackshirt, No. 36, December 30 1933–January 5 1934.

15 *Blackshirt*, No. 26, 14-20 October 1933. He was employed by the post office and wrote that he had been told being a Fascist was incompatible with his work. A full account of his activities can be found at National Archives, HO45/25570.

16 *Blackshirt,* No. 36, December 30 1933–January 5 1934, No. 75, 28 September 1934, No. 38, 12-18 January 1934, No. 43, 16-22 February 1934, No. 44, February 23–March 1 1934, No. 48, 23-9 March 1934, No. 51, 13-19 April 1934. A Home Office report of April reported that Woolhouse was in charge of Falmouth: National Archives, HO144/20140.

17 *The Western Fascist*, No. 16, 18 February 1934.

18 *Blackshirt*, No. 61, 22 June 1934 & No. 62, 30 June 1934.

19 *The Okehampton Post*, 27 January 1934.

20 *The Okehampton Post*, 21 April 1934.

21 Dorril, *Black Shirt*, 252.

22 *Western Independent*, 3 June 1934.

23 The Peoples' History Museum, LP/FAS/34/30.

24 National Archives, HO144/20141.

25 *Blackshirt*, No. 63, 6 July 1934.

26 *Saltash Gazette*, 14 June 1934.

27 *Saltash Gazette*, 28 June 1934.

28 *Saltash Gazette*, 6 September 1934; *Western Evening Herald*, 1 September 1934; *Western Morning News*, 12 September 1934. S/B/O Mason was promoted to Deputy Branch Officer in January: Blackshirt, No. 39, 19-25 January 1934.

29 *Western Morning News*, 14 September 1934.

30 *Blackshirt*, No. 36, December 30 1933–January 5 1934.
31 The People's History Museum, LP/FAS/34/100, 386, 207, 206; *Blackshirt*, No. 69, 17 August 1934.
32 *Blackshirt*, No. 43, 16-22 February 1934.
33 *Blackshirt*, No. 60, 15 June & No. 80, 2 November 1934.
34 W. G. Hoskins, *Devon* (Newton Abbot, 1954), 530.
35 Western Independent, 23 July 1933.
36 National Archives, HO144/20140.
37 *Evening Herald*, 22 February 1978.
38 *Western Independent*, 5 November 1933.
39 Wasley, *Devon At War*, 8; *Western Independent*, 5 November 1933.
40 *The Western Fascist*, No. 2, 4–11 November 1933.
41 H. Lewis played for Plymouth Albion from 1924 to 1925: *Plymouth Albion RFC* (Plymouth, 1976), 14.
42 *Western Morning News,* 22 November 1933.
43 *Western Independent,* 23 July 1933.
44 *Western Morning News,* 21 July 1933.
45 *Western Independent,* 23 July 1933.
46 *Western Independent,* 30 July 1933.
47 *Western Evening Herald*, 4 August 1933.
48 *Western Independent*, 6 August 1933.
49 *Western Evening Herald*, 18 August 1933.
50 *Western Evening Herald*, 25 August 1933.
51 *Western Evening Herald*, 31 August 1933.
52 National Archives, HO144/19070.
53 *Western Evening Herald*, 23 September 1933.
54 *Western Evening Herald*, 23 September 1933; *Plymouth Herald*, 22 February 1978.
55 *Western Independent*, 17 September 1933. The two men were noted in a report of the *Western Morning News* of October 12 1933. Cann's home address was printed in the Plymouth Post Office Directory for 1933 but the Voter's List for the following year shows he had moved from his home: Plymouth Central Library, Plymouth Voters' List, Mutley Ward.
56 *Western Morning News,* 15 September 1933.
57 *Western Evening Herald*, 6 November 1933.
58 *Western Independent*, 5 & 26 November 1933.
59 Stephen Dorril, *Black Shirt; Sir Oswald Mosley and British Fascism* (2006), 43-4, 51, 238; Karen J. Musolf, *From Plymouth to Parliament, a rhetorical history of Lady Astor's 1919 campaign*

(1999), 50, 184. He spoke at Mutley Baptist School, Lower Compton School, Palace Street Schools, Cattedown Road Schools and Lockyer Hall in November.

60 Maurice Collis, *Nancy Astor, an informal biography* (1960), 180-92; John Griggs, *Nancy Astor* (Feltham, 1982), 152.

61 Plymouth & West Devon Record Office, 186/18/44.

62 *Western Morning News*, 17 October 1934.

63 *Western Independent*, 17 December 1933.

64 *Western Independent*, 17 December 1933.

65 *Western Independent*, 17 December 1933.

66 *Western Morning News*, 30 December 1933.

67 *The Western Fascist*, No. 8, page 5.

68 *Blackshirt*, No. 38, January 12-18 1934.

69 Robert Benewick, *Political Violence & Public Order* (1969), 31, 240; Richard Thurlow, *Fascism in Britain; From Oswald Mosley's Blackshirts to the National Front* (2006), 34, 72; Thomas P. Lineham, *East London for Mosley; The British Union of Fascists in East London and South-West Essex, 1933–40* (1996), 117; Dorril, *Black Shirt*, 251; National Archives, HO144/20158.

70 *Devon & Exeter Gazette*, 7 March 1934. Similar warnings were given by another speaker at *Nottingham: Western Evening Herald*, 6 August 1934.

71 *Paignton Observer & Echo*, 7 June 1934; Dorril, *Blackshirt*, 250-1.

72 For instance, see *Western Morning News*, 5 November 1934 & *Express & Echo*, 18 September 1933.

73 *Action*, 12 February 1938.

74 *Tiverton Gazette*, 19 June 1934.

75 *Devon & Exeter Gazette*, 16 July 1934; *Western Morning News*, 20 July 1934.

76 *The Sidmouth Observer*, 14 February 1934.

77 *The Bideford Gazette*, 6 March 1934.

78 *Western Morning News*, October 1934.

79 *Western Independent*, 7 October 1934.

80 *Western Morning News*, 10 & 12 July 1934. The speakers were Captain J. F. Finn and Mr G. Easterbrook; Benewick, *Political Violence*, 289-90.

81 *Western Morning News*, 14 July 1934.

82 *The Crediton Chronicle*, 18 October 1934.

83 Devon & Cornwall Constabulary Museum, A2004.01930, 23 February 1934.

84 *Western Morning News*, 7 March 1934.
85 *Western Morning News,* 2 February 1934.
86 Dorril, *Blackshirt,* 250.
87 *Blackshirt*, No. 37, January 5-11 1934.
88 *Blackshirt*, No. 38, January 12-18 1934.
89 *The Western Fascist,* No. 16, 18 February 1934.
90 *Western Morning News,* 9 February 1934.
91 *Blackshirt,* No. 42, 9-15 February 1934 & No. 43 16-22 February 1934.
92 *The Western Fascist*, No. 16, 18 February 1934.
93 *Blackshirt,* No. 41, 9-15 February 1934.
94 National Archives, HO144/20140.
95 National Archives, HO144/20140.
96 *The Western Fascist,* No. 16, 18 February 1934.
97 *Western Morning News*, 16 February 1934.
98 *Blackshirt,* No. 45, 2-8 March 1934.
99 *Western Morning News*, 23 February 1934.
100 National Archives, HO144/19070.
101 *Blackshirt,* No. 45, 2-8 March 1934.
102 *Western Morning News*, 2 March 1934.
103 *Blackshirt,* No. 46, 9-15 March 1934.
104 *Western Morning News,* 9 March 1934.
105 *Western Morning News*, 6 April 1934; *The Bideford Gazette*, 10 April 1934; *Fascist Week*, No. 23, 13-19 April 1934.
106 *Western Independent,* 8 April 1934. A. K. Chesterton responded with a letter on the defence force on the 15th. In January S/C/O Bowden was promoted to be Company Officer from January 5: *Blackshirt,* No. 39, January 19-25, 1934.
107 *Blackshirt,* No 51, 13-19 April 1934.
108 *Western Morning News,* 9 April 1934; *Western Independent*, 8 April 1934.
109 National Archives, HO144/20143.
110 *Western Morning News,* 27 April 1934.
111 National Archives, HO144/20143.
112 *The Fascist Week*, – May 1934. Unit Leader Connolly had been promoted to be Section Leader in January: *Blackshirt,* No. 39, 19-25 January 1934.
113 *Western Independent,* 6 May 1934.
114 *Western Independent,* 29 April & 6 May 1934.
115 *Blackshirt,* No. 53, 27 April–3 May 1934.

116 *Blackshirt,* No. 53, 27 April–3 May 1934.
117 Plymouth & West Devon Record Office, 2834/76.
118 *Western Morning News*, 30 May & 1 June 1934; National Archives, HO144/29143; *Western Independent,* 6 May 1934; Nigel Todd, *In Excited Times* (Whitley Bay, 1995), 35.
119 *Western Morning News*, 28 May 1934.
120 *Western Morning News*, 1 June 1934.
121 *Western Morning News*, 10 July 1934.
122 National Archives, HO144/20143.
123 *Express & Echo*, 13 June 1934.
124 *Western Independent,* 17 June 1934.
125 *Blackshirt,* No. 61, 22 June 1934.
126 *Western Independent,* 17 June 1934.
127 *Blackshirt,* No. 61, 22 June 1934 & No. 62, 30 June 1934.
128 *Western Independent*, 17 June 1934.
129 *Blackshirt,* No. 63, 6 July 1934.
130 *Western Independent,* 17 June 1934.
131 *Western Independent,* 28 January 1934. Miss Spurrell had spoken at a meeting of the ILP at Newton Abbot in January 1934.
132 *Western Morning News*, 6 September 1934; Western Evening Herald, 5 September 1934.
133 National Museum of Labour History, LP/FAS/34/99.
134 National Museum of Labour History, LP/FAS/34/99i; LP/FAS/34/4i.
135 *Western Independent*, 17 June 1934.
136 National Archives, HO144/20141.
137 *Western Independent,* 17 June 1934.
138 *Blackshirt,* No. 74, 28 September 1934.
139 *Blackshirt,* No. 76, 5 October 1934.
140 *Western Independent*, 30 September 1934; Plymouth & West Devon Record Office, 2834/76.
141 Benewick, *Political Violence*, 265.
142 *Western Evening Herald*, 28 September 1934.
143 *Western Independent,* 7 October 1934.
144 *Western Evening Herald*, 1 October 1934.
145 I am grateful to Frank Gent for this information.
146 *Western Evening Herald*, 3 October 1934.
147 *Western Morning News*, 16 November 1934.
148 Benewick, *Political Violence*, 96, 115; Dorril, *Black Shirt*, 323, 229-30, 411, 515. A special Branch report of 17 December 1934

discussed Piercey's relationship with Mrs Joyce: National Archives, HO144/20144.

149 *Blackshirt*, No. 77, 17 October 1934.
150 *Western Morning News*, 6 October 1934.
151 *Western Morning News*, 8 October 1934; North Devon Journal, 11 October 1934.
152 *Western Evening Herald*, 8 October 1934.
153 *Western Independent*, 7 October 1934.
154 *Western Independent*, 14 October 1934.
155 *Western Independent*, 14 October 1934.
156 The *Western Weekly*, 20 October 1934.
157 *Western Morning News*, 12 & 13 October 1934; *Express & Echo*, 12 October 1934.
158 The *Western Evening Herald*, 15 & 15 November 1934.
159 *Western Evening Herald*, 15, 11 & 13 October 1934
160 *Western Morning News*, 17 November 1934. Mills gave his address as 2 Melrose Road, Smithfields and Piercy of 7 Cumberland Road, Barnes.
161 *Western Morning News*, 8 October 1934.
162 Thomas P. Lineham, *East London for Mosley; The British Union of Fascists in East London and South-West Essex, 1933–40* (1996), 171.
163 *Devon & Exeter Gazette*, 17 November 1934.
164 *Western Morning News*, 13 October 1934; Western Independent, 7 October 1934.
165 Nigel Copsey, *Anti-Fascism in Britain* (Basingstoke, 2000), 23-4.
166 *Western Morning News*, 17 October 1934.
167 *The Times*, 23 October & 10 November 1934
168 *Devon & Exeter Gazette*, 17 November 1934.
169 *Blackshirt*, No. 79, 26 October 1934.
170 *Western Independent*, 2 December & 14 October 1934.
171 *Blackshirt*, No. 81, 16 November 1934.
172 *Western Independent*, 2 December 1934.
173 Dorril, *Black Shirt*, 323-6; Dave Renton, *Fascism, Anti-Fascism and Britain in the 1940s* (Basingstoke, 2000), 16-18.
174 *Western Independent*, 2 December 1934.
175 National Archives, HO144/20142.
176 Hoskins, *Devon*, 527.
177 *The Exmouth Journal*, 12 August 1933.
178 *The Exmouth Journal*, 26 August 1933.
179 *The Exmouth Journal*, 16 September 1933.

180 Devon Record Office, Voters' List, Exmouth, 1933.
181 *The Exmouth Journal*, 23 September 1933.
182 *The Exmouth Journal*, 30 September & 4 November 1933.
183 The Exmouth Chronicle, 29 July, 26 August, 23 September, 30 September, 28 October 1934.
184 *The Exmouth Journal*, 4 & 11 November 1933.
185 *The Exmouth Journal,* 25 November 1933.
186 *The Exmouth Journal*, 10 December 1933.
187 *The Exmouth Journal*, 16 September 1933.
188 *Blackshirt,* No. 48, 23-9 March 1934.
189 *The Exmouth Journal*, 3 & 24 March, 21 April 1934.
190 *The Western Morning News*, 25 September 1934.
191 Hoskins, Devon, 533.
192 David Baker, *Ideology of Obsession: A. K. Chesterton and British Fascism* (1996), 73-6, 83-6, 107. Chesterton's successor was appointed in August 1934: *Torquay Times*, 11 August 1934.
193 *The Torquay Times,* 29 March 1929.
194 Baker, Ideology, 74, 121.
195 *The Torquay Times*, 12 May 1933. Spalding moved to Edghill, Meadford Lane in 1935.
196 *The Torquay Times*, 16 June 1933.
197 *The Torquay Times*, 25 August 1933.
198 *British Lion*, No. 11, January 1933.
199 Hoskins, Devon, 524.
200 *The Totnes Times*, 24 March 1934.
201 *Blackshirt*, No. 49, 30 March–5 April 1934.
202 *Western Morning News*, 2 November 1933.
203 *Paignton News – Brixham & Preston Chronicle*, 28 April 1934 & 2 June 1934; *Paignton Observer and Echo*, 7 June 1934; *Totnes Times*, 9 June 1934; *Blackshirt*, No. 55, 11-17 May 1934.
204 *Western Evening Herald*, 2 January 1935.
205 Blackshirt, No. 51, 13-19 April 1934. A Home Office report that month also noted a branch at Torquay: National Archives, HO144/20140.
206 The Peoples' History Museum, LP/FAS/34/293i.
207 Hoskins, *Devon*, 527, 530.
208 *Express and Echo*, 15 December 1933.
209 *Western Morning News*, 15 December 1933.
210 *Express and Echo*, 19 December 1933.
211 National Archives, HO144/21064.

212 *The Fascist Week*, 13-19 April 1934.
213 *Express & Echo*, 22 February 1934.
214 *Express & Echo*, 26 February 1934; *Western Morning News*, 27 February 1934.
215 *Express & Echo*, 16 January 1934. Ellis had been District Acting Officer but this was removed from him by the first week of January: *Blackshirt,* No. 37, January 5-11, 1934.
216 *Express & Echo*, 4 January 1935.
217 *Besley's Directory of Exeter*.
218 National Museum of Labour History, LP/FAS/34/55i.
219 *Blackshirt,* No. 48, 23-9 March 1934.
220 National Archives, HO144/21064.
221 Dorril, *Black Shirt*, 288.
222 Dorril, *Black Shirt*, 286.
223 *The Exmouth Journal,* 3 March 1934; *Pulman's Weekly*, 27 February 1934.
224 Hoskins, Devon, 524.
225 National Archives, HO45/23673.
226 *The Sidmouth Herald & Directory*, 3, 10 & 24 February, 3 10 & 17 March, 14 April and 19 May 1934; *The Sidmouth Observer*, 13 December 1933.
227 *Blackshirt,* No. 42, 9-15 February 1934.
228 *The Kingsbridge Gazette,* 6 July 1934; Census for 1901, William Ellis lived then at 61 Fore Street.
229 The Peoples' History Museum, LP/FAS/34/289i.
230 The Peoples' History Museum, LP/FAS/34/292.
231 *Blackshirt,* No. 60, 15 June 1934.
232 *Fascist Week*, No. 20, 23-9 March 1934.
233 *Blackshirt,* No. 48, 23-9 March 1934.
234 National Archives, HO144/20140.
235 The Peoples' History Museum, LP/FAS/34/290 & 291i.
236 *The Tiverton Gazette*, 8 May 1934.
237 The Peoples' History Museum, LP/FAS/34/294.
238 *Blackshirt,* No. 48, 23-9 March 1934.
239 *Blackshirt,* No. 74, 28 September 1934. Stanley Ion Murdoch was listed as a boarding house proprietor at Trentishoe: *Kelly's Directories*, 1935 and 1939. I am grateful to Margaret Reed for this information.
240 *Blackshirt,* No. 44, 23 February–1 March 1934.
241 *North Devon Journal,* 4 October 1934.

242 *North Devon Herald*, 11, 25 October & 18 January 1934.
243 *North Devon Journal,* 11 October 1934
244 *North Devon Journal,* 25 October 1934.
245 *Western Evening Herald*, 29 November 1934.
246 *North Devon Journal*, 25 October 1934; *Kelly's Directory*, 1939.
247 *North Devon Journal,* 4 & 18 October 1934, 8 November 1934.
248 *Western Evening Herald*, 8 November 1933. It was also reported in the *Express & Echo* on 10 November 1933.
249 *Pulman's Weekly*, 21 November 1933.
250 *Blackshirt*, No. 65, 20 July 1934.
251 *Fascist Week*, No. 11, 29–25 January 1934; Dorril, *Black Shirt,* 271.
252 Benewick, *Political Violence*, 98-104; Richard Thurlow, *The Secret State; British Internal Security in the Twentieth Century* (Oxford, 1994), 182; Renton, *Fascism*, 20-1.
253 James Fox, *The Langhorne Sisters* (1998), 424-6.
254 *Western Morning News*, 6 October 1934.
255 Information supplied by the *Western Morning News* library.
256 *North Devon Journal,* 11 October 1934.
257 Dorril, *Black Shirt*, 250.
258 *Okehampton Post*, 17 June 1933.
259 *Okehampton Post*, 7 October 1933.
260 *The Western Times*, 13 October 1933.
261 Hoskins, *Devon*, 533, 524.
262 *The Bideford Gazette*, 17 October 1933; *North Devon Herald*, 11 October 1933; *North Devon Journal*, 12 October 1933. See also editions for the 26th of October and 2 November.
263 *The Bideford Gazette*, 17 October 1933.
264 *The Bideford Gazette*, 17 October 1933; *North Devon Herald*, 26 October 1933; *North Devon Journal*, 31 May 1934; *Express & Echo*, 31 May 1934.
265 *The Western Fascist*, No. 5, 25 November–2 December 1933; Sheffield University, 119/A2/167.
266 *The Western Times*, 20 October 1933; *North Devon Herald*, 19 October 1933.
267 *The Western Times*, 22 October & 3 November 1933; *North Devon Herald*, 2 November 1933.
268 *The North Devon Herald*, 26 October 1933.
269 *The Bideford Gazette*, 31 October 1933.
270 *North Devon Journal*, 28 October 1933; *The Western Times*, 27 October 1933. Oxland also spoke at Stratton in Cornwall in April

1934 although no mention was made regarding his political affiliations: *The Bideford Gazette*, 10 April 1934.

271 *The Western Times*, 17 November & 1 December 1933.

272 *The Western Times*, 27 October 1933.

273 *The Western Times*, 1 December 1933.

274 *Western Morning News*, 22 November 1933 & 5 January 1934.

275 *The Western Times,* 22 & 24 November 1933; Hoskins, Devon, 523.

276 *Mid-Devon Advertiser*, 9 December 1933.

277 *Mid-Devon Advertiser*, 21 October 1933. The speaker was Mr G. C. Solby of Sandwich.

278 *Mid-Devon Advertiser*, 2 December 1933.

279 *Western Evening Herald*, 20 December 1933; *The Mid-Devon & Newton Times*, 16 & 23 December 1933; *The Times*, 21 February 1934.

280 *Fascist Week*, No. 8, 29 December 1933–4 January 1934.

281 *Western Independent*, 17 December 1933.

282 *The Times*, 21 February 1934.

283 *The Western Times*, 2 February & 26 January 1934.

284 *The Kingsbridge Gazette*, 16 February & 20 April 1934.

285 *The Tiverton Gazette*, 3 April 1934; *The Western Times*, 4 May 1934 & 29 March 1934.

286 *Fascist Week*, No. 19, 16 – 23 March 1934; *The Okehampton Post*, 27 January 1934. This was Mr Sam Johns of Tremeer in Lanivet.

287 *Western Independent*, 18 February 1934.

288 *Blackshirt*, No. 44, 23 February–1 March 1934.

289 *Blackshirt*, No. 44, 23 February–1 March 1934.

290 *Western Morning News*, 5 January 1934.

291 *North Devon Journal*, 11 & 18 January 1934. *North Devon Herald*, 18 January 1934; *Fascist Week*, No. 11, 19-25 January 1934.

292 *North Devon Herald*, 18 January 1934.

293 *Pulman's Weekly*, 15 August 1933.

294 *North Devon Journal*, 18 January 1934; *North Devon Herald*, 18 January 1934.

295 *North Devon Journal*, 18 January 1934.

296 *North Devon Journal*, 25 January 1934. Mr Turner had been concerned with campaigning for farmers since at least October 1926 when he chaired a meeting at Barnstaple: *The Western Times*, 22 October 1926; *The Bideford Gazette*, 1 May 1934.

297 *The Times*, 28 February 1934.

298 *Western Morning News*, 2 December 1933.

299 *North Devon Journal*, 4 July 1934; *Devon & Somerset News*, 7 September 1933.

300 For example, he spoke at Landkey in May 1935: *Express and Echo*, 29 May 1935.

301 *Tiverton Gazette*, 8 May 1934; *Devon & Exeter Gazette*, 4 May 1934; *The Crediton Chronicle*, 10 May & 15 November 1934; *Express & Echo*, 29 May 1935; *Tiverton Gazette*, 24 April & 8 May 1934. For some other letters see *Devon & Somerset News*, 31 August, 21 September, 12 October and 2 November 1933.

302 *Western Morning News*, 13 February 1934; *The Kingsbridge Gazette*, 16 February 1934.

303 *North Devon Journal*, 25 January 1934.

304 *North Devon Journal*, 15 March 1934.

305 *North Devon Journal*, 31 May 1934; *North Devon Herald*, 31 May 1934.

306 *North Devon Journal*, 14 June, 28 June & 12 July 1934. He also wrote to the *North Devon Herald*: 14 June 1934.

307 *The Totnes Times and Devon News*, 17 February 1934.

308 For example, see *Western Morning News*, 23 July 1934.

309 *Daily Gazette*, 21 February 1934; *The Times*, 21 February 1934; *Mid-Devon Advertiser*, 24 February 1934; *The Mid-Devon and Newton Times*, 24 February 1934.

310 *The Bideford Gazette*, 29 May 1934. Other reports appeared on 5 & 12 June.

311 *Western Morning News*, 30 May 1934; *Express & Echo*, 30 May 1934; *North Devon Journal*, 31 May & 14 June 1934; *Okehampton Post*, 9 June 1934.

312 *Express & Echo*, 1 June 1934.

313 John D. Brewer, Mosley's Men, *The British Union of Fascists in the West Midlands* (Aldershot, 1984), 117. Benewick, *Political Violence and Public Order*, 90; Dorril, *Blackshirt*, 250.

314 Dorril, *Black Shirt*, 409.

315 *Western Morning News*, 6 November 1933.

316 *Western Morning News*, 7 November 1933.

317 See page 203.

318 Benewick, *Political Violence*, 274-5.

319 Dorril, *Black Shirt*, 295-9.

320 *The Bideford Gazette,* 3 July & 6 March 1934.

321 *The Western Times*, 5 October 1934.

PART TWO

Fascism moves to Exeter, 1935 to 1939

Developments from 1935 to the Outbreak of War

1935

1935 was not merely a quiet year for fascism compared to the previous years but one with a phenomenal drop in political activity. It was no longer a new movement and was severely challenged by members from other parties.

The national party was reorganised because of a continuing crisis in membership. National headquarters closed and the building was sold. There were financial cuts and restrictions place on wearing the uniform; national headquarters dictated only those committed to door-to-door canvassing were entitled. This caused dissatisfaction in many urban branches but nothing is known about how Fascists in Devon reacted to this loss of uniforms. Money from Italy, the main source of financing, diminished and then increased once Mosley supported Mussolini's invasion of Abyssinia with the 'Mind

Britain's Business' Campaign which advocated staying out of Italy's involvement in Africa. The party presented this as a patriotic policy in Britain's own interests but the Home Office concluded it resulted from substantial covert funds from Mussolini. By the end of the year membership began to recover partly, it has been thought, as a result of the anti-war campaign.[1]

The issue which drew earlier local headlines rumbled on in Devon but the Fascist presence drew to a close. In late May 1935 there was a sale of distrained cattle in Landkey and both W. Down and F. S. Hooper, British Union members from near Tiverton, were on hand.[2] In June protest meetings took place after sales in the mid-Devon village of Chulmleigh of animals auctioned for non-payment of tithes. The main speaker was Mrs Rash, better known as the novelist Doreen Wallace. She had previously spoken to farmers in Somerset in 1933. In the audience was Captain Hammond, in uniform, who distributed copies of two Fascist publications, *Fascism to the Agricultural Worker* and *The Fascist Case Against Tithes*. Mrs Rash spoke at two sales about tithes and stated she was not a Fascist but agreed with them on tithes.[3] Hammond explained the party's views on agriculture and tithes but the issue was marginal in terms of fascism.

1936

In 1936 the party changed its name to the British Union of Fascists and National Socialists and had a new slogan 'If you love your country you are National, if you love her people you are a Socialist – Be A National Socialist'. This coincided with Mosley shifting the party's 'inspiration' from Italy to Germany which included even the choice of new uniforms for headquarters' staff of a coat, peaked cap, jackboots and an armband in red, white and black which was akin to Hitler's SS. Public apprehensions about Hitler were raised when his troops marched into the Rhineland but Mosley stressed there was no conflict between Hitler's union of German people and

Britain's future in empire. The party's main message was of peace with Europe. In 1936 Mussolini reduced his funding by more than two-thirds which created shortages only partly relieved by Nazi funds. Diana Guinness, then Mosley's main mistress, spent considerable time in Germany seeking financial assistance for the party. The party also adopted a more anti-Semitic tone, including plans to deprive British Jews of their citizenship, and largely concentrated efforts in building this as the major issue for support in London's East End where high-profile meetings and rallies took place. It unleashed a period of violent attacks on Jews in London but at one event, the famous Cable Street March, some 100,000 anti-Fascists turned out to demonstrate against the party. Within days of it Mosley married Lady Diana Guinness at the home of Josef Goebbels in Berlin, with Adolph Hitler in attendance. The wedding was kept secret from the British public. The year ended with a campaign to support King Edward VIII, who was attracted to fascism, shortly before he abdicated in December.[4] The loss of the king was a great blow for a party which had made loyalty to the monarch a main policy.

The party's focus was on events far from the West Country and Devon featured very little in propaganda. The general loss of publicity for the Fascists in newspapers makes it extremely difficult to discover the local state of the party. Nevertheless, the general situation can be ascertained along with the political climate in Devon. Speculation increased over war with Germany and war clouds were seen even from Devon. A good example of this was the flight of *Hindenberg* along the South Coast of Devon. Local people watched it pass.[5] Henry Williamson was on the North Devon coast when he saw it return from New York to Germany. He later wrote:

> *It was a wonderful sight! I could see the red emblem, with black swastika. It seems part of the summer sky, a cloud-phantom. 'Look!!' I said, to a man sitting near, blue reefer jacket and white flannels, Panama hat. 'The* Hindenberg*! Isn't she lovely?' They all stared into the sky over Morte Point. 'Humph!' said the man. 'Shouldn't be allowed to come over England like that, in my opinion. They're only spying, taking photographs for the next war'. 'But don't you think they*

> *might be feeling rather proud of showing their new airship to the English? They so earnestly want to be friends with us – just for the sake of old times' 'Well I'm damned if I'd trust them'.*[6]

The Western Morning News then had its 'waygoose', that is a sponsored staff outing, in early July to North Devon. The staff watched the vessel pass and one journalist noted 'details of her fabric, including the swastika on the rudder, were clearly observed'.[7] No doubt many of them recalled this sight as war drew closer and then when Nazi planes, with the same emblem, began to bomb local cities, towns and villages.

Williamson's political allegiances were made clear when he praised modern Germany at the Barnstaple Branch of the British Legion in February; a North Devon newspaper reported he said the Fascists were 'only putting their own house in order and, in his opinion, very efficiently'. Williamson concluded by explaining Nazi policies through a speech by Hitler.[8]

Concerns about war raised the spectre of enemy sabotage at Plymouth. The submarine L-54 had its main diesel engines tampered with at Devonport and MI5 was called in to investigate this incident as well as several others in other parts of the country. Five dockyard workers, allegedly with left-wing political sympathies, were later dismissed.[9] MI5 had other causes for concern in Devon. The previous year a German espionage agent had spent part of the summer in the county making notes of RAF bases. He was arrested and charged with offences against the Official Secrets Act. He served four years imprisonment.[10]

The dearth in newspaper reporting of fascism in 1936 is a great handicap but this is somewhat corrected by an amazing survival of a local collection of Fascist letters. The Saunders papers are the only ones of their kind: no other administrative papers for a Fascist District have yet been found for the rest of the country. The first letters begin in 1936 and reveal extraordinary details of the workings of the party in Devon. The papers themselves are principally concerned with Dorset but the originator, Robert Saunders of Friar Mayne Farm near Dorchester, worked closely with Rafe Temple Cotton, the lead Fascist organiser for Devon in the late

1930s. Saunders was appointed District Treasurer and subsequently District Leader for West Dorset. Of the surviving thousands of letters, books and pamphlets, more than 500 mention Devon. Following Saunders' death in 1993 they were deposited at the Special Collections and Archives of Sheffield University. Without these papers it would not be possible to understand the local state of the British Union of Fascists and National Socialists from 1936 to the outbreak of war. There is an Exeter bias in the letters which is understandable given the city's relative proximity to Dorchester. This is significant given Exeter was the chief focus of Fascist activities in these years. Even so, it would be useful to have more details of the party's workings in the late 1930s in other communities, particularly Torquay and Plymouth.

Photograph from Action of Rafe Temple Cotton as the party's Prospective Parliamentary Candidate for Exeter, 5 November 1936 (courtesy of Friends of Oswald Mosley).

1937

The year began for the British Union of Fascists and National Socialists with the Public Order Act on January 1st. The party had to make great changes: uniforms in public were banned as were controversial marches and public meetings, stewards were forbidden at open-air meetings and the party was demilitarised with a change of titles. It is thought the loss of uniforms gave the Fascists a less aggressive image which appealed to more middle-class voters. The result was that by the end of the year the number of members had increased. An acute financial crisis hung over the party's activities even with German and Italians funds. Michael Goulding, who had been sent in 1934 to agitate in Plymouth, became a British Union candidate for a council seat in London's East End. The campaign, with its heavy anti-Semitism and hundreds of meetings, dominated the party's activities. Even so, the party failed to win one seat. It has been suggested there was a great difference between the British Union's main focus in 1937, Jew-baiting in the East End, and the 'isolated, idealistic provincial Fascist branches' which were more interested in patriotism and found anti-Semitism embarrassing.[11] Yet there were many anti-Semitic party members in Devon such as Claude Duvivier of Woodbury who in 1937 was a founding member of The Link, a group which aimed for a German-British alignment.[12]

In March staff were cut from 143 to 30. All paid national speakers were dismissed; this had a considerable impact on Devon. They included prominent members John Beckett and William Joyce. Both had spent considerable time in Devon. This caused considerable dissention in the party and Joyce and Beckett shortly afterwards formed a new party, the National Socialist League. Although some members were bitter, the loss of Joyce would allow them later to distance themselves from him when he subsequently became notorious as Lord Haw Haw. Allegedly Joyce had informed Beckett that in any war between Germany and Britain he would fight with Germany because it was fighting against Jews.[13] In June the Metropolitan Police reported Mosley told his senior officers the movement's aim was to preserve its main strength in building contacts with workers and raise as much discontent as possible amongst them, possibly through covert help to the communists and other extreme elements.[14]

Events in Germany overshadowed the fortunes of British Fascists and their perception in the country. On April 16th the new German ambassador arrived at Torquay to inspect a German naval ship. Joachim von Ribbentrop was given a civic reception and stayed at the Imperial Hotel. In turn, the mayoral party was among a small group at dinner in the Marine Spa. Two days before his visit the

German sailors played a football match with Torquay United at Plainmoor and before kick-off the Germans gave the Nazi salute. The sailors repeated this when marching in the streets of Torquay and chanted 'Heil Hitler'.[15] In mid March there was a debate at Sidmouth on 'Dictatorship or Democracy' and Philip Donovan of the University College of the South West, later Exeter University, spoke in favour of dictators. Among his comments were 'Hitler was not out for his own ends'.[16]

By the middle of the year the party in great parts of the country, such as Liverpool, Manchester, Birmingham, Carlisle, South Wales and Lincolnshire, had no effective organisation.[17] Devon was, in comparison, fortunate in having Rafe Temple Cotton strenuously flying the flag in Exeter. One well-known Devon Fascist left the county. Henry Williamson moved to East Anglia[18] but continued to be a high-profile supporter. Finally, from November the British Union of Fascists and National Socialists became known as the British Union.[19]

1938

British Union began the year with further cutbacks and staff reductions. Membership was small with only 5,800 active members most of whom were in London. The party had become marginal in British politics and is thought to have lost working class support but an anti-war message appealed to the middle classes. Mosley's campaign to keep Britain out of war coincided with Hitler's march into Austria in March and his policy continued into 1939.[20]

The party adopted the Communist 'street-block-cell-system' in 1937 and this helped to build grass-roots support partly through the effort of members such as Branscombe's Rafe Temple Cotton. Membership began to grow and in Devon the party increased canvassing activities. British Union had been forced to diversify how it spread its message because it was largely denied public halls.[21] The Saunders papers reveal how the Blackshirts became innovative

Photographs probably taken by Rafe Temple Cotton of an outdoor meeting with Sir Oswald Mosley at Belmont Park, Exeter, date uncertain. The firm, Abbott & Munday located at 40-1 Clifton Road, can be seen on the edge of the park (Devon & Cornwall Constabulary Museum).

Masthead of Action, with stamp of the Exeter Branch headquarters (private collection).

but a few other sources, including Fascist publications, are also illuminating. 1938 was the year in which the party won its only election in any part of the country. In November it took a municipal seat in Suffolk: the party had 179 votes and won the fourth seat in a contest between five candidates. Interestingly, this was the area where tithe disputes had taken place four years previously.[22] In 1938 Exeter continued to be the centre of fascism but members in other parts of Devon were also active.

1939: the last eight months of peace

Anticipation of war polarised opinion on British Union. Some voters were attracted to the peace campaign but it convinced others the party was a front for Nazism. The highly publicised meetings with Hitler by the two Mitfords, Mosley's own wife, whom he admitted in November 1938 having married in 1936, and his sister-in-law Unity, further identified him and the party with German interests rather than Britain's own. Public anxieties were heightened with the Czechoslovakia invasion in March and the unveiling of the German-Soviet pact in August. Mosley's pacifist policy attracted new members and it is thought there were some 7,500 members in the provincial branches.[23] The sense of unease many members of the public felt about the loyalty of British Fascists to their own country can be understood when one reads a letter of March 1939 from Henry Jameson Dixon, a Fascist from Torquay, to H. R. Hoffman, head of a German propaganda agency in Munich. Dixon was free with his opinions and had he expressed them in Torquay they would have caused many fellow countrymen to question his allegiance:

> *The recent situation is great fun to we British Fascists. We see the funny side of the whole thing and the stupid fools we have to call a government. We hail with delight the way you have broken up 'the Jewish gang' in Czechoslovakia. Before our stupid democracy had time to swallow the shock the whole thing was all over. So much for prompt action, which has once again, thrown the warmongers into confusion. There is one consolation, Germany has countless true friends in Great Britain. If they try any war games on, it will be far different to 1914. Indeed, you may yet have time to come and help us, along with Italy and Spain, to clear up the SCUM... we are overjoyed with your English broadcasts. Let the lunatics have it, hot and strong. What you want now is to get some of our British Fascists to broadcast from Germany. I wish I had the opportunity.*[24]

His views on William Joyce's treasonable broadcasts a few months later are not recorded.

The number of Devon's Fascists is uncertain but the party was active. Exeter remained the centre with the organisation coordinated by Rafe Temple Cotton. There was one unusual event most likely associated with the anticipation of war. In April Ernest Fawcett Rover, then of Marldon Road in Torquay, was charged with vagrancy. He was on public relief having only recently arrived in the resort but he refused work. When answering the summons Rover stood up in court 'gave the Nazi salute and exclaimed *Heil Hitler*'. He subsequently remarked, in German, 'I am mute' which he translated for the court's benefit. Whether Rover was suffering from mental illness or was a Fascist is unknown. No connections have been found with British Union.[25]

By 1939 the party was associated with anti-Semitism but such views were not limited to it. The Conservative M.P. for Totnes, Major Ralph Rayner, made comments at Lustleigh which were heavily criticised as being discriminatory. He had expressed sympathy in early January for people driven out of their own countries and added:

> *no one deprecates an asylum to those who are flying from racial or political persecution, but it is a sentimental fallacy that because a man is a refugee from his own country he is a valuable addition to our numbers. The fact is that in Britain, and most especially in London, a host of foreigners have found homes who should never have been allowed in. Their ranks supply the drug traffickers, the keepers of low night-clubs, and an unduly proportion of the professional criminals in the capital. Even the more reputable foreigners soon forget that they have cause to be grateful to us. Without a qualm they elbow and intrigue Britons out of jobs and set up parasite trades such as pin-table saloons or bogus clubs that batten on the stupidity of our people.*[26]

Until 1939 anti-Semitism would have found little resonance in Exeter with its very small Jewish community. However, in April a small number of Jewish refugees were accommodated mainly in the University College. The Society of Friends provided a meeting room for them. Another woman worked as a domestic servant in Newton Poppleford.[27] Whether this small movement was used for political capital by Cotton is unknown.

There was increasing public talk of war through the year and Germany was a major topic of conversation. Allusions were made to Hitler in ways unthinkable when war broke out: the Reverend Johnstone, the vicar of St Marychurch at Torquay, announced a drastic need to reorganise his League of Youth and said he 'was going to be a bit of a Hitler that night'.[28] Efforts were made to influence public opinion. In April Lady Alexandra Harding, god-daughter of Queen Alexandra, came to Torquay to speak to the South Devon Debating Society. She was on a national tour to promote Germany. Her husband had been a member of the Grand

Council of the British Fascisti and she was a member of the Anglo-German Fellowship.[29]

One curious letter was written on April 22nd to Exeter's *Express & Echo*. The writer was the Marquess of Tavistock, whose family had been a major landowner in Exeter, and particularly in the town of Tavistock and West Devon, since the 1540s. His letter criticised the vicar of St David's parish for his definition of pacifism. The Marquess, the twelfth Duke of Bedford from 12 August the following year, was known for Fascist leanings and began a series of peace proposals to the Germans from September. What makes his letter particularly interesting is not that he publicly aired his views but that he did so in Exeter. He wrote from Sussex and is not known to have taken any particular interest in Exeter's affairs. It cannot be determined whether his own Fascist party, The British People's Party, formed the month Tavistock wrote his letter, was active in any part of Devon.[30]

The county's police continued to monitor foreign nationals and although talk of imminent war created suspicions of visitors from other countries the constabulary was only interested in the whereabouts of two men, who were both Americans, in connection with the Aliens Order of 1920. Cecil Dunn had landed without permission at Plymouth on the 4th of December and John Hector Subrenski alias Fisher had been released from H. M. Prison Exeter in February but had not been seen since. His last address was King's Hall, Longcombe near Totnes. *The Police Gazette* noted aliens from across the country transgressing the law but did not list any German or Italians connected with Devon.[31]

Exeter and the development of Devon

In October 1935 the Home Office determined Exeter Branch had only 14 members and 'the two branches are now disbanded. The few members hold occasional meetings. There has been no sign of increased activity and little or no interest is taken in the Movement, which is practically 'dead'.[32] The noting of two branches is curious. This may have included Exmouth. There were no other Devon reports but that year meetings were held in seven places although these appear sporadic. It would be difficult to argue the party's influence in 1935 had become anything but inconsequential. Captain Hammond of Kennerleigh, the county's Propaganda Officer, spoke at nearly every meeting. A telling piece of evidence is a note in *Blackshirt* that from March to May sales of Fascist literature in Devon had increased by thirty per cent. It is interesting no indication was given of what the sales were or how low they had been.[33]

National headquarters sent William Joyce to bolster the local scene in 1935 as well as 'the Black Prince'. This was the party's publicity car and it toured in the summer. Ilfracombe was intended to be visited on August 6, Torquay and Paignton on the 12th and Plymouth on the 13th. Westcountry members had donated the car[34] but what effect it had locally is not recorded.

There were only thirteen recorded Fascist meetings across Devon in 1935. The earliest received good local publicity. On the 30th of January the first meeting was held at Sampford Peverell in the War Memorial Hall. *The Tiverton Gazette* covered it with great enthusiasm; it printed a factual account of several thousand words detailing policies, notably on farming. The main speaker was Captain Hammond. In the audience were Frederick Hooper, W. Hawkins, H. Britton and 'a number of ladies'. Mr A. H. Down, a local farmer, was the chairman. The newspaper's headline was 'Britain First'.

Hammond admitted this was the village's first meeting but 'he could say definitely that it would not be the last. It was, he said, our intention to hold these meetings in town and village throughout the countryside until every man and woman, every boy and every girl is fully acquainted with the objects of our movement. What is the urge that causes these young men, who are the cream of our race, the stalwarts of our manhood, to stand flatfooted on the ground in face of organised hooliganism, and suffer physical violence at the hands of other men? It was a real awakening of the British spirit.'[35]

Hammond spoke across Devon. He was one of the two speakers on 6 June in the Crediton market place. The other was Assistant

Propaganda Officer R. J. Rodgers of Plymouth. They had an audience of about one hundred people.[36] As well as having William Joyce speak in Tiverton, there were two meetings in mid July and September at the Clock Tower. Hammond spoke on both occasions. In the autumn *Blackshirt* described the audience as large. It noted 'this rapidly increased to such a size that it blocked the traffic and the platform was accordingly removed to another pitch'.[37]

By late April Exeter's meetings were described as 'regular'. The only one known took place at Exe Bridge where Hammond and Rodgers spoke to a small audience.[38] On May 4th two hundred people heard Rodgers in Market Street. Curiously, a report in *Blackshirt* claimed growing interest amongst students from the University College of the South West, later Exeter University.[39] There was also a meeting in late September and Plymouth members travelled to hear the speaker.[40]

Anti-Fascist meetings continued in Barnstaple in 1935 judging from a complaint by Fascists in June[41] but there is no information on Fascist events in the town. Six months later, on December 5th, Hammond spoke at a public meeting in South Molton's market. Fascist literature was sold out.[42]

Finally, in addition to having William Joyce speak in October, Torquay was visited by Mrs Brock Griggs in early November. She also spoke in St Marychurch.[43]

William Joyce at Dorchester, Plymouth, Tiverton and Torquay

In 1935 the most prominent Fascist to visit the West Country was William Joyce and he spoke in Devon on three occasions. He also came to Dorchester in Dorset on January 28th when some 150 local people gathered in the Corn Exchange to hear him. Two years later he would be removed from the party and in 1945 was executed for his broadcasting as Lord Haw-Haw. The Dorchester meeting was peaceful. It attracted additional attention because the Fascists, both men and women, marched through the streets carrying banners and the Union Flag to the meeting.[44]

On March 28th Joyce spoke at Heathcoat Hall in Tiverton. The

WILLIAM JOYCE
(Director of Propaganda British Union of Fascists)
will Speak on
BLACKSHIRT POLICY
at the
HEATHCOAT HALL, TIVERTON
on
THURSDAY, 28th MARCH, 1935
at 7.30 p.m.

ADMISSION: 2/-, 1/- and 6d. Free Seating and Standing Room also available up to capacity of the Hall.
Reserved Tickets at 2/6 from Mrs. DOWN, Sampford Barton, Sampford Peverell
BRITAIN FIRST!

Advertisement for William Joyce's meeting at Tiverton (Tiverton Gazette, March 1935).

meeting was organised by Hammond and Captain Priestley at Plymouth.[45] Reserved tickets were available from Mrs Down, the wife of W. A. Down, at Sampford Barton in Sampford Peverell. The *Tiverton Gazette* covered it with a report of several thousand words and in great detail recorded Fascist policies. The report was glowing of the speaker.

The speech was a 'brilliant exposition of the policy of the British Union of Fascists'. Joyce spoke 'with eloquence and obvious sincerity for over 90 minutes' and held his audience's attention throughout a quiet hearing with the 'slight exception of one interruption'. There was 'at the end spontaneous and cordial applause [which] was a merited tribute from an attendance of all shades of political opinion to an oratorical *tour de force*'.

They heard the movement was one of patriotism and revolution and Joyce 'presented his points and criticism with moderation and fairness'. One topic was fascism's two enemies in communism and international Jewish finance. During an interval Hammond asked for questions but none were forthcoming. Dr E. Barrat Hines closed the meeting with a vote of thanks to Joyce and commented 'whether they agreed with him or not they owed him thanks for a very fair and fine address'. The meeting ended, as nearly every British Fascist meeting did, with singing the National Anthem. The paper noted it was exceptional by being 'rendered by all with unusual warmth of feeling'.[46]

In early July Joyce spoke at the Assembly Rooms in Devonport. *Blackshirt* reported the proprietor had been intimidated but still rented the hall to the Fascists. It noted he afterwards held a meeting with Plymouth Fascists, congratulated them on their work and reminded them the Communists had boasted no further Fascist meetings would be held in the port. This was the first public meeting to be held in Plymouth in more than six months. The police ban on street meetings remained.[47] Joyce may have spent some five weeks at Plymouth.[48]

Finally, on October 9th he came to speak in St Marychurch. *Blackshirt* reported 'the audience was attentive, the applause was frequent, and it was generally evident that the Fascist policy commanded the sympathy of those present'.[49]

The renewal of Exeter in 1936

A new chapter in Exeter fascism began in spring when the branch was reinvigorated three years after falling inactive in 1933. Captain Vincent Keens was sent from National Headquarters to help organise. Keens had been a party official in Newcastle-Upon-Tyne and in 1934 inspected and formed new branches throughout the country.[50] By 1936 he was Inspecting Officer Southern Administration. Initially he lived at 9 Powderham Crescent but by September moved to Bovey Tracey where he stayed with a farmer, T. F. T. Currer-Jones at Soldridge Farm. Currer-Jones was also a Fascist and advertised in *Action*. Keens was still there in January 1937.[51] Bovey Tracey had a small clique of Fascists during the war who caused concern to the Home Office and were on the list of those to be arrested if the country was invaded. It was Keens who interviewed Unity Mitford at Oxford in 1934 when she walked into the branch headquarters to join Mosley's Fascists.[52]

Keens reactivated the party in various ways, one of which was to meet each existing party member. The headquarters moved from 85 South Street to 7 Queen Street, near the Civic Hall, by late May but the party also used 22 South Street. Keens appears to have worked full-time in Exeter through to early 1937 and perhaps later. Exeter became Devon's centre of Fascist operations. In contrast, Plymouth had become inactive but in July Keens held an outdoor meeting there. This was, he noted, the first such meeting 'allowed for two years'.[53] The police must have felt there was no longer a danger of disorder.

One of Exeter's first activities in 1936 was a meeting by National Staff Officer Risden on electoral matters. Keens regarded him as an old friend and a 'great fellow' and on March 12th District Officers and Acting District Officers came to plan forthcoming election battles.[54] By early April there were outdoor meetings: 150 people attended one.[55] On a Saturday night in late July the branch held a sales drive. *Blackshirt* reported thirty-five papers were sold within an hour and the newspaper's circulation manager, F. D. Hill, 'and a party of London members on holiday lent a hand.'[56] In August Keens was 'rushed to death as usual' but told a colleague 'things going fine'.[57]

The next month he was even more upbeat in claiming 'we are beginning to make great strides in Exeter and surrounding districts'. A second national official arrived. On Saturday, September 19th, Bryan Donovan, the Acting Director General of Organisation, came to personally meet Devon's Fascists. This visit was, Keens felt, 'in the nature of another step forward'. He wrote 'next time – the Leader'. Exeter had firmly become the Fascist centre including in disseminating information: Robert Saunders noted in September 'Exeter was most interesting. I heard some astounding things from Donovan. I will tell you about them when I see you. They explain why the *Daily Mail* "dropped" fascism.'[58]

There was a sense of momentum felt by at least some party members. In October 1936 Saunders wrote to a colleague 'While we do not publish any figures I recently learnt the rough total of our membership. I was pleasantly surprised. We are almost as strong in proportion to our population as Hitler was when he came to power. Down here in the South West it is difficult to realise what progress the movement had made. The Leader believes that we shall be in power by 1940, I think that he is right.'[59] That month there was a successful meeting in Buller Hall in St Thomas which was 'packed to overflow' to hear A. Raven Thompson, a leading national figure.[60] There was also at least one meeting at Exe Bridge. In mid September Fascist Haynes spoke to an 'attentive audience. Successful sales drive.'[61]

Keens pooled the region's human resources and organised Sales Drives in mid November. Each branch sold *Action* and *Blackshirt* and Keens invited members from throughout Devon and Dorset to Exeter on November 14th for a joint effort. He asked the Acting District Officer Sales of Torquay (Mr Proud of 31a Castle Chambers in Torquay), District Officer of Totnes (George Shorland of Mardle Cottage at Coombe Bridge in Buckfastleigh), District Officer of South Molton (Captain Hammond of Kennerleigh near Lapford), District Officer of Tiverton (W. A. Down of Sampford Barton in Sampford Peverell) and the District Officer of Exeter (Rafe Temple Cotton of Branscombe). Members were expected in uniform with Fascist armbands being mandatory. A week later the same exercise took place in Torquay.[62] In mid December two carloads of party members travelled from Devon to Dorchester to help a sales drive there. A week later Dorset members came to Exeter.[63]

Increasing literature sales featured in Devon's reports in *Blackshirt*. It may be the level had been very low but in May they made a steep upward curve and one report specified Plymouth and Exeter had a fifty per cent increase in *Blackshirt* and *Action* sales. This appears to have been reliable. *Blackshirt* published a weekly Sales League and in the South Exeter was almost always listed in the top six places. In mid September it was in second place and Torquay was fifth.[64] Plymouth was never listed nor any other part of Devon.

At the beginning of December Rafe Temple Cotton gave his first speech at an outdoor meeting in Exeter and when Dorset members came two weeks later they held an open air meeting where four

Fascists spoke. According to Robert Saunders it was 'Quite a successful evening on the whole, but the meeting was not well attended. However, it gave us some practice at making ourselves heard above the traffic!' The format benefited both districts; a week later, on the 30th of December, Saunders again wrote 'on Saturday Exeter are again coming over to Dorchester for another sales drive. We must try to again break all records for papers sold. We have arranged to go to Exeter on every third Saturday in each month and for them to come here on every first. I hope that by working together in this way we shall move things in both towns.'[65] Cotton admitted to Saunders another reason why Fascists from outside Exeter were useful: Exeter members felt they would lose their jobs if their employers saw them selling Fascist literature and thus identified them as party members.[66] The presence of a large number of uniformed Fascists, selling literature and marching through the streets would have made a considerable impact on not just smaller Devon towns but in Exeter as well.

The Exeter sales drive on November 14th coincided with a meeting for female members. Mrs Brock-Griggs, Women's Administrative Officer for the Southern Zone, arrived from London to meet Devon women at the Queen Street headquarters. Brock-Griggs was a noted speaker, six months earlier she had travelled to Germany for the May Day celebrations and spoke in Dorchester in June. While the men sold Fascist literature the women listened to one of the movement's leading figures. The men were banned from the building to 'avoid having men running up and down these noisy stairs when Mrs Brock Griggs is holding her meeting of women. Our premises are rather confined.' A separate room was provided for men, after the street selling, at Berni's Continental Café in High Street.[67] The café was later the location for the arrest of an Italian who was interned during the war.[68]

The year ended on a high. On 27 November 1936 Mosley visited Exeter for the Leader's Conference for members.[69] The organisation was done in military style. A guard of honour greeted him. Those attending were in full uniform and when he arrived stood and gave a full salute. Keens introduced each officer. Late arrivals were ordered to salute and offer a full apology to Mosley. There was also guidance on what could be said:

> *Officers are advised to ask only such questions as are pertinent to the discussion, not to make speeches but to put their suggestions and complaints briefly and clearly.*

When Mosley departed the audience was required to stand and salute.[70]

Cotton had been District Leader in Honiton before he moved his attention to Exeter sometime before November 1936. He later claimed Claude Duvivier of nearby Woodbury had been in charge of Exeter and admitted to having him removed because he felt Duvivier was unsuitable. Duvivier was an occasional writer to *Blackshirt*.[71] An indication of how Duvivier had worked as Exeter's District Officer is indicated in one letter in which he urged readers to obtain a copy of Hitler's *Mein Kampf* which 'not only does it prove what a fine and interesting character Hitler really is, but one can pick up very valuable hints for propaganda, organisation and stewarding of meetings. With no better sentiment can one conclude but with the words 'Hail, Hitler!'[72]

1936 was a more active year than 1935 and there was considerable enthusiasm among at least some members. As Saunders wrote in September 'Up the Blackshirts!'[73]

Devon in 1936

A confidential Home Office report of late March noted 'the state of the movement in the remainder of the southern zone is causing concern for [Bryan] Donovan and headquarters in general. Almost without exception branches are numerically weak and fail to carry out active propaganda work. Only a few scattered groups exist in the West Country.'[74] This was presumably why Keens had been posted to Exeter and why Donovan and Mosley came there.

One of the few ways to uncover what happened in Devon is through the weekly listing in *Blackshirt* of meetings. It is telling that only eighteen were reported for all of 1936. Many occurred in Exeter but some took place in mid-Devon where Hammond was based. It is probable that as Propaganda Officer he sent more reports than Devon's other Fascist officials but it is as likely there was less to report in previously active places such as Plymouth, Torquay and in North Devon.

The mid-Devon events were diverse and reported under the heading South Molton where Hammond was also District Officer. In January a meeting took place at the Town Hall in Crediton and there was a Grand Dance in the village of Sampford Peverell. Mrs Down of Sampford Peverell assisted with the tickets. In March Anne Brock-Griggs, the national Women's Officer, spoke in Tiverton as did Clement Bruning. A district meeting was planned there in May. Another Crediton meeting took place in May, as part of what was called 'the Summer Campaign', and surrounding villages were visited. The following month a 'well-attended' meeting took place at Cheriton Fitzpaine and the audience was described as excellent. In July Torrington had 'a highly successful meeting' at which Hammond spoke and 55 copies of *Blackshirt* were sold. This was followed by an optimistic, and yet curious, report at the end of the month: 'National Socialism well-received by farm workers, good paper sales. Local people fed up with old parties.' Finally, there was a 'fine' meeting at Okehampton in August.[75] Given South Molton was dependent upon Hammond it is likely there were not many other events. His importance in Devon is also indicated by the places that received visits from the propaganda van with the 'Great British Union Countryside Campaign'. After it left Yeovil on September 18th it visited South Molton, Tiverton, Tavistock, Newton Abbot and Honiton.[76] Two of the five were within Hammond's area. It is interesting those parts of Devon which had attracted farmers in the tithe disputes in 1933 and 1934, and afterwards abandoned by the party, were not visited.

References to the rest of Devon are sparse. There was a public debate in March at Axminster and in May Honiton had a meeting. These too were organised by Hammond. 'Many' copies of *Blackshirt* were sold.[77] Exeter had reports of only three meetings but other sources show it was busier than *Blackshirt* suggested.

Exeter Branch in 1937

The Saunders papers show a continuing evolution in the local activities of British Union in 1937. Party members were busy throughout Devon but the centre remained at Exeter as it had been in 1936.

At the start of the year illness and family matters kept several key Fascists from helping canvas or lecture. The number of active members is unknown. There are references to Fascists in various newspapers, such as R. M. Hill of Furze Close, Woodbury Common in Woodbury. He corresponded to *The British Lion*, the 'official organ of the Unity Band, associated with the Legion of Loyalists and other patriotic organisations', and was a sympathiser if not a party member.[78] In January Cotton apologised to Robert Saunders for not seeing a party propaganda film at Dorchester with the excuse 'owing to [R.] Ingle being on the sick list and [Claude] Duvivier being occupied looking after his wife and his family. There is now no one but myself, and Mrs Cotton, to keep the flag flying in Exeter. The last thing I want is to give the people of Exeter a chance to say "those Blackshirts are fading out in Exeter".'[79]

Exeter remained the centre for organisational meetings. One was held on January 18th to learn about street canvassing. In the winter outdoor meetings were too cold and one was scheduled at a school for January 12th. Cotton hoped 'to have a couple more if the first is a success before February when the unemployment figures come out.' January appears to have been a frenetic month in Exeter and Cotton found one meeting particularly inspiring because of the speaker, William Joyce. Cotton wrote to Saunders on the 11th:

> *We had a wonderful time during the weekend. And also learnt much! About 25 at the school – a number which Joyce was very pleased with. Joyce was wonderful! Even those who use to think little of him now regard him as almost a demigod!! The least one can say is that he is a very remarkable man.*

It began in late afternoon on the Saturday and did not finish until late on Sunday. One Blackshirt was told 'apart from courtesy

Fascist discipline necessitates your prompt attendance please'.[80] The speakers' school was one of eight organised across the country.[81] Joyce was fired shortly afterwards.

The headquarters became active. Cotton wrote the:

> *New headquarters is a great success we had a very successful tea there last night for members' wives, friends & children & hope to arrange a regular fortnightly meeting & discussion with members & friends' people who are all interested but not members. This should be a useful addition to the open meetings which always contain an element of rowdyism which keeps many thinking people away. We are sorely hampered by lack of chairs, cups, furniture generally, it takes me nearly ½ a day with the van going all over the town collecting one or two from each member every time we want a meeting. So we are hoping to try and raise a chair fund and organise whist drives to help it along. I wish my business did not keep me quite so busy & I had more time to spare for all this and for additional meetings.*[82]

The Exeter and Dorchester branches continued to cooperate in attending meetings, helping in sales drives and giving lectures although the weather in January prevented travel. Saunders' anti-Semitism showed in an apology on one occasion: he wrote 'many apologies for not coming down to Exeter last night. The roads were still bad and the weather was so appalling that it seemed useless to attempt the journey. Even the clerk of the weather seems of late to have succumbed to Hebrew corruption! I hope, however, that he is still impartial enough to enable you to come to Dorchester next Saturday.'[83] George Wiltshire, a Weymouth official who was registered by Joyce as a party speaker,[84] was one member who came to Exeter and Saunders became a regular visitor over the next three years. The two branches raised funds in 1937 to buy a loudspeaker they planned to share. It was thought 'without amplification the meetings are hopeless'.[85] Exeter's District Treasurer was William Rowe of Combe Raleigh near Honiton. He was still raising money for the loudspeakers in September. Rowe kept the party funds in an account at Barclay's in Exeter's High Street.[86]

The decay of Plymouth Branch resurfaced in February when Saunders wrote to Vincent Keens then posted to Limehouse in London. Saunders informed him 'I have been in touch with a man named Bowden of Burton Bradstock. He is an ex-member and wants to rejoin. He was one of the Plymouth crew, where he was at one time in charge of the Defence Crew. He is going to write me full particulars, which are to be sent to NHQ for them to decide if they approve of his rejoining. Do you know anything about him?'

Keens instructed him 'Have NOTHING WHATEVER to do with BOWDEN!' without reasons.[87] In 1934 R. F. Bowden had been praised for his handling of the tithe war but reasons for his fall from favour remain unknown unless he had written the anonymous account of Plymouth Branch in 1935.

February was a good month in Exeter for fascism. Saunders wrote to another Fascist on the 22nd that in Dorset they sold great numbers of Fascist newspapers and:

> *We sold quite a number at Exeter and held by far the largest meeting yet. After waiting an hour while the Salvation Army were at work, I opened the meeting and received my first really bad heckling, from the members of the Young Communist League. They had been holding a meeting on the only other pitch – down by the river – where one of the number had been addressing two swans, three or four communists but no human beings. We, on the other hand, and thanks to their heckling, had a really large crowd in no time. After a bit I thankfully handed over to Capt. Hammond. He was at his best, and gave a fine speech. His biggest hit was when he said to a Communist woman, who had been keeping up a running commentary of heckling, 'I quite realise, madam, that your husband will not allow you to speak when you are at home, but that is no reason why you should inflict it upon me now!' It made the crowd roar with laughter and kept her quiet for quite five minutes! Now that we have active opposition in Exeter I think that we shall make great progress there.*[88]

There was a meeting in Market Street in May. The topic was war and it reportedly drew 'a large crowd'. Eight Blackshirts sold literature in the streets. The meeting was one of the few in Exeter in 1937 reported by the Fascist press: this was the first recorded for the year in any part of Devon. Two others held in May were also noted at Branscombe and Beer but only 'several' newspapers were sold there.[89]

In March Mosley came to Dorchester to speak and the local party dropped a flyer through every householder's door.[90] Devon members waited for him to visit Exeter in July but publicity was not so easily arranged. Saunders was excited at the prospect of having Mosley in Dorchester and wrote to Cotton, then the British Union Parliamentary Prospective Candidate, about the implications of the party leader coming to Exeter. He asked him:

> *When is the Leader going to introduce you to Exeter? Or don't you know yet? I must say that I admire, but do not envy you in your task. In Exeter, as in Dorchester, our job is rather like trying to set fire to green wood. Even green wood, however, will light if the flame is intense enough and the flame is held to it long enough. I believe that our own particular fire will become ablaze as soon as people feel the pinch of the next depression on their pockets. Meanwhile, our task, it seems to me, is two fold. First, by our propaganda to gain from the public a general, if somewhat vague, respect and sympathy for our movement. Secondly, to find, test and train members who will form the foundations of our organisation in the days when the public begin to stampede in our direction. When the fight begins in real earnest it will be necessary to have men and women who are not only experts at their jobs but can be relied on to carry them out.*[91]

The subsequent organisation for that meeting was intensive: detailed instructions were sent from national headquarters to ensure it was organised with military precision. Stewards were sought from local branches and requests made it clear only men were to fulfil this role.[92]

The state of the party in Exeter immediately before Mosley's July visit was discussed by Cotton who wrote to Saunders:

I am glad to hear you will be over for the Leader's Meeting, have you seen or heard about the advertisement the Daily Worker *are giving us? They have had big headlines for three days,* Mosley Speaks (he hopes to!) In Exeter July 3rd. *Symes is anticipating an imported red front as well as the local. Spent nearly all night last night with the chalk. Putting 'You can not' in front of their slogan 'Smash Fascism now' 'Civic Hall Saturday'. Things are looking lively!*

Could you bring any new leaflets you have to spare. I think we have enough 2d + 4d + 6d booklets anyway one does not usually sell very many at a meeting, we have lots of leaflets about 12 months old which ought to be got rid of. I am counting on your bringing your own Action *and* Blackshirt *to sell. If you have room no harm to bring a reserve of literature but I think we have enough. Glad you are getting noticed. Things terribly slow here still, except for these rather insignificant little imitators of Red Front. We meet [?] apathy on every side. Sort of 'why do you want to try and wake us up' attitude.*[93]

Immediately afterwards one Fascist wrote to a colleague:

The Exeter show was wonderfully good. About 1,500 people and no trouble. The Red Front had given the meeting plenty of advertisement by much chalking of 'Smash Fascism' etc. But when the time came their courage seemed to have evaporated and they were very subdued. Sunday needs no description from me. If it did nothing else, it gave a chance to those who had not seen them before, to inspect the Red Front at close quarters. And that can never do anything but good to fascism.

Clement Bruning, in charge of District Propaganda, came to Exeter from London from the 3rd to the 4th of July for speaker classes.[94] It was at this time that Cotton advertised in *Action* for

Fascist staff for his horticulture business at Branscombe. As in January, on July 24th he sought a 'married couple wanted or two women to take entire charge of house, help garden, able drive car. County people preferred'.[95] Canvassing and lecturing must have taken its toll on business activities.

In October 1937 the party celebrated its fifth birthday and a report was made of branch activities across the country. There were two from Devon. In Exeter 'R. Temple Cotton, the prospective candidate and [Hammond] the County Propaganda Officer for Devon are carrying out a big speaking campaign with good results'. The second report was from mid-Devon noting Hammond's 'meetings at the Clock Tower are showing that the people of Tiverton realise that only the British Union can carry on the great traditions of the British people – typified by the 'Men of Devon'.' No mention was made of the rest of Devon.[96]

The following week Exeter became problematic. *Blackshirt* reported a sales drive and meeting in which Hammond spoke in Market Street. Then the 'opposition rushed platform and succeeded in breaking up the meeting. Our answer is to announce two meetings next Saturday, and call for every Devonshire Blackshirt to rally and help in Exeter this week'. Meetings took place at Market Street and Belmont Road. Hammond spoke and 'the Reds made desperate efforts to smash the meeting with little success. They were prevented by local members rallying round the platform'.[97]

The brief Fascist account overlooked important details: Hammond's speech in October would result in a threat of legal action and Exeter's Chief Constable met with the Home Secretary in London to discuss it.

A police report noted:

> *Little was heard of the Fascist movement here from October 1934 until the latter end of 1936, but during that time occasional street meetings were held. During 1937, however, they increased and our records show that twenty-two meetings were held in various streets in this city in connection with the movement. This number included ten in Market Street, two in Gervase Avenue, four at St Annes, four at the*

Triangle, one in Belmont Road and one in King Street. The constables on the beats were invariably present, with supervision by the section sergeants, but no disorder was observed by the police at these meetings until October 1937.[98]

It was at this time Hammond made a speech which had great consequences for the Fascists and the Exeter police. The report further noted:

On Saturday, 8th October, a meeting was held in Market Street and addressed by a man named Hammond. P. S. Hooper reported that following the meeting a small disturbance occurred, through the crowd resenting what Hammond said, and it became necessary for the police to clear the street as the meeting closed.

On the following Saturday, 16th October, a meeting was held at St Anne's at 7.30 pm, but there were only about ten members of the public present and no disorder occurred. The speakers then proceeded to Market Street and the first speaker was Mr Cotton, the prospective parliamentary candidate for the city. He spoke until 9.10, and during that time there was no disorder. Immediately after this Mr Hammond of Kennerleigh, Lapford, with other Fascists, took the platform and Hammond commenced to speak. At that time between 200 and 300 persons were present. Immediately he commenced to address the assembly the crowd began to boo and shout, and it was five minutes before he could obtain a hearing. When he had been speaking for about twenty minutes a portion of the crowd attempted to rush the platform. A number of the Fascist supporters prevented them, and a sergeant and constable who were present at the meeting, were able momentarily to quell the disorder. Sergeant Hooper, who was again present, was apprehensive of the crowd, who were shouting and threatening the speakers, and fearing grave disorder he requested the speakers to close the meeting. Hammond addressed the crowd and said 'I am closing the meeting at the request of the police' and this was received with a loud cheer.[99]

The meeting was more akin to those at Plymouth in 1934 than anything Exeter had experienced. The police report added:

> *With considerable difficulty an Inspector and a number of constables who had arrived succeeded in getting the speakers and members of the movement to their head-quarters at 7 Queen Street. They were followed through the streets by a crowd, which had increased to between 400 and 500. The Inspector sent to the station for reinforcements and with their help the crowd were dispersed. Whilst the police were dispersing the crowd in Queen Street, Cotton and another member of the Fascist movement began distributing handbills amongst the crowd, but were stopped by the police.*[100]

The writer concluded it was Hammond the crowd disliked.

> *The sergeant and constable who were present in Market Street were of the opinion that the disturbance was caused by the crowd's dislike of Hammond. The sergeant reported that the disturbance was general throughout the crowd and not confined to one section of it. The sergeant, in reporting the incident, said he was apprehensive of disorder, and in his opinion had the police not been present in sufficient numbers and had Hammond continued to address the crowd, injury to person and property would have resulted.*[101]

The report was written by Albert Rowsell, then Chief Inspector and later Chief Constable. The consequences were serious for Hammond.

> *Following the report on this disorder you communicated with Mr Hammond and Mr Cotton, and informed them that in view of the apprehended breach of the peace Hammond*

> *could not be prevented to address further meetings in the streets other than in the open space at the Triangle.*[102]

As Devon's Propaganda Officer such a drastic curtailing of his ability to speak was disastrous. On October 30th a meeting took place in Market Street with some 200 people. It was orderly with only a small section which made continual interruptions. Nevertheless Cotton spoke for only ten minutes before he abandoned it. He left accompanied by his mother, two other women and Hammond.

> *Within a few minutes an incident occurred near where they were standing, and during it Mrs Cotton struck a member of the crowd on the face. This caused the crowd to surround the party and become hostile. The five people then left and walked to High Street, being followed by the crowd still acting in a hostile manner. In Fore Street two constables, assisted by some members of the public, threw a cordon across the street and stopped a portion of the crowd from following. By the time the Fascists had reached High Street, however, a crowd, which had apparently reached there by way of side streets, numbering 200, were following and shouting and showing signs of hostility towards the Fascists. A number of fireworks, which had been thrown, added to the confusion of the moment. A police inspector stopped the Fascists and advised Hammond to take shelter from the crowd, and on this advice they proceeded to the Royal Clarence Hotel nearby, and the crowd dispersed. There appears to be no doubt that on this occasion, as on the former, but for police action serious disorder would have resulted and there was grave risk of injury to person and property.*[103]

On November 6th, a Saturday night, up to 600 people gathered in anticipation of a meeting in Market Street. One hundred were thought to be boys. Members of the crowd told the police they were 'waiting for the blackshirts'. However, the Fascists did not show.

Hammond and Cotton began to write and call upon the Chief Constable to arrange meetings. Restrictions remained that Hammond only spoke at the Triangle. Meetings were held throughout the city including on 16 October at St Anne's in Blackboy Road, 13 November at the Triangle, 20 November in King Street, 27 November at Belmont Road, 4 December at the Triangle, 11 December in Market Street and the Triangle, and 18 December in Market Street. Rowsell noted the police had previously not interfered with political meetings in Gervase Avenue, Market Street, Goldsmith Street, Bedford Street, St Anne's and the Triangle. Other smaller meetings had taken place in King Street, Castle Street and Belmont Road. He also noted on weekend evenings the Salvation Army commonly held meetings in some locations and the police moved political ones to other venues. Rowsell also recorded there was no history of prohibiting meetings except involving the National Unemployed Workers' Movement during a Hunger March and another with the Kensit Preachers.

The Home Office asked for the justification of the ban. According to Rowsell the police feared congested areas such as Market Street with passing pedestrians, heavy vehicular traffic and commercial property with large glass windows were unsuitable for controversial meetings. On these grounds Hammond was banned.

The British Union of Fascists regarded the action as illegal and the Home Office agreed privately but did not admit this to the Fascists. A legal appraisal was:

> *It certainly seems as though the Chief Constable has overstepped the mark in failing to recognise that, because an individual has used provocative language or conduct on one occasion (apparently not sufficiently serious to warrant a prosecution under Section 5 of Public Order Act) he is not on that account justified in banning that individual from public speaking. Each particular case must be judged on its own merits and the Chief Constable cannot (and should not attempt to) in advance ban meetings addressed by a speaker with a record for provocation. An interesting parallel would be the Met. Police attitude to the notorious Jew baiter, Penfold . . . who was never prevented from speaking, but*

Exeter High Street where the Fascists were attacked in the autumn of 1937 (private collection).

> *who was carefully watched by the police and when he overreached himself, arrested and charged.*[104]

The ban began on October 19th 1937. As late at May 6th 1938 the Home Office was still fudging the issue. On that date the national headquarters of the party was informed the Secretary of State:

> *Is fully satisfied that there is no question of the police in Exeter having wished to discriminate unfairly against Captain Hammond or against Fascist meetings in general and taken measures to maintain the peace, that the Secretary of State has no powers to express an opinion as to the powers of police to take preventative action.*[105]

It is unclear when the ban finished. Meanwhile Cotton held his own meetings. In November one was in Market Street and another at the Triangle was described as being 'quiet and orderly'. The reports in *Blackshirt* changed: they become frank and lost their boastfulness. Two further meetings in early November were described as 'both fairly well-attended, and some interest though very few papers sold, and crowds mainly in opposition still'.[106] It is possible they were being written by Cotton and not by Hammond. Four weeks later a report concerned Cotton speaking 'to a group of young people at the Toc H Headquarters, by invitation, and answered a number of questions. Especial interest was shown in the Policy for Small Traders. Canvassing bringing some results at last. Paper sales taking place with quite good results. Enquiries made as to time and place of next meeting by members of the public. Interest is definitely aroused'.[107] Also in November Hammond advertised in *Action* for help from local members with a 'simple county propaganda scheme'.[108] What this entailed is uncertain but it may have been related to Mosley's second visit that year to Exeter for a conference on December 9th. Of it Saunders wrote to three colleagues:

> *We went to the leader's conference at Exeter last Thursday. He has now quite recovered from the Liverpool affair and is as fit as ever. Exeter has been having rather a rough time at the hands of the Reds of late. Their police have not, I am sorry to say, shown up too well. There is a possibility of a test case being fought against them in the Courts. We still make steady progress. The District's membership has increased exactly 150% in the last twelve months, which is not too bad. However, we have a long way to go yet . . .*
>
> *The leader's conference was great, and well worth going all the way to Exeter even with such bad road conditions . . .*
>
> *We went to the leader's conference at Exeter last Thursday. He is now quite fit again. The Reds have given the Exeter members a rough time of late. And their police have not been too good, I am sorry to say. We may be fighting them in a test case in the courts before long . . .*[109]

Saunders had, for some unknown reason, not been to Exeter often since the summer and the two districts had worked independently of one another. Their cooperation would once again change with the new year. Saunder's mention of a test case must have been a reference to Hammond's ban.

Devon and the Wessex Branches, 1938

As County Propaganda Organiser Hammond supported a national propaganda campaign with an appeal in *Action* in February 1938 'here in Devon we are weak in numbers, stronger we must be in spirit. Devon readers and members rally your friends and sympathisers by generous response to this appeal'.[110] Hammond remained busy promoting the party in Devon and also nationally. Among his letters to Fascist newspapers he wrote criticizing the Dean of Exeter for being anti-Nazi and pro-Communist.[111] Devon needed speakers and continued cooperation with the Fascist branches to its east proved useful to Hammond. Dorchester's Robert Saunders and Cotton continued to speak for one another and in February the West Dorset branch organised a pool of speakers, The Southern Speakers' Pool.[112] The organiser wrote to Saunders:

> *The spare copy is for the Exeter Branch, will you be so kind as to send it to them? If they take up the idea so much the better, even if they don't, the knowledge that other branches are working helps.*

Shortly afterwards Cotton was requested to canvas in Dorset. He spoke on April 2 at Weymouth, June 11 at Lyme Regis and August 20th at Bridport while Saunders was in Exeter on May 7 in Market Street,[113] July 9 at St Thomas School and September 24 again in Market Street. The plan varied speakers for audiences, made the movement appear larger and also increased the number of events. In March Exeter Branch was anxious to formally join the Pool. That month Saunders travelled to Exeter to address the branch Study Group. Cotton explained to Saunders he particularly appreciated help because there was no other branch nearby. By this date Plymouth Branch was still moribund as was probably the rest of Devon outside Exeter. Cotton wrote on March 2nd to Saunders:

Very many thanks for your most interesting letter and offer of help. Your meetings' campaign and speakers' school makes me green with envy. The lack of anyone within easy reach with whom to cooperate hits us very hard. Captain Hammond is still banned from speaking and the people of Exeter are getting tired of hearing me time and time again. Also, its confoundedly difficult to think of new things to say, speaking mostly in the same street one can't repeat the same speech and I have such little time preparing them. If only we could get someone else to come and speak they might take more notice, anyway it would give them the idea there is someone else in the movement besides Mrs Cotton & I. Our trouble is even our most devoted members who will always turn out and will go canvassing or delivering papers or chalking 3 or 4 times a week they are all engaged in some kind of trade which makes it a real risk of losing their jobs if they were to stand with me in the street selling Action.[114]

Cotton's first talk on April 2nd was 'a flop'. The meeting was held on Weymouth Sands but a cold biting wind stopped people lingering. His envy about the speakers' school was genuine. By mid May Exeter had established its' own; local Fascists were coached in communicating effectively.[115]

The canvassing plan was not just to reach the larger communities but to strike out into the countryside: the second phase was to exchange speakers and establish teams of 'raiders'. In March the Dorset Fascists organised a newssheet, *The Southern Speaker.* In that first issue it was noted 'to work in the dark is to loose [sic] all sence [sic] of companionship and direction and it is to promote companionship [and] light the road that this journal is published'. The editor, Ralph Jebb, recorded topics audiences were asking about including Spain, foreign affairs, farm workers' wages and slums. He offered some 'Hateful Hints' for village meetings in the April 14th issue:

The plan is simple and should be effective. The speaker and his transport take a pre-arranged road and stop at their allotted village. They ride through and see where there are

> *any people. They there and then address them. The meeting should be no more than half an hour and then the speaker should ride on to his next village. These quick raids are now being carried on in Oxfordshire most successfully.*

Cotton enthused about this style of speaking and manner of reaching the masses. Jebb explained in another issue:

> *Eighteen months ago Raven Thompson, at the height of the Abyssinian Crisis, spoke to an empty street in Bridport. Not one person stopped to listen to him. Today a National Socialist Meeting on that same spot will always draw a crowd. In the Southern Counties, National Socialism will come by mass suggestion and self-conviction. It will not come by personal conviction. It is because of the former factor that the Southern Speakers' Pool has been formed. The Southern Speakers' Pool exists for two purposes. One to 'Show the Flag', the other is to expound our policy. Each purpose is as important as the other.*

Another reason, which was not admitted, was each branch did not have enough men and women of sufficient calibre to cover the enormous area of Devon and Dorset.

Exeter in 1938

The Saunders papers continue to provide the framework for understanding Devon fascism in 1938. At the beginning of the year he asked Cotton how Exeter Branch and the new headquarters at 22 South Street were. Shortly afterwards he admitted his West Dorset branch, like Exeter, had difficulty in attracting active members. Even so it appears Cotton was actively canvassing votes in Exeter. In February Saunders came to Exeter to talk to members and friends. Interestingly, he won a public debate at Dorchester which asked whether fascism or socialism was better. The public voted for fascism. Devon had a similar debate later that year. Saunders wrote his debate 'created quite a sensation in the town': the result attracted controversy and publicity, some of which must have reached East Devon.[116] In late autumn Saunders debated at Exeter 'That it is in the interests of the people of Britain that the British Union, and not the Labour Party, be returned to power.'[117]

Early 1938 was busy. There was a sales drive on January 3rd and two days later Cotton had an evening party for members and their friends. He outlined plans for the year. On the 7th Fascists distributed a leaflet 'Why do food prices rise' in what was described as a 'workers' district'. Three days later they were handing out free copies of *Action*. Then, only a few days later, they were in the market square at Newton Abbot where there was a 'small but interested crowd'. Cotton, Hammond and D/D Leader Rowe spoke. Another evening meeting followed in Exeter with a sales drive. It was obviously a busy fortnight for local members.[118] The rest of the month there were more sales drives but bad weather hampered them.[119]

In March organised opposition appeared. The branch reported in *Blackshirt*:

> *Meeting held at Market Street with small interested crowd. Canvass started in the city with small band of helpers. Usual sales drives organised. County Propaganda Officer [Hammond] opened first study group meeting at District Headquarters.*[120]

However, Cotton wrote to Saunders on the 20th:

> *Could you possibly come to Exeter some day other than Saturday? The reason is that I am particularly anxious to have a good meeting in the St Thomas district of Exeter. We have been canvassing two wards there and had a large number of people showing a desire to learn more about us and then the local labour candidate has heard of our efforts and has had a meeting down there to try to counter our results. This district of Exeter lies on the West of the Exe and there are no cinemas or Woolworths or market places there and therefore it is almost deserted of a Saturday night. If you could manage Monday or Tuesday May 2 or 3rd or 9th or*

> *10th any of these four days would be good and almost any day better than Saturday. I am sorry to ask you to change but this attack by the labour party has made it essential to return with a meeting there as soon as possible and as I have explained Saturday is not the best day for this district. Let me know what day you can do. Of course if you are too booked to change it we can get a fair audience for a certain at any of 3 places in the city on Saturday but I can do that myself. I would like to have you in the ward. I shall write and try to get the local school, Montgomery Street School, directly I hear from you.*[121]

On May 5th Cotton wrote once more asking if Saunders could come to the meeting in St Thomas on May 20th. In it he revealed his contempt for democracy:

> *I can get the schoolroom in our canvas ward for that night. I am sorry not to have been able to let you know when I wanted you before this. The reason is that under the good old democratic system the committee take a fortnight to let me know the room was let for other purposes on the days I asked for. I don't know how we shall do at all but with luck we should get an audience and if we do it should do some good as we have come across quite a bit of interest in this ward, people who are quite willing to anything you give them and judge for themselves, but I don't know if they will even bother to turn out for a meeting. Still nothing ventured, nothing won. We must try and see what happens.*[122]

That meeting seems to have been successful. The branch reported in *Blackshirt*:

> *Quite a good meeting was held at Montgomery School, Exeter, and many questions were put to the speaker. These were ably answered and apart from interference by a gang of noisy youths, were received very favourably by the majority of the audience. Policy Class at District Headquarters and other meetings at Queen Street and Market Street.*[123]

Cotton had some unusual help during Easter but the results did not justify the effort.

> *We had three Blackshirts in camp here for Easter weekend and as this was more than halfway from Exeter towards the villages which Jebb has asked me to raid under the Southern Speakers' Pool scheme we decided it was an opportunity not to be missed & set off on Monday Bank Holiday. Unfortunately the boys had to be back in Exeter that night so we had to go about teatime and during the afternoon we could not find an audience to address anywhere. I think if we could have stopped till about 8.00 we might have had results, also of course the holiday was probably against us.*

The four men managed to distribute several hundred leaflets and newspapers and Cotton planned to return.[124] This form of publicity had results but created problems as well. In April Cotton admitted to Saunders of uncertainties:

> *Do you usually obtain police permission for these raid meetings? Is it permitted to chalk the road where the meeting will be held? We did this in North Devon with the police watching us doing it and in fact holding up the traffic. But in Beer we did it in the middle of the night & arrived to find a crowd of 200 or so & an irate village constable. I think if it is permitted it is the best possible advertisement, just chalk on the road Blackshirt (or British Union) Meeting here at 7.30 Saturday and it seems to collect a crowd. If this is permitted I could drive out and do it about the Wednesday beforehand. If it's against the local byelaws I think we had better not, who is the authority for this area?*[125]

Eventually the organisation for these 'village raiders' comprised seven teams from branches at Exeter, Dorchester, Bournemouth and Salisbury.[126] Exeter benefited from the new arrangement and in late April received another boost with the arrival of A. G. Woodgate from Uplyme near Lyme Regis. Woodgate had moved from Lancashire to Lyme Regis in 1935 and later to Yeovil. He was about

30 years old and was later described as tall and a good speaker.[127] Within a month of his arrival in 1938, when he lived at 58 Oxford Road, Cotton reported 'Woodgate is doing grand work for us now, glad to hear of your progress. We are having good meetings. I have one every day for a week as Moir is staying here to help us.'[128] On May 9th Woodgate wrote to Saunders:

> *As you will see from the above address, I am now in Exeter and I have every reason to believe that I shall settle down here, so I suppose I had better be transferred to this branch.*
>
> *I have already made contact and have twice had the pleasure of speaking for the B.U. here, last Saturday we held a meeting and after I had been speaking for some thirty minutes there came along a bunch of the supporters of Millwall who had been playing football here. Well, they commenced to make themselves heard and at first I welcomed them, for within a few minutes a crowd of some 300 had collected, but then one commenced deliberately to urge the crowd to attack us, and it is a sad commentary on Exeter justice that the police, instead of arresting him as they should have done, made us close our meeting.*
>
> *However, we shall try again next Saturday, and in the meanwhile I believe Cotton is to hold a meeting in Whitchurch Canonicorum this week. I will speak to Cotton about Lyme Regis and I hope we shall be able to go along there.*[129]

Exeter had a great increase in meetings in May. A report was sent to national headquarters and printed in *Action*.

> *Nine Meetings in ten days. A period of increased activity has been undertaken by the Exeter District of British Union. Nine meetings have been held in ten days addressed by different speakers. Patrick Moir has also spoken at most of these and also Saunders of Dorchester. Meetings have been held in the streets at Jarvis Avenue, Belmont Road, Market Street, and Burnt House Lane, a well-known Labour Stronghold. All were attended by interested audiences, and there is strong support*

> *for the British Union policy of 'Britain First'. In addition contacts have been visited and a fine meeting took place at the Buller Hall addressed by Patrick Moir. There was some opposition from a few Reds, but the majority of people were very keenly interested in the British Union's policy. Exeter is determined to carry on the good work, and are looking forward to further successful meetings.*[130]

The Saunders correspondence for 1938 is thin for the summer months. An interruption might be due to Cotton having left for a German holiday. By early July he had returned as he had organised a farmers' meeting. He had earlier spoken in Market Street to an audience of between 200 and 250 people where 'a small noisy opposition were repeatedly told to shut up by the rest of the crowd'.[131] In September Cotton brought his loudspeaker with him to one East Devon town. The innovation in the genteel resort of Sidmouth provoked indignation. The editor of *The Sidmouth Observer* wrote:

> *We do not know what the law is regarding the use of loud speakers in a public place, but the police should certainly have power to prohibit their use when they become a nuisance and to a large number of people in a wide areas surrounding the Market place on Monday night they were most annoying. Actually there was no need for the use of a loudspeaker apparatus. Anyone standing in the Market Place can address a large number of people without any artificial aid. The use of this amplifying apparatus flung the voice of the speaker over a considerable area. The noise penetrated into homes where children were trying to sleep, where people were trying to read or listen to the wireless programmes. From just after 8 until ten minutes to ten a torrent of words poured forth. By all means let anybody who wants to speak in the Market Place but for goodness sake cut out the loud speakers.*[132]

Three days later *The Sidmouth Herald's* editor joined in when he wrote:

> *Promulgation of the gospel of fascism as well as that of any other 'ism is, we presume, admissible in the Market Place, but we certainly agree with the protest made by our contemporary against the use of a blatant loud speaker such as was the case at the meeting held there on Monday evening.*[133]

By October Cotton had at least two loudspeakers for his outdoor meetings.[134] It may have been fortunate he used only one in Sidmouth.

The target set in February for the Southern Speakers Pool was 5,000 people but by September they had reached 11,000. Jebb attributed this to the use of loud speakers. The Westcountry branches also extended the use of machinery. They sought funds to

Wall, probably in Devon, daubed with Fascist slogans possibly by Rafe Temple Cotton (Devon & Cornwall Constabulary Museum).

buy a van and used a trailer for the loudspeaker. They also chalked slogans and daubed walls with paint. In several issues of *The Southern Speaker* there are references to 'PJ', the initials which signified Perish Judah. In one instance he wrote 'The Exeter P. J. hounds have abandoned chalk for the glue pot, the new national headquarters' strip posters tease the boycott front'. The Fascists had to be imaginative to obtain publicity given they had little newspaper coverage or use of the BBC.[135] Jebb calculated the first phase of the Pool resulted in 70 meetings across the region. Exeter had 'a sound record of progress, new members, improved paper sales and best of all the tireless Cottons have lit the torch in Plymouth, Paignton, Totnes and Kingsbridge.'[136]

The activity at Totnes was reported in *Action*. On April 13th, what was apparently the first such meeting in the town, termed a 'Pioneer Meeting', was held at the Commercial Hotel. Hammond spoke and new contacts were made. Five weeks later there was another meeting. *Action* noted there was a 'demand for literature. An example of the increasing interest in National Socialism is shown by the fact that at a small indoor meeting in Totnes, a considerable amount of British Union literature was sold. A year ago probably only a quarter of this amount would have been sold at such a meeting. But then the tide was against us. Now it is beginning to turn in favour of National Socialism'.[137] *Blackshirt* noted 'new ground is being opened in the Totnes area. Dundas and others distributing 'Ten Points' throughout the town. Local people have been sent copies of 'Tomorrow We Live'. As the result of last meeting several assurances of support have come in'.[138]

How the meeting on April 13 was described as the first is difficult to square with George Shorland of Buckfastleigh having been District Officer for Totnes only two years previously. Presumably another local member was 'J. B. of Totnes', a letter writer to *Blackshirt* in 1933.[139]

In the days leading up to Chamberlain's visit on September 29th 1938 to reach the Munich Agreement, Hitler's peace pledge, there were attempts by many to flee London and escape war to the safety of Devon. In Sidmouth estate agents were 'bombarded' with requests for information on letting houses and the trains from Waterloo were packed with would-be refugees.[140] In early

November Saunders spoke in Exeter and he sent his speech to *Action* for possible propaganda purposes. It is one of the few Exeter speeches to have survived. Saunders began with a discussion about the Munich Agreement. He told Exeter it was a British diplomatic failure and humiliation because Britain had made promises to other countries and then had to back down when its bluff was called. Saunders said two unimportant countries, Germany and Italy, had defeated Britain which had an empire comprising a quarter of the world because they had a modern form of government in Fascism while Britain kept its 'outworn and inefficient system of Democracy'. Only a national union government, which erased party politics, could meet the challenge of Mussolini and Hitler. He ended by invoking the empire. He said:

> *That spirit which enabled our forefathers to build the greatest empire in the whole of history and which, when rekindled, will enable this generation to take that empire and to build from its vast resources a civilization beyond the wildest dreams of man. We ask you, our fellow Britons, to join with us in this enormous struggle. A struggle which we can, and will, win by building up this, our own movement; by fighting elections and returning men and women to parliament from among the most ardent and reliable of our workers, and finally be returning to power our own government. A government lit by this spirit of the people, will sweep away the blunders, the inefficiencies and the humiliations of the past and then go forward to ensure that Britain again be great.*[141]

No doubt it was a stirring speech.

At this time there was discussion of Cotton withdrawing as Exeter's prospective parliamentary candidate to move to West Dorset but Cotton refused.[142] The closeness of the two districts helped the diminished party. There are no objective reports about how the Fascists were received by the public when they suddenly appeared in small villages and towns in Devon but there is one illuminating report from the Fascists themselves. On May 20th Saunders informed Jebb of his experiences at a village on the counties' border. He wrote:

Edmonds and I were extremely lucky not to have been beaten up and our equipment smashed at Charmouth – of all places! – last night. A rather hostile crowd gathered as soon as we stopped. We played a record and just as it finished a retired Colonel type of Tory came up, frothing at the mouth saying we have no right there and that he had been unable to hear his phone call in a box several hundred yards up the road. I told him we had as much right to hold a meeting as he had to make a phone call. He then told us that we should have gone further down the road, away from the phone-box. I pointed out that if we had done so we should have been right outside another box. He then asked for my name and address so that he could write to Mosley and report me! When he found I lived locally it rather took the wind out of his sails, and by that time he was beginning to realise that he was making a fool of himself. He drifted away, and Edmonds started to speak.

Then a bright fool put a dog down one of the loud-speakers. I moved him away and then a couple of real thugs arrived. They threatened to beat us up if we did not close the meeting. When we refused to do so, one of them punched me on the ear . . . I nearly hit back. Had I done so, we would have been for it, as the crowd were nasty, and there was only Edmonds and I. As it was I talked to them for ten or fifteen minutes, and then took over the mike – Edmonds had stopped speaking sometime before – and after a good deal of heckling, got most of them listening for about half an hour. All well, that ends well, but last night did not look like ending well at one time!

The Raiders planned programme was to visit rural villages during the summer and then from November in the towns. For five months they were instructed to 'work the streets, then at the end of March, again set out with an entirely new form of attack upon the villages. When do we rest? When we die.'[143] Their promotional work took a turn in 1939 and particularly in the last few months before war.

Across Devon in 1939

Little is known of activities in Plymouth where Edward D'Alessio was District Leader but he later claimed the branch was inactive. In East Devon the Southern Speaker's School continued working including Cotton taking a meeting at Lyme Regis in Dorset on March 18th. The year was somewhat fragmented by his four-week holiday with his mother and brother to Germany and Austria. The trip had repercussions when war broke out.

In May Cotton travelled to Barnstaple where he sold literature and gave out enrolment forms to four interested parties. It was, he

A scene in Germany or Austria where Rafe Temple Cotton had several holidays (Devon & Cornwall Constabulary Museum).

wrote, a good meeting. Cotton also went to Taunton where he used a new way to gain support. He wrote to Saunders:

> *Have you any Western National Bus men on strike in your area? I expect so, at Bridport anyway. They are very discontent with their union not backing them up, they are beginning to see that their union leaders are hand in glove with the capitalists and this gives us a wonderful line of attack. At Taunton we got one of them to state their case from our platform and I went on to say what's the good of a*

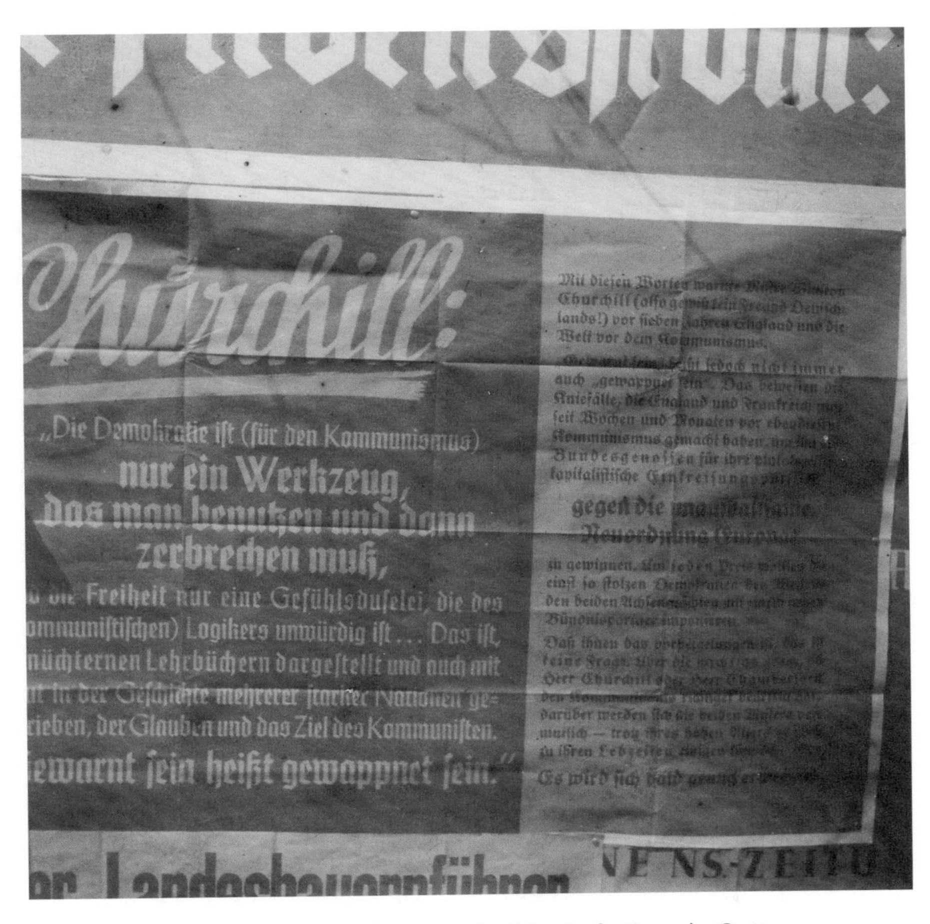

A German poster photographed by Rafe Temple Cotton, probably summer 1939 (Devon & Cornwall Constabulary Museum).

Four Fascists having a picnic possibly in North Devon. The Fruit & Flower Farm van from Branscombe is in the background and Rafe Temple Cotton on the far right (Devon & Cornwall Constabulary Museum).

> *union which you know to be hand in glove with the enemy. Join British Union for power action. We gave out hundreds of transport leaflets & Power Actions, we have great hopes of some of these men. There are of course some Reds after them too.*[144]

Cotton resigned as District Leader but continued as Prospective Parliamentary Candidate. The Temporary District Leader was Jack Forward of Park Road. Even so, Cotton continued to organise Exeter Branch. He arranged speakers to cover his absence because the Branch's own men, and possibly women, could not appear publicly because of their 'business reasons'. He asked for Saunders to come from Dorchester and although Cotton wanted to target three places he knew where he could get an audience, at Exe Bridge, Market Street and Goldsmith Street, there were logistical problems.[145] Cotton found the National Unemployed Worker's Movement and several religious groups, including another militaristic group, the Salvation Army, competed for the same sites. He was annoyed and wrote to Saunders 'I am very keen that they shall not get the idea that they can dispense with us like that'. Saunders came on June 3rd but he was warned by the new District Organiser 'I will try to have as many members as possible present at this meeting in order to prevent the National Unemployed Workers' Movement members getting too frisky. Police close down our meetings at the slightest

A Fascist meeting, possibly in Devon, date unknown (Devon & Cornwall Constabulary Museum).

hint of trouble these days.'[146] Saunders was late in arriving due to car trouble and later wrote to Ralph Jebb:

> *We, of course, arrived late, but the police turned the Reds off our pitch, so that was ok. I had quite a bit of heckling and a really good audience. The police had changed their attitude and were standing no nonsense from the Reds. One man was warned by them for pushing his cap down the loudspeaker, and later when he tried to climb onto the van, they arrested him. The Exeter members seemed quite pleased with the meeting and with the new policy of their police.*[147]

Jebb was also at Exeter giving a talk that month. He was even more enthusiastic and praised it as an extraordinary event:

> *My Exeter meeting was great, the Communist rival meeting had an audience of none. They then came on to heckle me and left amid giggles from the crowd. Our crowd stayed for an hour and five minutes, a wonderful meeting the best I have ever had anywhere. The work Temple Cotton has done is at last bearing fruit. The police expressed themselves as pleased with the rout of the Communist Leader who they said was a pest.*[148]

Some enthusiasm may have come from excitement in speaking in a city after months in villages: Saunders wrote it was a pleasant change after having audiences of only two children and a cat.[149]

W. A. Down of Sampford Barton was arrested and his case highlighted in *Action*. Down, a longstanding and active member of British Union described as 'a stanch follower of Mosley', was noted in a feature article as being 'of good old Devonshire stock'. Down farmed in the small Mid-Devon village of Sampford Peverell. His dispute harked back to the heady days of the Tithe War. In November 1938 some of his stock had been sold on refusal to pay tithes and in June he was arrested over his failure to meet his contractual obligations with the Pigs Marketing Board. *Action* compared him with the Tolpuddle Martyrs who had been imprisoned over their principles. It called him a 'son of Devon, who suffered imprisonment rather than surrender to justice'.[150]

Cotton returned to Devon full of enthusiasm for Germany and Nazi Austria. It is probably from this holiday that photographs were taken which subsequently found their way into the custody of the Devon Constabulary. Cotton wrote at length about his admiration for Nazi Germany:

> *Had a glorious holiday. The German people are intensely friendly to British, they have extreme confidence that the Fuhrer can settle any differences between us without war. Nowhere was the war scare evident as it is here, though Belgium seems to have a good bit of the usual democratic gutters.*
>
> *German school children in particular were especially friendly, they crowded round our car trying off what they had just learned at school! Good afternoon, beautiful car, etc. These are being taught to hate us by their Nazi leaders? The A.A. told us before we left that we should have a most unfriendly reception that whatever we had experienced before now the whole attitude of the Nazi party & propaganda was turned against us. Absolute lies! In Innsbruck I lost some luggage and failed to make the railway understand, an SS man at once came to the rescue & went out of his way to be helpful! The police & SS & frontier guards were all of them helpful & polite in the extreme.*
>
> *In the Aulberg I was at one time the centre of a large mock battle, troops all around & exercises with machines & [?]Boen guns going on. We were told it was extremely dangerous to go in any zone occupied by military, I went where I wanted, got the cheery welcome 'Heil Hitler! Guis Gott Englander!' from the soldiers themselves & I took pictures too!! We were told there were anti-British notices on all the hoardings in Germany. We saw notices saying that the youth of Britain was rising against conscription & foreign entanglements 'While every German will realise that the youth of so great a country would leave her in the lurch <u>were Britain or the Empire</u> attacked the nearby photograph shows a*

demonstration of London youth against conscription and foreign wars'. This is as near a translation as I could make of the most common notice referring to Britain. It ended by saying that we 'Germans too do not want war with Britain', and was accompanied by a picture not of our march but one I think by the Civilian Militant Patriots or some such body. There was also on many notice boards a poster about our dear Whinnie the Poo! Headed just 'Churchill says' then it quoted two of his speeches, 1928 that peace would never be secure till the Bloodthirsty regime in Russia were overthrown, 1938 to save peace Britain must unite with Russia. The only comment was 'Does the Britain-Russia alliance intend peace?' Anti-British posters my hat! Our car with circle and flash badge got a good many salutes but the badge was not as widely recognised as I expected. One man in Alberg asked after the movement & said he hoped for everyone's sake we would soon get the Jews out of office in Britain. He was an old guard Nazi and the Jews line of attack seems almost identical on us as on Hitler before he came to power.

In Austria we had a long talk with a woman who had taught my brother German (in 1929) she had always been a supporter of Adolphus & she had no hesitation in criticising the Nazis when and where she thought fit (according to our papers she would have been in concentration camps from what she said to us quite openly & she said she had no fear, she said just the same to the Nazi leader of her village!). But even she had to agree with all the Nazi principles, her criticisms were merely that they had been a little too violent to the poor class Jews, that anti-Nazi government officials had been sacked since the Auchloss and that the Germans still came to Tyrol to buy butter and cream, so it proved they were short of food hence it was all lies they said in their propaganda about feeding the starving Tyrol peasants but that criticism does not cut much ice! London people come to Devon to buy cream & yet there is supposed to be no shortage here & yet again the Devon Farm Labourers' children are certified under-nourished by the M.O. at our schools here in Honiton.[151]

In mid July Cotton, with other Devon members, heard Mosley at Earl's Court.[152] This was his last great rally: some 20,000 people heard him call for peace and say he could not let British men 'die like rats in Polish holes'.[153]

Cotton also set about reprinting in Exeter an article by Henry

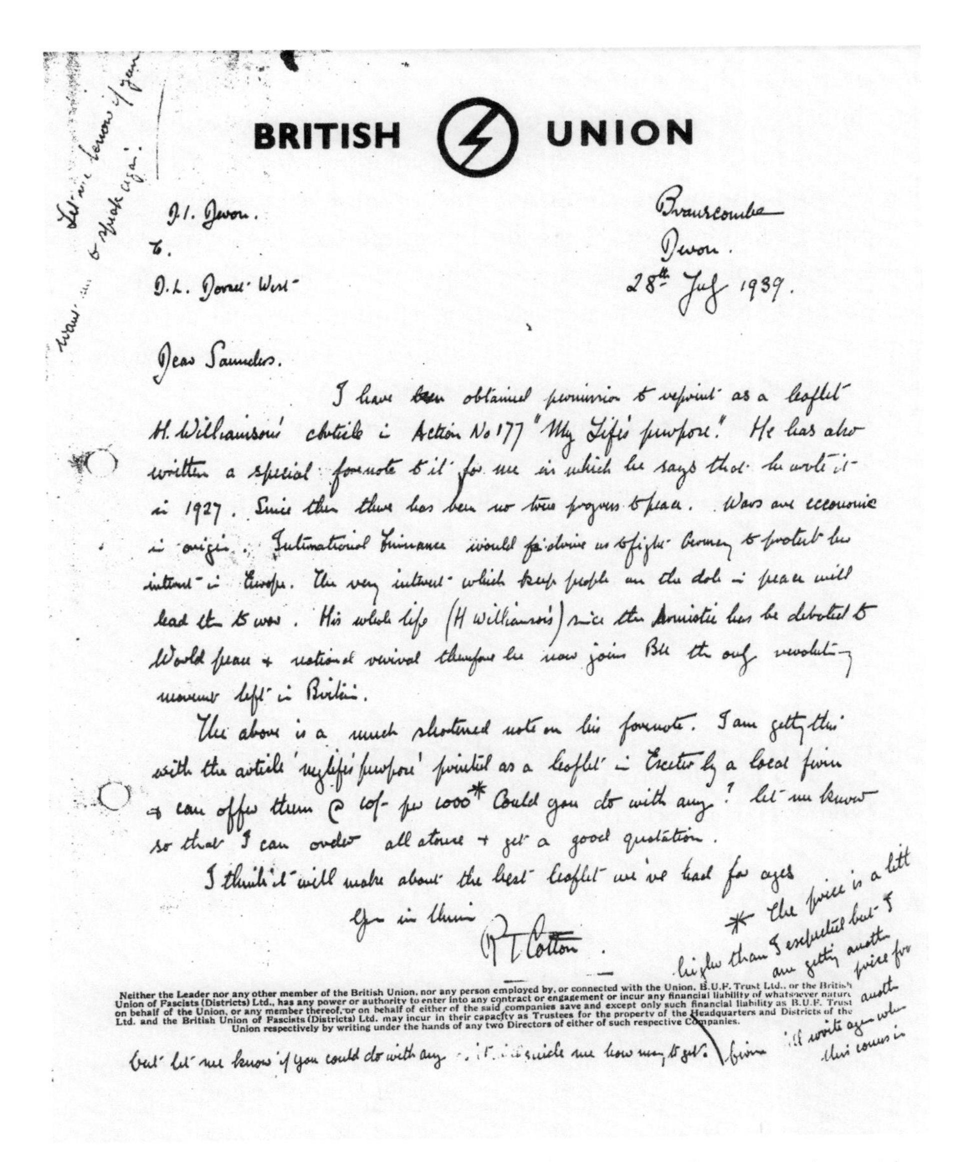

BRITISH UNION

D.I. Devon.
to.
D.L. Dorset West

Branscombe
Devon.
28th July 1939.

Dear Saunders.

I have ~~been~~ obtained permission to reprint as a leaflet H. Williamson's article in Action No 177 "My Life's purpose." He has also written a special foreword to it for me in which he says that he wrote it in 1927. Since then there has been no true progress to peace. Wars are economic in origin. International Finance would fain drive us to fight Germany to protect their interest in Europe. The very interest which keeps people on the dole in peace will lead them to war. His whole life (H Williamson's) since the Armistice has be devoted to World peace + national revival therefore he now joins BU the only revolutionary movement left in Britain.

The above is a much shortened note on his foreword. I am getting this with the article 'my life's purpose' printed as a leaflet in Exeter by a local firm + can offer them @ 10/- per 1000* Could you do with any? let me know so that I can order all at once + get a good quotation.

I think it will make about the best leaflet we've had for ages

Yours in thein [illegible]

R T Cotton.

* The price is a little higher than I expected but I am getting another price from another [illegible] + will write again when this comes in

Neither the Leader nor any other member of the British Union, nor any person employed by, or connected with the Union, B.U.F. Trust Ltd., or the British Union of Fascists (Districts) Ltd., has any power or authority to enter into any contract or engagement or incur any financial liability of whatsoever nature on behalf of the Union, or any member thereof, or on behalf of either of the said companies save and except only such financial liability as B.U.F. Trust Ltd. and the British Union of Fascists (Districts) Ltd. may incur in their capacity as Trustees for the property of the Headquarters and Districts of the Union respectively by writing under the hands of any two Directors of either of such respective Companies.

but let me know if you could do with any [illegible] guide me how many to get.

Let me know [illegible] & speak again.

Letter from Rafe Temple Cotton of Branscombe to Robert Saunders with news of printing a leaflet by Henry Williamson, July 1939 (Sheffield University).

Williamson. The well-known North Devon author had written 'My Life's Purpose' in 1927 and gave his permission for it to be a leaflet. He wrote a special foreword. Cotton explained Williamson's life since the Armistice of 1918 had been devoted to peace and that he had joined British Union because he considered it the only party capable of keeping the country out of war.[154] Shortly afterwards, in the last days of August, Williamson suggested to Mosley he could fly to Berlin and appeal to Hitler to stop the war. Mosley told him it was too late. As he left Williamson noticed the news hoarding 'Nazis Seize Danzig'.[155] Cotton continued speaking in the summer including Weymouth on July 20th and Salisbury not longer after.[156]

Some party members were left bewildered by the announcement Hitler and Stalin had signed a cooperation treaty. For many their support for fascism was tied with the struggle against communism and could not reconcile this with the main Fascist country allying itself with the Soviets. It was also difficult for communists. Some committed anti-Fascists left their party[157] and in Devon one Fascist felt unable to continue with British Union and resigned: Edward Ronald D'Alessio of Plymouth left in disgust even though he had been an active Fascist for many years.

Plymouth, from regional capital to redundant branch

While in 1935 the national party attempted to reorganise and focus its attention on campaigns removed from the West Country, such as supporting unemployed Lancashire cotton workers, local Fascists were left more to themselves than previously. The Plymouth headquarters was demoted with the national change of administration and the club closed with staff moved or made redundant. There was no longer a 'Western Area' and across the country the social clubs were shut down. The May reorganisation changed branches to conform to parliamentary jurisdictions and became known as

District Branches.[158] An indication of the dwindling of Plymouth Branch was fascism was defended in local newspapers from London and not local members.[159]

There were repercussions for redundant staff. Cyril William Roy Cann, Western Area Administration Officer for the party in 1934, and Arthur Reeve had intended to establish the Devon and Cornwall Car Hire Company. Cann used a garage behind the Lockyer Street headquarters for the Fascists and was sued for non-payment of the subsequent telephone bill for the proposed company. In legal deliberations held January 17th 1935 Cann admitted the party no longer employed him. The closure of the building was probably responsible for the loss of his would-be business. There is another possible element to this venture. Cann and Reeve may have been responsible for some curious anti-Semitism in August 1933. An unidentified garage owner insisted customers wishing to hire cars had to sign a form they were not Jewish. They were also not allowed to be undergraduates, in the armed forces, publicans, turf accountants, musicians, actors or jockeys.[160]

The national loss of momentum in 1935 was felt in Devon. There was a marked lack of coverage in local newspapers. This was due to at least four factors. First, the afore-mentioned political pressure would have denied the party publicity. There is also a specific factor in relation to *The Western Morning News*: the editor made good his threat of October of 1934 to boycott the party's activities. James Palmer promised he would 'close its columns' and did.[161] Second, the Fascists may have stopped being newsworthy with the novelty factor worn off after two years: violence was the only distinguishing factor between their and other political party events. Third, there was less activity to report with a diminished presence in the county and finally, the police ban on street meetings continued into the new year.

The loss of the Plymouth club and meeting places, withdrawal from tithe fighting, reorganisation and firing of staff, and exclusion from the *Western Morning News* was bad enough but on January 6th the party suffered its greatest blow. That day the *Western Independent* published 'The Rise and Fall of Fascism in the West Country' written by a former local officer. It was a devastating indictment of the movement and national headquarters.

The writer's identity was not revealed: most likely it was R. Bowden. This 'kiss and tell' account from the movement's Plymouth beginnings in August 1933 to the club's closure is extraordinary. A. K. Chesterton, the former Torquay newspaper editor and then propaganda officer for the party, responded with a letter and dismissed the revelations as being from a disgruntled former employee. However, the anonymous Fascist's account was straightforward in its facts and is collaborated by other evidence.

He claimed to have been one of the first to join at Plymouth in the summer of 1933. There was then no office, membership stood at twenty, and meetings were held outside the Post Office on the pavement. Numbers of non-active members gradually increased, helped by sales of *Blackshirt* of between 1,500 and 2,000 a week and the opening of the Lockyer Street office saw active members rise to some 340. Even so, members at parades stood at about 200. By December 1933 he thought there were one thousand non-active members. This would have made the number of overall members some 1,340, a staggering number to achieve in four months.

The writer claimed to have been in charge of the Defence Force at the time of Mosley's meeting and wrote the police congratulated him on the tone of the meeting. He suggested the stewards, all local men, were tactful with the hostile element of the crowd and the police had congratulated him on the way it was handled. He also noted the tithe issue was then raging and the local party had enrolled, in only a few weeks, over 100 farmers in the British Union of Farmers. In February 1934 he wrote they had asked national headquarters for financial help with supporting farmers in the large geographical area of Devon and Cornwall. Farmers were still subscribing to the new Union but, he wrote, 'here came the first sign of trouble'.

His account would not have been disputed. However from this point on the writer was extraordinarily critical of the manner in which national headquarters dealt with the Western Area. Mosley had, he said, returned to London after the Plymouth Guildhall meeting and told officials to go to Plymouth to see how a branch should be run. These men were not pleased and it was with them the writer took exception.

London took up the attitude that the expenditure of the Westcountry had been excessive and the local organiser was superseded by an organiser sent by the national headquarters at Chelsea. When this change took place we were the strongest branch in the country. Our expenditure was in the region of £30 a week, inclusive of the rental of the Lockyer Street headquarters which amounted to about £30 monthly.

When the local organiser resigned, a Court of Inquiry was held in London, six members from Plymouth attending. The findings of that court have never been promulgated, although the audit proved that all the monies had been properly expended.

Up to this time the relations between Plymouth Fascists and the police and the public had been admirable, but a change began to come over the scene. During last summer [1934] meetings became very rowdy, there were frequent fights, and what followed was a gradual breaking away of old members who disliked being associated with these scenes.

We who left the British Union of Fascist considered that the Westcountry and the East End of London were two totally different places and what applied to the East End did not apply to us.

The meeting at the Corn Exchange was not a tenth of the size of the successful Guildhall meeting, yet the Fascists lost control of it and the police were forced to restore order, as the stewards and the anti-Fascists were fighting all over the hall. The meeting was handled badly and the stewards too aggressive and provocative.

At this period London administered another blow to the branch. It decided that all activities in connection with tithe should cease, and the British Union of Farmers was disbanded practically with the stroke of a pen. We were left flat and lost many members in consequence.

London had no sympathy with the West Country and showed itself completely out of touch with the provinces. We could not make them understand the farmers or how strong our tithe campaign was making up in the country districts.

By last September, out of the 200 Blackshirts who paraded for Sir Oswald Mosley's Guildhall meeting only about ten were left. The non-active members have declined until they have almost reached vanishing point. I should think that 50 would be a generous estimate of their present members.

For the Leader's meeting in the Drillhall in October the Plymouth Branch was unable to find sufficient men to steward the meeting, and London had to send down a special squad. The result of that meeting was disastrous.

It led immediately to a further reduction in membership. There were still up to this time a few prominent businessmen who were on the non-active roll, but the scenes in the Drillhall, and afterwards in the Market Square, led them to tender their resignations.

At present the British Union of Fascists in the Westcountry is composed only of men who are employed either on full-time or part-time terms, number about ten Blackshirt members.

There are three paid members of the BUF in Plymouth. There are no activities. The sale of the weekly paper has dropped to insignificant figures.

The closing of the Club in Lockyer Street was rendered necessary by the falling off in strength. Yet at the end of 1933 we were taking £50 a week for drinks and refreshments!

Fascism has failed in Plymouth because of London officials who have no sympathy with the provinces and believe that Fascism can only come about in London. It was impossible to ever bring a complaint to the personal notice of Sir Oswald Mosley.

Although I have left the Blackshirts, I still believe in the Fascist policy, and there are hundreds like me in the Westcountry. I don't think fascism has any chance now unless there is a return to constitutional methods, the cutting out of a lot of this elaborate showmanship, and a policy of getting at the public in the same way as the orthodox parties.[163]

Chesterton was dismissive and unconvincing in his criticisms. He blamed the changes on the need to correct bad management, that decent members had been dismayed by the number of men 'lounging about' at Lockyer Street and that the branch was being 'restored to health'. Most interesting of all, he revealed the party had agreed with the police not to hold any meetings in January.[164]

The defector's inside view explains how Plymouth Branch imploded and how different the priorities of London politics were from those in Devon. If his account was accurate, then the machinations of the national headquarters were responsible for the collapse of fascism in Plymouth. It never recovered.

The party in Plymouth was not yet completely dead. In mid February there was an effort to revitalise it with the appointment of Captain H. E. V. Priestley, an Inspector of Branches and a self-described 'live wire' sent from London to take charge of Devon and Cornwall. He regarded his job as that akin to a commercial traveller and had to 'go out and get the business'. Priestley refocused efforts in targeting the wealthy instead of the mass meetings hitherto a feature of the local party: he planned on having 'Fascist teas' in the region's country houses as he had done in Sussex. Targeting the general public would have been difficult given the ban on outdoor meetings in Plymouth. Nevertheless Priestley claimed he hoped to be able to rent halls in 'all the towns and villages' of Devon and Cornwall beginning with Torquay. He was a comparative novice having joined the party only fourteen months previously.[165] The ban continued for several years.

The rest of the year saw further changes to the way the party was run locally. First, an event took place in August which would have been unheard of before. The party invited a socialist to debate at the headquarters. There is no hint of any violence or disorder. The meeting even appears to have been amicable.[166] There is one report of violence: in August a story appeared in *Blackshirt* that six Jews attacked a Plymouth Blackshirt selling literature in a street.[167] Literature was generally on sale on five locations on Friday evenings; this was at the post office at Westwell Street, Derry's Clock, Regent Cinema, Gaumont Cinema and in the market place.[168]

In August the party tried to circumvent the street ban by placing a notice board outside their headquarters on which they placed Fascist literature. It was a desperate move but *Blackshirt* optimistically reported membership was rising.[169] The following month, on the 15th, they had another innovation: a public meeting was held in the headquarters. This was part of Mosley's peace campaign over the Italian invasion of Abyssinia. The meeting was successful enough for the branch to plan on holding further sessions in the building.[170] A month later two further meetings took place and the public were welcome to visit the building on Wednesday and Sunday evenings.[171] The party's inability to hire halls and the ban on holding outdoor meetings resulted in their having to open their own doors. It implies a lack of opposition which might reflect a general feeling among the anti-Fascists that fascism was a 'spent force'.[172]

The Lockyer Street building was finally given up in November 1935, two years after it opened with a fanfare. The new headquarters was 10a Union Street in Stonehouse. The branch hoped to carry out a programme of sales drives, canvassing and meetings.[173] The British Union of Fascists did not offer Parliamentary Candidates in the General Election and Plymouth members were reduced to touring polling booths and handing out Fascist literature to electors casting votes for other parties.[174] Perhaps the most positive event of 1935 was the opening of a Fascist bookshop at 5 Queen Anne Terrace.[175]

The inactive state of the party in Plymouth and elsewhere is confirmed by regular reports sent by the police to the Home Office. In February a note on the most important centres in the country had no information on the South West. The early May report noted the only active area outside London was Lancashire whereas 'Bristol, Gloucester and other west of England districts are stationary'. There was a positive note for the party in 'it is the considered opinion of a well-informed and impartial observer that, although the actual membership of the movement has dwindled, the amount of sympathetic support, especially from the middle and upper middle classes, has increased'.[176] Another report, of 'secret information', dated 24 October 1935 noted 'most of the south coast towns have now merely a book membership – the whole work is carried on by one or two persons for each unit. The only exception of note is Southampton, which had improved its position.'[177]

In 1935 there was some activity in Devon but the level was low and the regional centre of local fascism moved eastwards to Exeter for the rest of the 1930s. At the end of October 1936 the police sent 'Secret Information' to the Home Office that Vincent Keens 'receives all correspondence' for Plymouth at the Exeter office.[178] It would appear that in Plymouth the party was inactive despite an assistant district officer, S. E. Underwood, having been appointed in March.[179] One hint of activity comes from a legal case between two men over a property in Union Street, where Plymouth branch was relocated. *Blackshirt* reported the case as part of a Jewish attempt to develop a block of property. It was also perceived as being inspired by Mr Nelson, a pawnbroker whose previous name was Blomberg. Roberts, a New Zealander, was being sued by another Jewish man for improperly housing commercial goods and through a Plymouth solicitor contacted British Union national headquarters for legal advice. It is not known whether Roberts was a Blackshirt nor why he felt he needed Fascist advice.[180]

Little is known of any activity in Plymouth in 1937 but Rear Admiral W. E. R Martin of Saltash wrote to *Action* 'I am glad to tell you that *Action* is sold out every week at the bookstall at Millbay Station, Plymouth'.[181] This shows some level of activity at least in the port. Plymouth is absent from any mention of sales figures of Fascist literature in *Blackshirt* nor were there any reports made of meetings for that year.

Fascist holidays

The classified columns of the Fascist press are a surprisingly rich source of information about Devon Fascists. Local members placed considerable numbers of advertisements in *Action* and *Blackshirt* offering goods and services. For instance, in 1934 Fascists visiting Devon were invited to purchase local honey from Honey Coombe

Apiaries at East Worlington near Crediton. Captain Hugh Brounscombe Hammond was the apiarist who advertised in *Blackshirt*.[182] He and Miss Elizabeth Hammond, presumably his sister, lived at Coombe Cottage since at least 1926. In 1935 he advertised for two strong young Fascist women to help in his business.[183] Hammond was then Propaganda Officer for Devon. It is not known whether the sales or recruitment were successful or how active other advertisers were in Devon.

Another classified advertisement came from the Globe Inn, now the Kingfisher, in Colyton. The Fascist there sought a saxophone[184] while an individual named Langdon of 7 Windsor Terrace in Exeter, tried to sell a vacuum cleaner in May in *Blackshirt*.[185] There was also Theodore Francis Taylor Currer-Jones at Soldridge Farm outside Bovey Tracey who in 1936 offered terrier puppies for sale to Fascist readers of *Action*. The following year Currer-Jones hosted Vincent Keens who had been sent from headquarters to organise fascism in Devon. Another dog breeder was Mrs Dorothy Beadon of Crossways in Lympstone who had miniature poodle puppies on offer.[186]

Rafe Temple Cotton advertised in connection with his business as a nurseryman in Branscombe. In September he offered British bulbs for sale from his nursery. Cotton had competition from a Fascist bulb seller in the Isles of Scilly. In the following month he placed another advert for a young male Fascist to work with him.[187] Later in the year, in December, Mrs Cotton sought help from a couple or two women and then in January 1937 Rafe Cotton placed another advert still seeking a couple to act at cook/housekeeper and handyman.[188] It may have been due to the amount of time Cotton

SITUATIONS VACANT

MARRIED COUPLE wanted, or two women, to take entire charge of house, help garden, able drive car. County people preferred. Temple Cotton, Flower Farm, Branscombe, Devon. 75

Advertisement for fascist help at Branscombe (Action, 24 July 1937).

spent on Fascist business that necessitated his employing additional staff.

A curious advert related to the Lobster Pot, a floating restaurant in Dittisham, which the owner, with the coincidental name of Oswald Moseley, tried to find a financial backer. No evidence has yet been found that he was related to Sir Oswald Mosley although it had been a family name since the eighteenth century. The coincidence could hardly have been lost on him or anyone who knew him.[189] His full name was Oswald Feilden Moseley and he lived at Lobster Pot Cottage.[190] There were many other advertisments but the greatest number concerned accommodation.

Throughout the late 1930s Blackshirts were targeted for holidays in Devon. A variety of establishments on both the north and south coasts, as well as others in inland places, sought Fascist patronage. With thousands of members across the country, and abroad, it is not surprising enterprising party members wanted to share their businesses and homes with fellow Fascists. Moreover, Blackshirts were probably given a warmer welcome than that awarded to other guests. There was a considerable range of accommodation on offer throughout Devon.

In the summer of 1934 Fascists had a choice. 'Superior' accommodation was offered at Birtles in Waterside, Paignton, while at 37 Cliff Road also in this seaside resort a lady offered part or full time board in her modern cottage. Likewise, Fascists were welcomed at Despard, a house at Trevarrick in Combe Martin.[191] No doubt all owners were members of the British Union of Fascists.

In 1935 shrewd party members hoping to capitalize on the movement included George Shorland of Mardle Cottage at Coombe Bridge near Buckfastleigh who throughout the summer placed an advert in *Blackshirt* that Fascists were particularly welcome to stay in his cottages and caravans. In June and at Christmas Shorland placed another advert selling clotted cream in the same newspaper. Shorland later lived at Brook Manor.[192] Thomas Rogers of Cliftonville in Salcombe also wanted party members to holiday in his furnished cottage. He also hired out boats.[193] It is likely Rogers was the man of that name described as the local organiser for the Fascists at a Salcombe meeting in 1934. 'British Union Fascists Welcome' was part of the advertisement for the Globe Hotel in Colyton.[194] Yet another opportunity for Fascists was Sanctuary Farm in Woodbury. Mr and Mrs Claude Duvivier welcomed guests to stay for bed and breakfast. Duvivier, a leading Exeter Fascist, regularly wrote to *Blackshirt*.[195] Fascists must have responded to the advert to stay at Despard, the house near Combe Martin, in 1934 because the owner again took out adverts in 1935.[196] One Fascist who did come on holiday was District Officer Thomas of East Grinstead who spent his time in and around Kingsbridge selling Fascist literature.[197]

In 1936 the county continued to advertise Fascist holidays. Colyton's Globe Hotel once again offered itself: the advert stated '*Blackshirt* readers welcome'. Readers of *Action* were also invited by the proprietor, William Hill.[198] For a second year Claude Duvivier also solicited Fascists to stay in 'glorious sunny Devon' at his farmhouse in Woodbury Salterton[199] as did Thomas Rogers, of Salcombe, in his furnished cottage by the sea.[200] In South Devon Blackshirts could expect a warmer welcome than usual from Mr Trevio at Parkham in Brixham.[201] They had a choice in Teignmouth: the owners of Havenhill and Coventry House particularly wanted party members.[202] In North Devon Fascists could expect a warm welcome from Mrs Prouse in her home with a sea view at Stoneycroft in Braunton.[203] One holiday maker who came down was J. P. J. Chapman, probably from Bournemouth. In his opinion the move in Exeter to fascism was 'remarkable'. He wrote 'on every side one hears the remark, better fascism than the reds'.[204] Fascists who were not able to come to Devon could always avail themselves of the services of George Shorland at Mardle near Buckfastleigh: he again offered to send them Devon clotted cream.[205]

In 1937 Fascists continued to come. The Globe Hotel once again advertised with 'many *Action* readers enjoyed last year's visit, will come again. To new visitors a good time assured.'[206] The proprietors, William Arthur Hill and Clara Wilhelmina Hill, must have been party members.[207]

The following year saw yet more advertisements. Three different locations, all on the south coast, were on offer in 1938. Paignton was one. An advertisement appeared for three weeks in May for 'Paignton bed and breakfast 40/. Detached residence in select neighbourhood, close to sea and station, ample garage accommodation.' The accommodation was Newbold House at 43 Totnes Road in Paignton,[208] a building since demolished. The notice did not give the name of the proprietors but the Voters' List for 1938 reveals they were Frederick and Winifred Essery.[209] In 1934 the Essery family had been in residence at the building which served as the Exmouth Branch headquarters.

Salcombe was again on offer. Spring advertisements in *Action* appeared for accommodation in the seaside resort. A 'delightful old world cottage, well furnished, all modern improvements and sanitation' was on offer. It had four good rooms and the garden sloped to the water's edge for boating. There were also rooms to let in a private house.[210] Most likely this was Thomas Rogers who had previously advertised. Finally, there was also a summer camp on offer for Blackshirts at Branscombe. Rafe Temple Cotton offered party members to camp out in July[211] and it may have been at Branscombe that a male cyclists' camp was organised for August.[212]

In the last season before war broke out at least five separate parts of Devon offered holidays specifically for Fascists. In June and July accommodation at Ilfracombe was advertised in *Action*. Mr Poyner of 21 Oxford Grove invited Fascists to stay at his bed and breakfast apartments in the north coast resort. Also, Mr Syndall of Blatchcombe Road in Paignton advertised 'board residence, bed & breakfast, every comfort, modern convenience, garage available'.[213] For three weeks, during which war broke out, there was another advert for the Globe Hotel in Colyton as 'fully licensed, excellent accommodation and food, garage, glorious country 2½ miles sea, proprietor member'. The proprietor continued his adverts during the war itself in May 1940.[214] The Castle Inn at Lydford on the western side of Dartmoor, carried a similar advertisement for six weeks from August through September. It offered itself as 'fully licensed, board residence, bed & breakfast, modern conveniences, moderate terms including bath and garage'.[215] Given the date of the advertisements it is possible the Globe Hotel and Castle Inn were appealing to party members in other parts of the country who had particular needs to leave their own homes. Each of these is surprising but not nearly so much as the advert for Dartmouth.

Dartmouth had a particular welcome for Fascists. It began with an attempt in March 1939 to invite the German warship *Schleswig*

Dartmouth with the Royal Castle Hotel on the far left (private collection).

Holstein, then about to sail from the Cornish port of Falmouth back to Germany, to the South Devon port. The mayor consulted leading locals who agreed this was not an 'opportune' time for a goodwill visit. The editor of the *Dartmouth and South Hams Chronicle* questioned the reasons and a lively debate took place in the correspondence pages on the lost benefits to the town: it was argued it have generated considerable national publicity and a great deal of money would have been spent by German seamen.[216] The proposal was made by Lt Colonel David J. Smith of Abovetown in Dartmouth, a frequent writer to the newspaper who in 1938 suggested the port solicit visits by cruise ships run by the German workers' movement *Strength Through Joy*. Again, this resulted in comment by other readers. One questioned political reasons for the suggestion. Smith wrote to the German embassy and received a positive response although the ships did not subsequently visit. It may be Smith was a member of the British Union although he did not admit this in the correspondence. He expressed concerns about refugees taking advantage of Britain but there is little else to explain his interest in Germany.[217]

What makes these moves to bring German ships into Dartmouth particularly interesting is the offer made to provide supper to the officers of the *Schleswig Holstein* at the Royal Castle Hotel, the premier hotel in the port. This was made by Commander Tillotson.[218] William Peel Tillotson began managing the Royal Castle in December 1937. In January 1938 he was successful in his application for the license at Dartmouth's Police Court. Tillotson had been in the Royal Naval Reserve from 1914 to 1930 and was a section commander in the Lancashire Special County Constabulary. He took possession of the hotel in March 1938[219] and a year later proposed hosting the *Schleswig Holstein*.[220] What would have made him of particular interest to German officers was his membership in British Union. It was at this very time he chose to advertise the hotel in *Action*. From the 25th of February until the 11th of March 1939 Tillotson inserted the following advert:

> *The Royal Castle Hotel, Dartmouth, Devon. This hostelry, which combines modern efficiency with ancient tradition, now offers hospitality to those desiring a holiday by river, sea and scenery. The hotel is owned and staffed by British Union Members, thereby ensuring disciplined attention. Forty bed-rooms, fitted with hot and cold water, electric fires, etc., a yacht motorboat and 2 dinghies are available for visitors. Trips can be made up the River Dart or along the Start Bay coast. Write for terms, then come and see how British Union works in practice.*[221]

Only six months later the country was at war. His advert may have alerted the local authorities to his political leanings.

According to the Voters' Lists of 1938 and 1939 there were also present in the hotel Harry Evans and Ethel B. Large, presumably the Fascists mentioned in the advert. Dartmouth was nationally known for its Royal Naval College and would shortly become equally renown for the American naval ships there during the second world war.[222] It was a sensitive location and no doubt there were concerns about a Fascist running the premier hotel. It has been suggested that Tillotson was interned during the war but nothing has yet been learned of the subsequent histories of Mr Evans or Miss Large. A history of the hotel shows the owner during the war years was a Mrs Morgan and that one Captain Rivers ran the hotel. In 1941 it was taken over by the 1st and 5th Commandos, then training for a raid on France which took place in March 1942. By then Tillotson had left Dartmouth.[223]

Tillotson had joined Mosley's party soon after it was founded and was the Area Organiser for Manchester. His Home Office report noted him being well-acquainted with Mosley and William Joyce. Tillotson left the party in 1935 because, he later claimed, it had gangster methods, but rejoined in 1937 or 1938. While at the Royal Castle he expressed pro-Nazi views and reportedly entertained Germans. He later claimed he left Dartmouth at the outbreak of war to avoid his creditors and the Home Office noted he had been involved in a number of doubtful business ventures. He was declared bankrupt in August 1940 and was then living at Washford in Somerset. Tillotson was interviewed and claimed to no longer be a Fascist. Three months later suspicions were aroused by his visiting the neighbourhood of the cable relay station at Sennen at night. By the 11th of October 1941 he was on the list of suspects to be arrested in the event of a German invasion. He was then living at Lychgate at Budock Vean in the Cornish parish of Constantine near Falmouth and was assistant manager at the Manor House Hotel. He told a guest in confidence he was still a Fascist and boasted he had 'drawn rings round Major Maude' in his interview. Tillotson told another he wanted Germany to win the war and had many Fascist friends working towards the same cause. By 26 June 1942 Tillotson had moved once more, to Bangor in Wales. However, he remained on the list.[224]

Armchair Fascists

Members spread fascism in various ways. One of the most effective was writing for the letters columns in newspapers. There is little known of some individuals except their letter writing. They include G. Eldon Manisty of Budleigh Salterton and J. H. Skinner of Tiverton who both wrote to *Blackshirt* in 1935.[225] In 1939 in particular dozens of letters were written to Devon's newspapers. Not all newspapers published them. *The Western Morning News* printed letters from a broad political spectrum and a small group of Fascists wrote incessantly that year. They included Claude Duvivier of Woodbury, H. B. Hammond of Kennerleigh, Revd Ellis and Miss Winifred Roberts of Ipplepen, Frank Scutt of Mansfield Terrace in Budleigh Salterton, Henry Jameson-Dixon of Torquay and Ernest Watkinson of The Godfreys on East Hill in Ottery St Mary as well as Cornishmen W. E. R. Martin of Saltash and R. P. Cobbold-Sawle of St Austell.

Topics included the party's policy against national chain stores and many were anti-Semitic but most stressed the positive qualities of Mussolini or of Hitler. Miss Roberts, for example, wrote in March 'is it not time for us to make a serious effort to understand that remarkable social experiment going on in Germany and take home some useful lessons to ourselves when we think of a country where there are no unemployed?' Scutt thought in April 'simply expressed, Bolshevism is actually Jewism. Fascism and Nazism are the opposition to it. Which is it to be, Britain for Britons or Britain for the Jews? It is up to us!' Duvivier also wrote in April 'I am sure that I speak on behalf of Messrs Scutt, Watkinson, Martin and others when I say that we resent and repudiate the charge of Nazi Propagandists just because we dare to warn our fellow countrymen of what we firmly believe to be the truth.' On that particular day, April 14th, Watkinson warned of a plot to destroy the Empire and Hammond inveighed against the Jews. It is not known whether this was a coordinated campaign or if these individuals merely responded to each other's letters.

There were also a number of letters written by others with similar views. For example, W. Gooding of Portland Square in Plymouth wrote an anti-Semitic letter but it is not clear whether he was a British Union member.[226] There were also peace campaigners such as Rudolph Messel of Drewsteignton of the Devon branch of the Peace Pledge Union, an organisation which included a number of Fascists. Messel urged readers who objected to conscription to write to E. C. Maddox of Newton Abbot.[227] There was also Mr Lomoff, a White Russian in Plymouth, who wrote anti-Semitic letters.[228]

Much of this was anti-Semitic but other correspondents attacked fascism including 'Disgusted' of Saltash. He asked 'do those individuals really think that their misrepresentations of fascism can dupe the British mind as to German and Italian intentions? Do they really believe that in classing devilish fascism and Nazi-ism as Christianity they are going to befuddle the British mind against facts which are coming to light daily?' Equally, H. E. T. Wilkinson of St Minver in Cornwall wrote 'your correspondents' anti-Jewish propaganda appeals only to those of a low class of intelligence. They predict a world war and urge us to join Fascism, but even if this great catastrophe should come, and if they win it, it will be our victory to have sided with the losers.'[229]

Other letters give insights into happenings throughout the county. Lancelot Dickens of Weeks-in-the-Moor Farm at Okehampton thought socialism and fascism agreed in many of their policies towards agriculture. He considered they both wanted to revive the industry, increase production, restrict imports, fix prices, suppress the middleman's profit and increase the purchasing power of the masses to create a greater market. Intriguingly, he asked 'is it, then, any wonder that socialism, and indeed, fascism, are recruiting in larger numbers the support of our farmers, small holders and farm workers?'[230]

Reverend Ellis Roberts and Winifred Roberts of Ipplepen

Two Blackshirts from Ipplepen seem to have done most of their work through newspapers and their letters and articles reveal some of their thoughts about fascism. The Reverend Ellis Roberts of Ipplepen, who been a Fascist for more than ten years, was a regular contributor to *Action*. He was interested in the question of race and one of his publications was a pamphlet entitled *Chosen Race and British Union*. In 1937 he was 77 years old. Like many older Fascists he had connections with the empire. He had retired to Devon in 1931 after having been a teacher at Noble College in Masulipatam in India in the late 1890s. He was invalided in 1901 and three years later became the vicar at Newbold on Stour. Roberts was there until 1912 when he moved to Alberbury where he stayed for the next seventeen years.[231] In 1931 he and his daughter Winifred moved from Shropshire to 'Orleigh', a semi-detached bungalow in Ipplepen situated near the church. The Roberts remained there during the second world war and their political leanings were known in the village. One resident recalls 'the Roberts were suspected of signalling to enemy aircraft at night with lights' and another remembers 'Oh! I didn't know the name Roberts, but there was a rumour that the other half of our building was occupied by people suspected of being spies.' The letters and articles reveal some of the thinking of ordinary members of the party.

Roberts joined Mosley's party in 1935. He wrote that December he had recently joined 'and when I add that I am seventy-six, almost blind, and a semi-invalid from chronic bronchitis, it will not be set down as want of interest that I am a non-active member'.[232]

Winifred Roberts was also a longstanding Fascist and regular contributor to *Action*. Among her letters in 1937 were 'One Honest Man' in which she wrote 'the following was told me by a friend who recently attended a public dinner. Here he found himself next to an engineer whose long and wide experience had brought him into contact with many politicians, at home and in the Colonies. His verdict was that in all the political world he knew of only one honest man. That man is the leader of the British Union.' She also contributed 'Forward Democracy' in which she wrote while British women were filling in forms regarding food consumption 'meanwhile we fight for Freedom and for Bread!' In December she even offered to bake for Christmas: she wrote 'if any district wishing to give a Christmas party among the poorer members would like to have a cake for the purpose, please apply to address below, first applicant will get it.[233]

In January 1938 Reverend Roberts' theme in *Action* was Ulster and the British Union. He wrote of the lack of any conflict between fascism and Christianity: 'let them turn to their bibles, as we used to do, and compare what they find there with the pronouncements of the British Union, and I believe they will find them in complete harmony. I have done this myself, and if the result had been otherwise I should not have joined its rank.'[234] Roberts was not the only Fascist cleric but he penned many letters. He wrote in another issue of *Action* 'when one hears and reads the scathing indictments raised against the 'Fascist' countries, and especially the 'religious persecutions' in Germany, it may surprise some to hear that the first and foremost reason for my support of Sir Oswald Mosley and the National Socialist cause is on religious grounds. It is because I am a padre, and firmly believe in the Christian religion that I welcome and thank God for what has already been achieved by Mussolini and Hitler, and look forward to the time when Mosley may be equally successful.'[235]

In 1938 Winifred Roberts commented on many subjects in 1938 including the Conservatives and the British sense of humour, holidays for workers and the Jewish conspiracy to bring war to Britain.[236] One of her letters has an odd insight into Ipplepen in 1938. Under the heading 'We need British Union' she wrote:

> *Two incidents have come my way this week which would, I think, have made me join the British Union, if I had not already been a member. First, an ex-service man came to my door selling lavender. After I had bought a packet, we got into conversation, and suddenly the poor fellow's feelings were too much for him, and, finding he had a sympathetic hearer, he began pouring out the bitter resentment he felt of the way in which he and his like 'the old 1914 men' as he said, had been treated by the country; at seeing swarms of alien refugees allowed in, and money collected for foreigners, while they thought themselves lucky if they could eke out existence by such ways as his. He wound up by saying that our politicians would not get him to fight for them again; he would rather be shot for refusing. The other was of a young couple who came to this village something over a year ago; they had been married a few months on the strength of a supposedly safe job. The man was a traveller for one of the large firms. His round proved a particularly heavy one, so that he often reached home thoroughly exhausted. At least, a short time ago, he asked to be put on a lighter round – and received a week's notice. He, his wife, and their four month's old baby, have had to give up their little home and go back to their friends. Yes, we want British Union and the sooner, the better.*[237]

In December she wrote of the 'decline of pantomime' and seasonal good will:

> *The article on this subject in* Action *for December 17, might had added to its just criticisms the abuse of pantomime from a source of harmless entertainment to a venting of petty, but venomous, political spite. At least, last year I can testify that in a performance otherwise pretty and pleasing, witless sneers at Mussolini were introduced without the slightest connection with anything that had gone before or that came after, and by persons who were either ignorant or supposed their audience to be ignorant, even of the pronunciation of the word 'Duce'. Probably, this year, snarlings at Hitler, and outpourings of sob-stuff for Iky* [Jews] *will be more in favour. It is almost impossible, today, for tired brains to find innocent relaxation anywhere, so noisy and so untiring is the chorus of hate.*[238]

The Roberts moved from Ipplepen to Silverton after the war to live with Henry Jameson Dixon, a Fascist from Kent, and his wife. Reverend Roberts remained a party member through to his death in 1947 and Miss Roberts was active into the 1950s.

The Fascist Uncle Tom Cobleigh of Widecombe-In-The-Moor

One writer who used his pen to promote fascism was H. E. Crocker, possibly a Devon man. By his efforts throughout the summer of 1936 the Dartmoor village of Widecombe-In-The-Moor became a Fascist community. Crocker wrote a series of articles entitled 'Fascism In Our Village' which appeared in *Action* from May through September. Uncle Tom Cobleigh had joined the Blackshirts.

> *Life has stirred suddenly and swiftly in our village and the cause of it all is old Uncle Tom Cobleigh. Judge of our surprise when he turned up at the Dog and Duck last night*

in a black shirt and, in answer to our excited inquiries, explained that he had joined Mosley's Fascists.

'Whatever made you do that?' asked Jan Stewer, rattling his empty pewter in an inviting manner.

'I heard one of the Blackshirts last evening', began old Tom Cobleigh. 'It was at a meeting at Westbourne, and the speaker had something sensible to say about farmers, so I stayed behind and asked him a few searching questions about what the Fascists would do for us farmers. I must say that that young fellow had a ready answer to all I asked him and didn't try to fob me off with silly answers like so many of these political folk. I thought it over last night and talked it over with the missus and this morning I ran into Westbourne and joined up, and here I am in my black shirt.'

Each week over the following months Fascists from throughout the country heard fascism explained through the words of Uncle Tom Cobleigh. In the first episode Jan Stewer and Peter Gurney learned about the Fascist policy to farm prices. As Cobleigh concluded:

That's good enough for me, and so I joined up and I wear the black shirt. Mosley's good enough for me.[239]

Notes

1 Dorril, *Black Shirt*, 332, 336-7, 352, 361, 368; National Archives, HO45/25385.
2 *Express & Echo*, 29 May 1935.
3 *Devon & Somerset News*, 14 December 1933; *Tiverton Gazette*, 2 July 1935.
4 Dorril, *Black Shirt*, 374-407.
5 *The Sidmouth Observer*, 19 August 1936.
6 Henry Williamson, *Goodbye West Country* (1937), 221.
7 *North Devon Journal*, 9 July 1936.
8 *North Devon Journal*, 27 February 1936.
9 Nigel West, *MI5; British Security Service Operations, 1909–1945* (Trowbridge, 1981), 47.

10 West, MI5, 94.
11 Colin Cross, *Fascism in Britain* (London, 1961), cited in Dorril, *Black Shirt*, 411.
12 Dorril, *Black Shirt*, 424.
13 Benewick, *Political Violence*. 288; Thomas Lineham, *British Fascism 1918–1939; Parties, ideology and culture* (Manchester, 2000), 110-111; Renton, *Fascism*, 20.
14 National Archives, HO144/21063.
15 Wasley, *Devon At War*, 11-12; *Torquay Times*, 16 & 23 April 1937.
16 *The Sidmouth Observer*, 24 March 1937.
17 Lineham, *British Fascism*, 112.
18 See Henry Williamson, *Goodbye West Country* (1937).
19 Julie V. Gottlieb, *Feminine Fascism; Women in Britain's Fascist Movement, 1923-1945* (2000), 85, note 48.
20 Lineham, *British Fascism*, 113; Dorril, *Black Shirt*, 430-47.
21 Copsey, *Anti-Fascism*, 71, 74.
22 Benewick, *Political Violence*, 284.
23 Dorril, *Black Shirt*, 448-65.
24 National Archives, HO45/25568/864023/12b.
25 *Western Morning News*, 21 April 1939.
26 *Dartmouth Western Guardian*, 12 January 1939.
27 *Express & Echo*, 7 April & 8 May 1939.
28 *Torquay Times*, 5 May 1939.
29 *Torquay Times*, 7 April 1939; Gottlieb, *Feminine Fascism*, 307.
30 *Express & Echo*, 25 April 1939; Simpson, *Odious*, 97, 138-9.
31 *The Police Gazette*, Supplement C, No. 21, Vol. XXIII, 24 May 1939.
32 National Archives, HO45/25385.
33 *Blackshirt*, No. 110, 31 May 1935.
34 *Blackshirt*, No. 119, 2 August 1935. Weston-super-Mare, Minehead, Falmouth, Penzance and Newquay were also on the tour.
35 *Tiverton Gazette*, 5 February 1935.
36 *Blackshirt*, No. 113, 21 June 1935.
37 *Blackshirt*, No. 116, 12 July 1935 & No. 127, 28 September 1935.
38 *Blackshirt*, No. 105, 26 April 1935.
39 *Blackshirt*, No. 108, 17 May 1935.
40 *Blackshirt*, No. 129, 11 October 1935.
41 *Blackshirt*, No. 112, 14 June 1935.
42 *Blackshirt*, No. 138, 13 December 1935.
43 *Blackshirt*, No. 134, 15 November 1935.

44 *Dorset Daily Echo*, 29 January 1935; *The Western Gazette*, 2 February 1935; *The Southern Times*, 2 February 1935.
45 *Blackshirt*, No. 102, 5 April 1935.
46 *Tiverton Gazette*, 2 April 1935.
47 *Blackshirt*, No. 116, 12 July 1935.
48 Wasley, *Devon at War*, 8.
49 *Blackshirt*, No. 129, 18 October 1935.
50 Todd, *In Excited Times*, 35; *Fascist Week*, No. 15, 16-22 February 1934.
51 Sheffield University, 119/A1/181 & 119/A2/154, 119/A2/175. Keens gave his telephone number as Buckfastleigh 68 which was Currer-Jones's number: *Kelly's Directory* for 1939. Number 9 Powderham Crescent was the home of Bessie Bragg. Presumably she rented a room to Keens: Devon Record Office, Exeter Voters' Lists, 1939.
52 David Pryce-Jones, *Unity Mitford, a quest* (1976), 71.
53 Sheffield University, 119/A2/182.
54 Sheffield University, 119/A1/184, 119/A5/114 & 119/A1/263.
55 Sheffield University, 119/A1/393. The letter is dated 7 April.
56 Blackshirt, No. 171, 1 August 1936.
57 Sheffield 119/A2/177.
58 Sheffield University, 119/A2/176-7.
59 Sheffield University, 119/A6/643.
60 *Blackshirt*, No. 184, 31 October 1936.
61 *Blackshirt*, No. 171, 1 August 1936.
62 Sheffield University, 119/A2/169.
63 Sheffield University, 119/A2/133 & A6/260-305, letter of 13/12.
64 *Blackshirt*, No. 160, 16 May, No. 162, 30 May, No. 178, 19 September 1934.
65 Sheffield University, 119/A6/260-305, letters of 23 & 30/12.
66 Sheffield University, 119/A2/134.
67 Sheffield University, 119/A2/134; Gottleib, Feminine Fascism, 288.
68 Gray, *Exeter Remembers The War*, 140-1.
69 'Secret information' was provided by the police that Mosley's autumn tour included a conference at Exeter on 27 November at 8 pm: National Archives, Ho144/21062.
70 Sheffield University, 119/A2/168.
71 *Blackshirt*, No. 144, 24 January 1936.
72 *Blackshirt*, No. 141, 3 January and No. 144, 24 January 1936.
73 Sheffield University, 119/A6/241.

74 National Archives, HO144/20147.
75 *Blackshirt*, No. 143, 17 January, No. 150, 6 March, No. 153, 28 March, No. 162, 30 May, No. 165, 20 June, No. 169, 18 July, No. 170, 25 July, No. 171, 1 August 1936.
76 *Action*, No. 30, 10 September 1936.
77 *Blackshirt*, No. 153, 28 March, No. 162, 30 May 1936.
78 *The British Lion*, Vol. 6, No. 3, May 1937. Also see the issues for June and August 1937.
79 Sheffield University, 119/A3/44.
80 Sheffield University, 119/A2/171.
81 National Archives, HO144/21063.
82 Sheffield University, 119/A3/44.
83 Sheffield University, 119/A6/199.
84 Sheffield University, 119/A2/260-305.
85 Sheffield University, 119/A6/197.
86 Sheffield University, 119/A3/77, C11/120 & C10/142.
87 Sheffield University, 119/A2/167.
88 Sheffield University, 119/A6/147.
89 Blackshirt, No. 211, 8 May 1937.
90 Sheffield University, 119/A6/223.
91 Sheffield University, 119/A6/199.
92 Sheffield University, 119/A3/183.
93 Sheffield University, 119/A3/45.
94 *Action*, 5 June 1937.
95 *Action*, 24 July 1937.
96 *Action*, No. 232, 9 October 1937.
97 *Blackshirt*, No. 233-4, 16 & 28 October 1937.
98 National Archives, HO144/21064.
99 National Archives, HO144/21064.
100 National Archives, HO144/21064.
101 National Archives, HO144/21064.
102 National Archives, HO144/21064.
103 National Archives, HO144/21064.
104 National Archives, HO144/21064.
105 National Archives, HO144/21064.
106 *Blackshirt*, Nos 236-7, 6 & 13 November 1937.
107 *Blackshirt,* No. 241, 11 December 1937.
108 *Action*, November 1937.
109 Sheffield University, 119/A6/43.
110 *Action*, 5 February 1938.

111 *Action*, 12 February 1938.
112 Sheffield University, 119/A7/105.
113 Sheffield University, 119/A7/104.
114 Sheffield University, 119/A3/42.
115 *Southern Speaker*, Vol. 1, No. 3, 15 5 1938.
116 Sheffield University, 119/A7/106 & 105.
117 Sheffield University, 119/A7/ 105 & 92-3.
118 *Blackshirt*, Nos 245-6, 15 & 22 January 1938.
119 *Blackshirt*, No. 247, 29 January 1938.
120 *Blackshirt*, No. 249, April 1938.
121 Sheffield University, 119/A3/40.
122 Sheffield University, 119/A3/38.
123 *Blackshirt*, No. 251, June 1938.
124 Sheffield University, 119/A3/38.
125 Sheffield University, 119/A3/38.
126 Sheffield University, 119/A3/40i-ii.
127 Sheffield University, 119/A3/396i-ii, 397 & C12/120; *Blackshirt*, No. 117, 19 July 1935.
128 Sheffield University, 119/C11/126, C12/120, A3/37.
129 Sheffield University, 119/A3/396.
130 *Action*, No. 119, 28 May 1938.
131 Sheffield University, 119/A7/98; *Blackshirt*, No. 252, July 1938.
132 *The Sidmouth Observer*, 21 September 1938.
133 *The Sidmouth Herald*, 24 September 1938.
134 Sheffield University, 119/A3/94.
135 Sheffield University, 119/A3/114b. The Southern Speaker, Vol. 1, No. 7, Sept. 1938.
136 Sheffield University, 119/A3/114a. The Southern Speaker, Vol. 1, No. 9, no date.
137 *Action*, 21 May 1938.
138 *Blackshirt*, No. 251, June 1938.
139 *Blackshirt*, No. 16, 5-11 August 1933.
140 The Sidmouth Observer, 5 October 1938.
141 Sheffield University, 119/A7/6.
142 Sheffield University, 119/A7/92.
143 Sheffield University, *The Southern Speaker*, Vol. 1, No. 4, 15 6 1938.
144 Sheffield University, 119/A4/25.
145 Sheffield University, 119/A4/25.
146 Sheffield University, 119/A4/27 & 48.
147 Sheffield University, 119/A8/102.

148 Sheffield University, 119/A4/98.
149 Sheffield University, 119/A8/34.
150 *Action*, No. 173, 17 June 1939.
151 Sheffield University, 119/A4/26.
152 Sheffield University, 119/A4/25.
153 Dorril, *Black Shirt*, 457.
154 Sheffield University, 119/A4/24.
155 Dorril, *Black Shirt*, 464-5.
156 Sheffield University, 119/A4/25.
157 Copsey, *Anti-Fascism*, 73.
158 Lineham, *British Fascism*, 100-102.
159 Western Evening Herald, 18 January 1935. The letter was written by A. K. Chesterton.
160 *Western Independent*, 3 August 1933.
161 *The Western Morning News*, 6 October 1934.
162 Benewick, *Political Violence*, 194.
163 *Western Independent*, 6 January 1934.
164 *Western Independent*, 13 January 1935.
165 *Western Independent*, 10 February 1935.
166 *Blackshirt*, No. 105, 26 April 1935.
167 *Blackshirt*, No. 121, 16 August 1935.
168 *Blackshirt*, No. 128, 4 October 1935.
169 *Blackshirt*, No. 122, 26 August 1935.
170 *Blackshirt*, No. 126, 21 September 1935.
171 *Blackshirt*, No. 128, 4 October 1935.
172 Nigel Copsey, *Anti-Fascism in Britain* (Basingstoke, 2000), 71.
173 *Blackshirt*, No. 135, 22 November 1935.
174 *Blackshirt*, No. 136, 29 November 1935.
175 *Blackshirt*, No. 139, 20 December 1935.
176 National Archives, HO144/20144.
177 National Archives, HO144/20145.
178 National Archives, HO144/21062.
179 National Archives, HO144/20147.
180 *Blackshirt*, No. 149, 28 February 1936.
181 *Action*, 3 April 1937, page 8.
182 *Blackshirt*, No. 67, 3 August 1934.
183 *Blackshirt*, No. 119, 2 August 1935. The Hammonds are noted in the Voters' Lists and in *Kelly's Directories*: Devon Record Office, East Worlington Voters' List, 1935 and *Kelly's Directories*, 1926 & 1935.

184 *Blackshirt*, No. 79, 26 October 1934. See also subsequent issues for 2 & 9 November.

185 *Blackshirt*, No. 106, 3 May 1935.

186 *Action*, Nos. 36-8, 24 & 31 October and 7 November 1936; *Action*, No. 41, 28 November 1936. Dorothy Ayre Beadon was listed as a voter as was Currer Jones: Devon Record Office, Lympstone Voters' List, 1936 & Bovey Tracey Voters' List, 1939.

187 *Action,* No. 31, 10 September 1936. This was Read of Garrison Street on St Mary's; *Blackshirt*, Nos 178-9, 19 & 26 September 1936 & No. 182, 17 October 1936.

188 *Action*, No. 43, 12 December 1936 & 46, 2 January 1937.

189 *Blackshirt*, No. 129. 11 October 1935. The adverts continued through to the 15th of November. Mosley also tried to sell fresh fish. His full name of Oswald F. Mosley was given in *Kelly's Directory* for 1939; Dorril, *Blackshirt*, 3-4.

190 Devon Record Office, Dittisham Voter's List, 1937 & 1939. The difference in the spelling of his name with that of Sir Oswald Mosley was noted in the Voters' List.

191 *Blackshirt*, No. 63, 6 July 1934. The advertisements continued through the season.

192 *Blackshirt*, No. 111, 7 June 1935 and No. 139, 20 December 1935. He was at the Manor by 1939: Devon Record Office, Buckfastleigh Voters' List, 1939.

193 *Blackshirt*, No. 109, 24 May 1935. The advert was also in the following issue.

194 *Blackshirt*, No. 112, 14 June 1935. The advert also appeared in the following two issues.

195 *Blackshirt*, No. 112, 14 June 1935. The advert also appeared in the following two issues. Duvivier's letters were printed in the 25 January, 8 March, 22 March and 1 November issues.

196 *Blackshirt*, No. 98, 8 March, No. 99, 15 March and No. 100, 22 March 1935.

197 *Blackshirt*, No. 121, 16 August 1935.

198 *Blackshirt*, No. 168, 11 July 1936 and also see the following three issues; Action, No. 21, 9 July, and the issues through to 10 October.

199 *Blackshirt*, No. 154, 4 April and the following three issues. He also advertised in *Action* from the 16th of April through to 9 July.

200 *Blackshirt*, No. 157, 25 April. See also the issues for 2 & 9 May. Thomas Herbert Rogers of Batson was listed as a voter: Devon Record Office, Salcombe Voters' List, 1936.

201 *Action*, No. 19, 25 June 1936. See also the next two issues.
202 *Action*, No. 20, 2 July 1936. See also the issues through to 27 August.
203 *Action*, No. 18, 18 June 1936.
204 *Action*, No. 26, 13 August 1936.
205 *Blackshirt*, No. 141, 3 January 1936. See also the following five issues.
206 *Action*, 8 & 22 May 1937.
207 Devon Record Office, Colyton Voter's Lists 1939; Devon Record Office, Axminster Rural District Council, R7/8/T/70.
208 *Action*, 14, 21 & 28 May 1938.
209 Devon Record Office, Paignton Voters' List, 1938.
210 Action, No. 109-111, 19 & 26 March, 2 April 1938.
211 *Action*, 2 & 30 July 1938.
212 *Action*, 9 July 1938. It was subsequently held closer to London: *Action*, 23 July 1938.
213 *Action*, Nos. 172-3, 10, 17 June & Nos. 177-9, 15, 22 & 29 July 1939.
214 *Action*, Nos. 183-5, 26 August and 2-16 September 1939. See *Action* for 2-16 May 1940.
215 *Action*, Nos. 180-5, 5 August – 16 September 1939.
216 *Dartmouth Chronicle*, 3 March 1939.
217 *Dartmouth Chronicle*, 14 January 1938. There are many other letters from him throughout 1938 and 1939.
218 Wasley, *Devon at War*, 16-17; *The Dartmouth Chronicle*, 3 March 1939.
219 *The Dartmouth Chronicle*, 7 January 1938 & 4 March 1938.
220 *The Dartmouth Chronicle*, 3 March 1939.
221 *Actions*, Nos 157-9, 25 February–11 March 1939.
222 Communication by Jeff Walder of Friends of Oswald Mosley.
223 Ray Freeman, *The History of The Castle Hotel, Dartmouth* (Dartmouth, 1995), 40.
224 National Archives, HO45/25569-70.
225 *Blackshirt*, No. 112, 12 July 1935 & No. 106, 3 May 1935.
226 *Western Morning News*, 21 January 1939.
227 *Western Morning News*, 17 May 1939. See also his letter of 24 April.
228 *Western Morning News*, 4 & 14 January, 22 April 1939.
229 *Western Morning News*, 11 April 1939.
230 *Western Morning News*, 13 April 1939.
231 *Crockford's Directory*, 1940.

232 *Blackshirt*, No. 139, 20 December 1935.

233 *Action*, 16 January, see also 18 September, 30 October and 9 December 1937.

234 *Action*, January 1938.

235 *Action*, 16 Oct. 1937, p.3

236 *Action*, 5 February 1938, 9 April 1938, 20 August 1938. See also 26 November and 10 December 1938.

237 Action, 2 July 1938.

238 *Action*, 31 December 1938.

239 *Action*, No. 12, 7 May 1936 and see the issues through to 17 September.

PART THREE

The Second World War: 3 September 1939 to 2 September 1945

The crossing of German soldiers into Poland on September first and Britain's declaration of war a few days later heralded the end of British Union although it staggered on for several months before closing. Amidst the public anxiety there was widespread questioning of the loyalty of British Fascists and an identification of them with the Nazis. Their public meetings continued but some turned violent even though hostility from traditional foes had ceased with the signing of a German/Soviet peace pact. A truce had occurred between British Fascists and Communists and for the first time Fascists did not face left-wing opposition but it came instead from the public.

Through the autumn and winter months Mosley continued to call for a negotiated peace with Hitler and met figures from other far right groups. This furthered uncertainties about Fascist loyalties to the government and to Britain itself. Some leading Fascists were arrested on the declaration of war but it was not until May, seven months later, that Mosley himself was arrested. Over the next month other members were apprehended and interned. Later in the war Fascists from other parts of the country found refuge throughout Devon but were still being monitored by the state in the event of a German invasion.

The Phoney War

With the outbreak of war people from throughout England began to arrive in Devon. They assumed it would be safer than their own homes. In the first few days of September thousands of evacuees arrived. There were also refugees, those who left on their own initiative and without state sponsorship. Among them were Jews who considerably increased the relatively insignificant Jewish population. This would have enraged some local Fascists and confirmed views the Jews were taking over the country. It was probably from one such individual, possibly Henry Jameson-Dixon, that *Action* received a copy of a local advertisement regarding 'a large influx of Jews' in Devon. The newspaper noted kosher meat was sold at the Torquay Co-op.[1] There was also one curious episode in the south coast resort in mid September when a local man was arrested over a drunken incident involving breaking a window. He claimed 'I saw two Jews having an argument about England, and being an Englishman I intervened, and one of them knocked me through the plate glass window'. The defendant also said 'two cars loaded with luggage stopped near me and not liking the conversation of the occupants – having always done my duty to my country – I struck a match to find their identity and was immediately backhanded by one of them into the window'.[2]

Not surprisingly Fascists were among the newcomers. Exeter Branch welcomed them: it advertised in *Action* for Fascist evacuees willing to help to write or call into the South Street headquarters on Friday or Saturday evenings.[3]

War had long been anticipated but even so some Fascists found it difficult when their country was at war with a Fascist state. Robert Saunders confessed to Rafe Temple Cotton 'I don't know how the declaration of war affected you, but if found it a great shock, and hardly knew what to think for several days. But now things seem clearer, and, in spite of everything, I look to the future with optimism.'[4] Public opinion turned against them in Bournemouth where the Branch windows were smashed and the landlord terminated the lease. The Branch, comprising only women since the men were conscripted, continued to operate but from new basement premises.[5] It is likely Devon opinion turned against British Union.

One member, Ida Shortland, of Lustleigh, encountered great hostility. In a curious letter she wrote:

> *because I am honest and outspoken I was subjected to a most merciless political persecution early last year and my life was made an absolute misery to me. However, my solicitors settled my slanderers satisfactorily for me and I am now able to live in peace and quietness, which is all I desire. Mr Douglas Bishop of Fairfield, Dawlish knows me well and I feel sure he would vouch for me, should you care to question him about me. The reason I have given you these details about myself, is to enable you to ascertain for yourself that I am responsible and reliable. I practically went out of politics last February [1940] and I entirely gave them up last May, but I have never resigned from British Union. After the war, if we are reinstalled? I shall vote for our candidate, if I ever have the opportunity of doing so, but I very much doubt if I ever take an active part in a Political Career as I consider it most upsetting to one's health and temperament.*[6]

In the last week of May 1940 Shortland wrote to Lucy Temple Cotton 'do you think as things are, it would be best for your son to destroy the list of contacts I sent him? I do not want anyone to be implicated through me and I can always let him have a fresh one later on when things get back to normal'. She added as a postscript 'in any case I'd rather the list was destroyed'.[7] Shortland had moved from Hemel Hempstead sometime after November 1936.[8] After the war she continued Fascist interests: in 1947 she wrote at least one anti-Semitic letter to the *Western Morning News*.[9]

In the South West the number of Fascist meetings dropped dramatically but the party planned on resuming village meetings in the spring of 1940.[10] Before that happened two local Fascists attracted widespread negative publicity.

Sending information of use to an enemy: Claude Duvivier of Woodbury and William Crowle of Devonport

The local party's fortunes suffered a blow when in January 1940 two longstanding members, Claude Felix Pierre Duvivier and William Alexander Crowle, were arrested on suspicion of aiding the enemy.

Duvivier farmed at Sanctuary Farm in the village of Woodbury near Exeter. He had been a Fascist from at least 1936 and in 1937 was a founder member of The Link,[11] a highly anti-Semitic organisation which was a propaganda vehicle for the German government.[12] Duvivier was Belgian and became British through naturalisation. When formally charged he was described by one local newspaper as 'a tall young man, slight and of smart appearance, and who wore a light overcoat over a plus-four suit, is well known in the Exmouth district. He was formerly interested in the activities of the East Devon Gliding Club and has frequently written letters to the Press on political subjects'. He was also an active member of 'the Fascist organisation'.[13] Crowle lived at 83 Cardinal Avenue in Devonport where he was an electric welder in the dockyard. He was described as 'a shorter and apparently younger man, wearing a light lounge suit and spectacles'.[14] Crowle joined the party in 1933, resigned that year and rejoined in 1939.

Duvivier was charged with possessing a document containing information which might be directly or indirectly useful to an enemy and of acting preparatory to the commission of an offence under the Emergency Powers (Defence) Regulations. Crowle's charge was he 'did unlawfully between January 1st and January 8th, 1940, communicate to another person, to wit, Claude Felix Pierre Duvivier, information which would be directly or indirectly useful to any enemy'.[15] Crowle was also charged with unlawfully recording information of use to an enemy. They pleaded not guilty.

Duvivier and Crowle testified they met at Exeter on May 7th 1939 en route to the May Day demonstration in London. Crowle stated he sat in a railway carriage with men wearing Fascist badges. One was Duvivier.

I told him that I was interested in the party and that while in London I was going to a Labour demonstration in Hyde Park and to a meeting of the Fascist party in the evening. He asked me to come to the Fascist headquarters in Smith Street and I spent the whole day with the Fascists. Duvivier seemed to be well known to some of the leaders of the party. Going up he told me he had a letter from a woman in Plymouth, who had got into communication with him as a result of one of his letters in the Morning News and she had told him of the activities of some of the Red agents in Plymouth.

Crowle had a letter from Duvivier a fortnight later. He rejoined British Union. Duvivier introduced him to Bryan Donovan, the Assistant Director, who asked whether Crowle had read a recent article about Leslie Hore-Belisha, the Devonport M.P., and asked him for any information about his past. Crowle later visited Duvivier in Woodbury.

It was shown in court Duvivier wrote to Crowle on September 28th 'whenever you have an interesting spot of news drop me a line. Yours till the day, D.V.' Crowle responded on the 23rd of October referring to Winston Churchill as 'Winnie' and noted 'you can draw your own conclusions from what I am going to tell you now. The *Repulse* is at Devonport. My sister corresponds with a young sailor aboard her and she received two letters from him but since the sinking of The *Royal Oak* has not received a line'. Weeks later, on the 12th of December Duvivier wrote a post card asking 'why no news from you?' Crowle wrote back 'I lost my cousin on the *Rawalpindi*, and I can tell you it is from good authority that I know a line of ships was flung across the North Sea to catch her [the German ship]. But she took refuge in a North Russian port. As you know, in the Arctic Circle you only get one hour daylight and she got away in the night'.

Two days later, on December 14th, Duvivier wrote his last letter.

Now what about this naval engagement in the South Atlantic? You must be especially interested, as I was. In your previous letter to me you said you had done two years on the Exeter. Well, according to all accounts, she was put out of

> *action. As usual, I suppose we shall not be allowed to know the extent of the damage or the number of casualties, although the Germans claim that she received 11 hits, had developed a bad list, and finally ran aground on a sand-bank. Neutrals mention she has had at least 100 casualties.*

He wrote with astounding frankness given they were in the midst of war:

> *The poor old B.B.C. tell us she only got one hit, yet the one hit was sufficient for her to drop out of action. Of course, as usual, we shall never know the truth, as both sides claim it as a victory, and being a National-Socialist, I prefer to believe the German version. It was a three to one battle, and I should have like to have seen matters reversed. Three pocket battleships versus the Repulse. What then? You know the answer as well as I do. My heart goes out to those men on the Graf Spee – heroes fighting for the cause, every one of them. Now there is the whole might of the Allied Fleet waiting for them outside – waiting for one crippled enemy. Where is the traditional sportsmanship and chivalry of the British Navy now? What does your dad think about it? To me it just makes me sick'.*

Even more devastatingly he wrote:

> *I believe she will fly home. There is a rumour from Rome that reinforcements and submarines are on the way. Let's hope so, otherwise I see no hope for the Graf Spee. If she does get away, boy, it will be a victory for the cause, and will go down in the annals of history as an epic for National-Socialists. And what of the Bremen? Oh boy! What a smack in the eye for Churchill! Of course, there was a British submarine stalking her all the time; but for humanitarian reasons – a grand story, what?'*

Crowle concluded 'you are right, old boy, justice will prevail. Our cause must win. I admire your determination and spirit. Keep it up.

It will be a hard struggle.' Their correspondence took an extraordinary turn when Crowle wrote in early January.

> *Many thanks for your card and letter. I am writing this letter to you mainly to see if you can help me out in getting some exclusive story for Action. I can tell you quite definitely it is a very startling indictment of the principles for which this country went to war. I have the papers actually in my possession – it will create a sensation and rip the freedom myth wide open . . . Winston Churchill is very largely implicated in this affair. It is his work. I believe that only his hands could have directed the scheme. Can you tackle H. Q. and find out if it will be possible to get an official down to see me . . . Don't ask him to come yet, but only when I ask. There are a few more details to clear up. I tell you I know it will be a delight to get this scoop, as it will prove beyond doubt that this government's acts savour of the O. G. P. U.*

It was said in court the remainder of the letter referred to the condition and location of Royal Navy ships.

A few days later, on January 8th, police officers visited with search warrants. They found a sealed envelope addressed to A. Raven Thompson in care of *Action* in London. In it was a letter from Duvivier vouching for the authenticity of Crowle, 'one of their most enthusiastic members in Plymouth'. Crowle claimed he acquired his information from rumours in hospital and in the town. Duvivier stated he felt it was unimportant and said 'I acted entirely in the cause of peace and believe in the necessity of friendship with Germany. My idea in forwarding this correspondence was merely to assist in providing a story for *Action*.' On January 16th charges were preferred against them at Exmouth and the trial was heard on the 30th. Part of the trial was heard in camera 'in the interests of public safety' and when it resumed in public the men changed their pleas to guilty.

Crowle felt he was being victimised because he was a member of British Union and that he had been discharged from the dockyard for the same reason. The two were given the maximum sentence the court could impose; each was sentenced to six months' imprisonment with hard labour under the Emergency Powers (Defence) Regulations. The chairman of the Bench said, during sentencing, 'this country is at war today with an aggressive nation and you have chosen to endeavour to obtain information which may or may not have been useful to the enemy . . . every man was entitled to his own political views, but no man had the right to use those views against this country when at war'.[16]

The editor of the *Exmouth Journal* commented:

> *They will expiate their crime in gaol but that obviously cannot be the end of the story. The authorities certainly cannot afford to let such fellows run loose at the end of the term. Public safety demands that they must be kept under strict surveillance. In the case of Duvivier, he has violated the oath he took, and surely must be held to have forfeited the right and privilege of British citizenship. We feel sure that the authorities, who have brought them to brook, will see to it that they have no further opportunity of exercising their peculiar brand of 'loyalty to King and Country'. They have chosen 'the mark of the beast' and thoroughly deserve the consequences of the action.*[17]

On 31 January British Union expelled them and issued the statement 'for a long period before the war we expelled any member who was known to feel or to behave like a German or member of any foreign nationality. The membership of two men involved in a recent case has been terminated for conduct incompatible with membership of this movement'.[18]

Further details of Duvivier were subsequently revealed during the questioning of Rafe Temple Cotton. He testified he helped in removing Duvivier as Exeter's District Leader. Cotton was asked 'how well did you know him – just as a fellow Fascist?' He replied 'Yes, I have been to tea with him once or twice. He is a fellow farmer as well as being a fellow Fascist.' Cotton said Duvivier's home was convenient as he lived on the road he travelled home from Exeter. When asked if Duvivier was his senior he replied 'When I first joined he was over me but then I found he did not do much active work in the furthering of the British Union movement and so I suggested at headquarters he was not a suitable man for a District Leader and I also said that he was half Belgian and that sort of thing, so I suggested it would be better for a British Movement not to have him as District Leader. I was instrumental in his not being District Leader'.[19]

It is not known what secret evidence was presented in court but it is possible it was later used against Cotton. The file of their interrogation along with MI5's summary have survived but one page has been substituted with information blacked-out for 'national interest &/or security'. Cotton's telephone had been tapped and operators at Seaton and Exeter overheard a conversation between him and Bryan Donovan, the Assistant Director General at British Union Headquarters. MI5 suggested Cotton used codes to communicate information but this he denied. The report recorded 'the caller from Hill Arrish asked for Captain Donovan. The caller then gave letters and figures and references to documents, quoting paragraphs. Bearing in mind that Duvivier was known to be the channel for passing naval information from Portland to British Union headquarters and having regard to Temple Cotton's position in the movement, we do regard this with suspicion. The statement that Duvivier's defence was supposed to be subscribed to by the Temple Cottons is derived from [blacked out] a conversation between Temple Cotton and Donovan on the 15th January 1940 when Cotton called up Donovan.' Cotton had asked 'did you get my message' to which Donovan replied 'Yes, did you get my letter to Duvivier?' Cotton said 'yes, is there anything you can advise?' to which Donovan answered he could recommend legal advice but it would be very expensive. He also said 'we mustn't commit ourselves as the charge is very vague'. Cotton answered 'Duvivier and I are willing to pay anything within reason' and Donovan suggested that a local solicitor would be suitable at present.[20]

Cotton stated he visited Duvivier's wife on several occasions when she was seeking legal aid for her husband. He also said he had seen Duvivier once while waiting for his trial and that British Union headquarters suggested he find representation in Cathcart Street in London.Cotton said he first met Crowle on a train to London 'a long time before' Crowle was arrested but their only subsequent association was a letter. M15 made a secret copy of it on 19th November 1939. It read:

> *Dear Mr Crowl, We have not heard from you for a long time? How are you and how goes public opinion in Plymouth? I have got to come to South Devon next weekend and could come on to Plymouth if it would do any good on Sunday 25th November. I would be very glad to meet you and any other members or hopeful contacts in Plymouth. Please write me at once if you would like to meet me. It is time something was done in Plymouth for BU. Have you seen this week's Action yet – it's a corker! Yours in Union, out for Britain first and peace.*

Cotton claimed Crowle's sister had responded her brother was seriously ill in hospital and that he was an ordinary member and the only one in Plymouth.[21]

Lucy Temple Cotton was also questioned whilst being interned. She was asked 'did you not think they were pro-German?' and answered 'I knew Duvivier was, that is why we never let him do anything in the movement if we could help it.' She was also asked if she contributed to Duvivier's defence and said 'no, we just helped his wife all we could but naturally we should do that.' In a summary by MI5 she was quoted as regarding 'him as a very foolish young man and [she] had no idea of any of his activities. It was a profound shock to her to read of the evidence in that case. She did not attend the trial and contributed nothing to his defence. She had had nothing to do with any of the work of Duvivier.'[22]

Another British Union member, Edward D'Alessio, also provided information in the summer of 1940. He was also interned and stated he had been annoyed to learn of Crowle's existence through the trial when he himself had been appointed Plymouth's District Leader. D'Alessio said he was aware of Duvivier through letters to the *Western Morning News*.[23] Duvivier was a prolific letter writer. Many were about Jews and others were against war with Germany ('we are animated by a strong patriotic desire to prevent our country being rushed blind-folded into a ghastly, senseless war, from which nothing but destruction and misery can ensue for all') or generally supportive of Hitler ('Hitler springs from the people and is a working-class superman, a front-line hero of the world war').[24]

It was through *The Western Morning News* that another Fascist connected to Duvivier came to the attention of MI5. On May 19th C. J. Palmer, editor of *The Western Morning News,* wrote of Robert Dundas 'you may like to see the enclosed – in confidence. I have not seen his stuff for a long time. As far as I remember he did not write from Totnes before. This Fascist was tied up with Duvivier, of Exeter, who you remember was arrested recently.' Dundas' letter was sent to the newspaper from The Old Manor in Littlehempston near Totnes and dated the 17th of May. He headed it 'This Fifth Column Nonsense' and wrote 'we have been called in our time most of the vile adjectives – we have been called slugs, hooligans, society degenerates. We have suffered the more dangerous veiled abuse that attacks under the cover of impartiality'.[25] It does not appear Dundas was interned. He was friendly with two Fascists living near Totnes at Ipplepen,[26] Reverend Roberts and his daughter Winifred, and they were most likely members active in Totnes where Dundas organised the party. How Dundas was acquainted with Duvivier, who lived some distance away, on the opposite side of the Exe Estuary, has not been determined. It may have been through Exeter Branch or possibly The Link.

Duvivier and Crowle were interned after serving their sentences. Duvivier appealed for his release and later reflected 'I personally did not entertain much hope, but I thought I would have a good try, especially as Crowle had been successful. I did so merely because I am fonder of my wife and children, than I was of kicking my heels in an Internment Camp, one only had to 'spin em a yarn', promise to be a good boy' and out you went. But no! The evidence against me is too patent, and in writing. You cannot deny what you have written so easily as you could the spoken word, and my result, of course a foregone conclusion was 'further detained'.' Duvivier was not released until 26 July 1944.[27]

The case of Duvivier and Crowle bears some relation to that of Hubert Fyrth, a left-wing student at the University College of the South West, later Exeter University. Fyrth received a copy of a British Expeditionary Force document from his brother and sent it to the *Daily Worker*. The letter was intercepted, the Fyrth brothers were arrested and Hubert Fyrth served twelve months for treason. Finally, although it has been argued Duvivier was treated severely another Devon man was treated far more harshly. Duncan Scott-Ford of 3 Pym Street in Plymouth was only twenty-one when he was executed for treason in 1942. A few months earlier he agreed to send information of British shipping movements to a German agent in exchange for the payment of an IOU for a bar bill of some £18.[28] There is one other Devon connection: a wing at Dartmoor Prison, Camp 001, was used for potential double agents.[29]

Fascism and the Battle of Britain

Fascist outdoor meetings continued in the spring of 1940 but there was a decidedly different atmosphere with British men and women risking their lives overseas and with the bombing of Britain. The party continued to call for a negotiated peace.

By April 1940 Exeter Branch was short of active members with Fascists called up for service. This probably explains why a firm was employed to put up posters; in February and March 150 British Peace posters were in Exeter and North Devon and another 100 in Torquay and South Devon. Meetings continued. In late March Cotton spoke to some 150 people in Exeter and planned another for the first week of April and in Exmouth on the 11th. Cotton and fellow Fascists distributed 2,000 peace leaflets in a few weeks. Cotton and Cecil George Brooker spoke in Honiton on April 19 at an 'excellent meeting' and gave peace leaflets. The following day they were in Exeter's Market Street. Saunders arranged with Dorchester Town Council to use Maumbury Rings, the open-air amphitheatre, for May 14.[30] This was Cotton's last public meeting but not a success. The audience of 300 included 150 soldiers. According to the police 'the speakers were heckled all throughout the meeting but not in an offensive way, and at times they could not carry on for singing and shouting'. Afterwards some soldiers made several attempts to overturn the Fascists' van. Four Fascists managed to push it away.[31] Three weeks later Cotton was arrested.

The invasion fears generated by the fall of France in early summer raised concerns of spies particularly among the great number of refugees then coming into England. Rumours became rife. One story current in Plymouth in early June concerned a woman and her young son travelling by rail to London. The boy dropped his toy in the carriage and this was picked up by one of the two nuns who were on the train. The mother noticed she had a hairy arm. She reported this to the police who caught two German spies and she received £10 as a reward. A variant of the story was that the two men were disguised as nurses. Two Plymouth council workmen were reported for taking levels for the Engineer's Department and a woman waving goodbye to her son at the train station was accused of giving the Fascist salute.[32]

There were also fears collaborators would hasten Britain's defeat. By then a great range of individuals were under suspicion and arrested. Fascists were only one of the groups of people targeted.

This led to some unlikely prosecutions. For instance, Stanley Hake of Sweet Brier Lane in Exeter was arrested and all charges were later dropped except the judges found him guilty of making statements likely to cause alarm or despondency. What makes this so extraordinary is his alibi: he described himself as a medium under the control of an astral spirit named 'The Arrow', at the Church of the Holy Spirit, who channelled information from 'Hawk', a 300-year old native American chieftain. Hake claimed not to be responsible for information he received including regarding the movements of the Expeditionary Force then still fighting on the continent nor for details of the enemy bombing of the South West. The Bench believed otherwise.[33]

Aliens were arrested and interned in a similar manner to during the first world war. Anthony Marsh was sent to prison for two months in June 1940 for not notifying the authorities in Paignton of a change of address. Marsh was also known as Karl Frederick Mertz; the twenty-five year old had been born in Dusseldorf to an English mother but had been in England since he was a toddler. He considered himself 'British in thought and deed' but his parentage made him a person of questionable allegiance.[34] Mrs Maria Stokes of 2 Preston Villa in Laira at Plymouth was placed on the list of those to be arrested in the event of an invasion in October 1941 for comments she had recently made. She was German by birth and married a British man in 1929. Her visits to Germany had been frequent and she returned from Germany only a day or two before the war. When questioned by police where her loyalties lay she answered 'her heart was torn in two'. The police decided she would aid the Germans and added her husband's loyalties were also questionable.[35] Mrs Brigitta Riorden, of 9 Argyle Terrace, Huntiscombe Road, Plymouth and later of 5 Davy Villas also in Plymouth, was placed on the Suspects List in October 1940. She was also German-born, married a British man in 1920 and the Home Office noted he was a drunkard who relied upon her salary as a midwife. Reports from colleagues, patients and anonymous sources all testified to her anti-British views.[36]

On 10 January 1941 Eric A. Weber of the Laurels, 19 Woodland Park, Paignton was placed on the Suspects List for 'words recently spoken'. At the time of his questioning the fifty year old had lived in Paignton with his wife and elderly father-in-law from 1938. Weber was a former German solider of the first world war who had previously been married with two sons in the German forces. He divorced his first wife and met his second, a British woman, in South Africa. They moved to Torbay and his Home Office report noted he supported the German invasion of Czechoslovakia and treatment of the Jews. He had also said Lord Haw Haw's news reports were as accurate as those of the British. It was decided he held pro-German views and was arrested and interned in June 1940. Weber was released six months later on the condition he did not travel more than five miles from his home and reported his activities to the local police each week.[37]

Another foreign national was Mrs Margaretha Venner who was also placed on the Suspects List. By 4 January 1944 her address was 10 Sussex Terrace in Ford at Devonport but she had moved to 18 Fore Street in Saltash seven months later. Venner was Austrian-born and British by marriage. She had come to England in 1937 for employment, worked as a domestic servant and at the beginning of the war was arrested and interned on the Isle of Man. While there she expressed anti-Jewish and pro-Nazi views. On one occasion a German plane flew overhead and with tears in her eyes Venner said 'the Germans are sending someone to deliver us'. She was released in June 1941 and two months later travelled to Plymouth where she married Fernley Venner, a local bricklayer. He had proposed to her before her arrest but she had refused him. Her Home Office file suggested she married to become a British national. The marriage was not a success and in April 1943 she enquired of the police whether a divorce would result in her regaining her Austrian nationality. A few months later she wrote to an Austrian friend she would give up her husband and home in order to return to Austria. It was at that point she was placed on the Suspects List. She remained, however, in the Plymouth area through 1944.[38]

Mrs Alice Caroline Parnell is a puzzle. She had three local addresses: the vicarage in Peter Tavy, the Old Cornish Arms in Cornwall Street at Bere Alston and at Campel Haye Cottage in Launceston. In October 1941 she was placed on the Suspects List for recent comments. Parnell was born in 1906 in France to a British father and a German mother, Alice Jacobs. She claimed in a police interview to be loyal to Britain but had been arrested and deported from the Channel Islands for sketching the roads to the local airport. While it may not be surprising she was reported for pro-German comments ('she agreed with everything the Nazis were doing, the occupation of the Channel Islands by them was a good thing and that the people under Hitler were happy and not starving as was so often stated') and that she was emotionally torn in regard to her family in Germany (her brother was in the Luftwaffe and she burst into tears when she overheard Plymouth people say they would kill any downed German airman without compunction) it was her revelation that she was a Jewess that makes her views so surprising.[39]

After Italy declared war on Britain in June 1940 Italians were rounded up. In 1931 there had been nearly 30,000 Italians living in the United Kingdom, most had been born in Italy.[40] Anti-Italian incidents occurred and rumours swept through Devon including at Plymouth there were stories of rifles being found under the floor-boards or bombs in the kitchen of a 'foreign café'. There were small demonstrations outside Italian cafés in Plymouth but apparently the only activity was the booing of women who had bought ice creams. Signs explaining the cafés were under new management ended the trouble.[41]

One of those arrested worked at Berni's Continental Café in Exeter. Interestingly, the café had been used by local Fascists several years before.[42] Victor Marriot was another. His original surname was Mariotto; both parents were Italian and although he was born in London he had dual nationality. In August 1940, at the age of 25, Marriot was arrested and then released ten months later on a suspension order. The Home Office noted he spread anti-British views although another civil servant recorded there was actually little evidence of it. The government tried to assess where his sympathies would lie in the event of an invasion and concluded he had no British friends, most of his spare time was spent in Italian social clubs and he was 'the type of person . . . to take advantage of his Italian nationality' in a German invasion. In June 1943 he moved to The Mill in Upottery in East Devon by which time he was on the Suspects List.[43]

Louis Anthony Bucchini alias Buchanan of 168 King Street, Plymouth, was put on the Suspects List on 22 November 1940. He moved to St Austin's Priory, Ivybridge, on 16 July 1941. Bucchini was born in Plymouth in 1898 to Italian parents. He served in the Royal Engineers' Signal Section as a Sapper in the first world war and for fifteen months until August 1940 he was a civilian wireless operator at RAF Mount Batten until he was released for pro-Fascist views and for being 'a staunch supporter of Mussolini'. The Home Office noted reports were received that Morse code was heard coming from his bedroom and apparatus was discovered there. He was also in possession of Italian Fascist material and a transcript of a German radio broadcast on British shipping movements and losses. Bucchini had said fascism and Nazi-ism would rule the world.[44]

One of the more curious Italian cases involved a hotel worker from Poole in Dorset. Alfred John Buffete Catford was 25 years old when he was arrested in Plympton in November 1940. An intelligence report on him noted:

> *Catford has a number of convictions for crime. He is a worthless type of individual who has had opportunities to go straight but has failed to take them. He may be slightly 'mental' but not to the extent of being mentally deficient. This man seems to have a predilection for Italians. He was friendly with two Italians at Poole who were there for six*

> *months in charge of a yacht. They left and one of them obtained employment on a yacht at Southampton and Catford shortly after obtained work at the same boat. This was in July 1939.*

In November Catford was arrested at Plympton, Devon. He was posing as an Italian and gave the name Danti Zinero Barletti; he tried to register as an alien. A map or maps was found in his possession showing vulnerable points in the locality. MI5 took part in the case and it is understood that Catford knew a number of Italian Fascists in the Portsmouth area. It may be that Catford's extraordinary behaviour is due to his mental condition but even if this is so, it is clear that he is unscrupulous and has some unusual interest in Italians. Thus in the event of an invasion, he might well give aid to the enemy and his detention in such an emergency is recommended'.[45] It is not known if Catford alias Barletti had any further involvement in Plympton.

In addition to German and Italian nationals, there were other foreigners in Devon who were watched. Robert Grosfills was a Belgian civil servant who fled his country when it was invaded by Germany. His membership of the Belgian Fascist party, and its collaboration with the Nazis, caused concern in the Home Office as did his close friendship with Joseph Hague, a prominent Belgian Fascist. In letters he expressed admiration for the moderate nature of German government over occupied Europe, was dismissive of Churchill and was delighted by Lord Haw Haw's broadcasts. Grosfills and Hague considered escaping from England in a Belgian fishing boat from Brixham or from Dittisham. He had lived at La Casita in Malden Road at Sidmouth by 1941 and was placed on the Suspects List.[46]

There was also a French woman under suspicion. In 1940 Ida Marie Joseph Pinson had been living at the Palm Court Hotel and the Manor Hotel in Exmouth and was the subject of a report from the county's chief constable. He wrote she made anti-British statements and supported the Vichy government. She had said 'the English have no morale and when the Nazis invade they will have a bad defeat. France will rise up and become more glorious once more and will be more powerful than England has ever been'.

Name:- MENTETH, Blanche Yvonne

Address:- (Last known) c/o Major Hole, "Parke", Bovey Tracey, Devon. (July, 1941.)

British, born Brighton, 4.8.1894.
Parents born in Channel Islands - both dead.
Special Branch report that Miss MENTETH was a member of the British Union for 3 months in 1937, but does not appear to have had anything to do with the Party since then.

Prior to 20.3.40, MENTETH was employed as Manageress of the Milton Hall Guest House, Chalfont St. Giles, Bucks, where she is alleged to have told her employer that she had met and shaken hands with Hitler. From 20.3.40 - 17.5.40 she was Manageress of the Spanish Ladies Cafe, Saltdean, near Brighton, where she excited suspicion by her pro-German views. From 6.6.40 - 14.6.40, she was employed as cook by a Mrs. Hancock at Exmouth. Here also she was reported to have expressed pro-German views.

In a variety of employments in different places, MENTETH was reported for her pro-Nazi views wherever she went.

In June, 1941, MENTETH was employed as cook by Mrs. Rhoda Marshall, of Fullaford House, Buckfastleigh, who signed a statement that she did her best to influence the rest of the staff to the prejudice of the State. Two other maids at the same establishment have signed statements that the following remarks were said by MENTETH during her employment with Mrs. Marshall :-

"I am sure Germany will win". "Hitler will only negotiate peace terms with Sir Oswald Mosley, who will be dictator of Britain". "My brother is in the German Army". "The English did not help the Channel Islands when they were invaded." "If invasion takes place it will be through Ireland by way of Port Rush and without opposition from Mr. De Valera." "Churchill is a butcher and a murderer." "Anthony Eden is the lady with skirts." "The English Government paid the I.R.A." "The Duke of Hamilton knew about the arrival of Hess". "The English have a law for the rich and a law for the poor." "They were never prepared in any way." "The Royal Family have a house ready in Canada to flee to in case this country is invaded." "The English Government have made no attempt to arrange things in blitzed towns." "The English Government dropped bombs on Eire to draw the Irish into the War." "Hoare Belisha sold this Government". "Goebbels is a marvellous

/man

Intelligence file on Blanche Yvonne Menteth of Bovey Tracey (National Archives, HO45/25570).

Fortunately she moved to Wales before MI5 took steps to have her deported.[47]

It was not just foreign nationals who were suspected. Blanch Yvonne Menteth was born in 1894 in Brighton and her parents were from the Channel Islands. In 1940 she worked for a brief time as cook for one Mrs Hancock of Exmouth and in June 1941 went to work for Mrs Rhoda Marshall at Fullaford House in Buckfastleigh. Marshall appears to have been a newcomer to the village and what her political views were has not been determined. While in their employ, and in many other places, Menteth was reported as having pro-German views. She claimed to have met Hitler and having shaken his hand. She alarmed fellow servants and complete strangers in Buckfastleigh by saying 'I am sure Germany will win', 'My brother is in the Germany Army', 'The British did not help the Channel Islands when they were invaded', 'If invasion takes place it will be through Ireland via Port Rush and without opposition from Mr De La Vera', 'Churchill is a butcher and a murderer', 'Anthony Eden is the lady with skirts', 'The Royal Family have a house ready in Canada to flee to in case this country is invaded', 'Hitler will only negotiate peace terms with Sir Oswald Mosley, who will be dictator of Britain', 'Goebbels in a marvellous man and highly educated', 'I will get Nazi armlets to wear when the invasion comes and I shall give the Nazi salute' and 'The Nazis are perfect gentlemen'. In October 1941 she was placed, on the advice of Devon's Chief Constable, on the Suspects List. Menteth did not keep her jobs for long and her other addresses that year were Parke, then the home of Major Hole in Bovey Tracey and currently the headquarters of Dartmoor National Park Authority, and St Gabrielle's School at West Ogwell near Newton Abbot.[48]

Charles Frederick Mallard was also under suspicion. He was 70 years of age by 29 December 1943 when he was described as 'an old, bad tempered, most opinionated man, with a grievance against the world in general'. Mallard moved from Ivybridge to Croyde on 23 November 1942 but quit his job there and returned to 3 Highland Street, Ivybridge, on 2 April 1943. He had previously lived in Bristol. The Exeter and Plymouth police had concerns about his loyalties. He had been a frequent traveller to Germany before the war and it was reported he retained pro-Nazi views and was a danger to the public good.[49]

A yet stranger case is that of Anthony Le Sueur, a teacher in Woodbury. He too was on the Suspects List. Anthony Burnley Clement Chuttwell was born in London in 1916 and changed his name by deed poll to Anthony Andre Ahmed Le Sueur in 1941. Le Sueur was his mother's maiden name. He was educated largely by private tutors and at the age of 18 went on the stage. He worked in a theatrical company at Hastings and various other repertory

SECRET

P.A. 863056

F.3.c.2.
WAR OFFICE,
WHITEHALL,
S.W.1.

Region 5/26C 11 JAN 1943 BRITISH

Head Office Reference P.F. 64555 Released Detenu.

Special Branch Reference:

Anthony Andre Ahmed LE SUEUR,
The Garrick Hotel, Charing Cross Road.

This young man was born in London in November 1916. His name was then Anthony Burney Clement CRUTTWELL; it was not until December 1941 that he changed it by Deed Poll to Anthony Andre Ahmed LE SUEUR; (LE SUEUR was his mother's maiden name). He was sent to Marlborough, but remained only two or three terms, as he developed double mastoid and was seriously ill. When he recovered he was sent to Bradfield College, Berkshire, but ran away from that school after one term. He was subsequently educated by private tutors. At about 17 years old he went to the British Institute, Paris, but would not settle down there. He went on the stage at about 18, and worked in a Company at Hastings from 1935 to 1937. He then had successive engagements with various Repertory Companies until October 1939, when he joined the R.A.S.C., and later volunteered for service in Finland. His health broke down while in training, and about July 1940 he was discharged from the Army on medical grounds. The opinion of the Army Medical Board at that time was: "This soldier has ability, amounting almost to genius; the impossibility of reconciling diverse elements in his make-up caused him such anxiety that he is of little practical use in peace and none in war".

LE SUEUR returned to the stage, and joined a Repertory Company at St. Annes-on-Sea, Lancashire. It was at this time that he met Miss MORRIS, who was a member of the same Repertory Company. Some time in the autumn of 1940 he became converted to the Mohammedan faith. In the summer of 1941 LE SUEUR joined the Anglo-French Corps (now known as the British Volunteer Ambulence Corps), and was stationed at Morpeth, near Newcastle. He had to leave this Corps because of his health, and entered the London Clinic in December, 1941, where he received mental treatment.

On leaving the Clinic, he obtained an engagement at the Play House, Jesmond, Newcastle. In March, 1942, he began to make astounding statements to other members of the Company; for instance

/event

Intelligence file on Mr Le Sueur of Woodbury (National Archives, HO45/25570).

companies until 1939 when he volunteered for service in Finland. However, his health broke down while he was training and he was discharged on medical grounds. The opinion of the Army Medical Board was 'this solider has ability amounting almost to genius, the impossibility of reconciling diverse elements in his make-up causes him such anxiety that he is of little practical use in peace and none in war'. Le Sueur returned to the stage and worked in Lancashire. Sometime in 1940 he converted to Islam. In 1941 he joined the Anglo-French Corps, also known as the British Volunteer Ambulance Corps, near Newcastle. In December he left the service in order to receive mental treatment in London. Shortly afterwards Le Sueur returned to Newcastle to appear on stage but began to make statements which astounded his fellow actors. He refused to fire-watch because, he said, 'I do not recognise the law of this country. I am in sympathy with the Nazi movement, and have been a member of the Nazi party for some time.' In his opinion Hitler was 'greater than Christ'. Most serious of all was his comment that in the event of an invasion he would help the Germans. This prompted an interview with the police and he then made further extraordinary statements. Le Sueur claimed to have joined the army and ambulance corps to obtain information 'to help the cause of national socialism, in the event of an invasion of this country, when I should take my place with the storm troopers'. He said he joined the Nazi party in Germany in 1937 and later associated with Nazis in France and in the Channel Islands. He was 'heart and soul a Nazi, and shall do all in my power to further that cause'. The Home Office received contradictory professional opinions on Le Sueur's views but he was detained in June 1942. Six months later he was released and then took up his post teaching history at St Peter's School in Woodbury. He remained on the Suspects List.[50]

There were also arrests of those who refused to fight. As during the first world war, there were great public debates over Conscientious Objectors. Many claimed religious convictions precluded their fighting and Fascists were suspected of not fighting only to weaken the national war effort. There were also many on the left who agitated for peace. The case of Stanley Rosenweig of Paignton demonstrates the range of such people. He stated he had no religious objections but asserted 'I have registered as a C.O.

because I refuse to fight under a capitalistic government whose aim in this war is to enrich themselves with the blood of the working man; a government composed of the biggest hypocrites and the heads of the largest munitions factories. I refuse to fight because I would be helping such a class, a class who put Hitler into power in 1933. This country, with France, established Hitler. . . . I would prefer death here in England before going out to kill a man of my own class'.[51]

A more striking example is Edward Gundry West of Malahat in Salcombe. The clerk of Salcombe Urban District Council wrote to the Home Office concerned the port would be seen as lacking in patriotism. It had, he added, an unblemished record. He wrote on 27 December 1939:

> *This man has resided in Salcombe for the past ten years, he is of independent means and is a Pacifist, a Quaker, a member of the Peace Pledge Union and a District Commissioner of the Boy Scouts. There is nothing known against him other than that he is somewhat of a crank . . . it would appear West is the most active member of the local pacifist group, and others known are Canon William Llewellyn Herford of Berry Ridge, Salcombe and Mrs Evelyn May Hartree of Sandhills, Salcombe, no public meetings have been organised since the war but I understand that private meetings are held at Mrs Hartree's house.*

Devon's Chief Constable added West knew a German alien but admitted there was nothing to suggest subversive actions.[52] In the spring of 1940, at the height of invasion scares, one local columnist acknowledged public uneasiness about pacifists but noted a judge's comment they were 'reputable citizens and honourable men however mistaken'.[53]

In the midst of war, with the widespread bombing in Britain and the threat of invasion, a great range of people were under suspicion.

Fifth Columnists?: the internment of British Union members

Many Fascists were also arrested and interned as Fifth Columnists, the enemy within. There had been disagreements in the government between MI5 and the Home Office over the legitimacy of the threat from British Fascists but with the fall of France the Cabinet became alarmed by the threat of invasion, an uneasy public and a critical report made by MI5. It stated by the start of 1940 Mosley had some 8,000 paying members with perhaps as many as three times more 'whole-hearted but non-paying sympathisers', that war was being presented as a Jew's war, defeatist rumours were circulated and young men were helped in avoiding subscription. Intelligence agents placed in the party reported up to half of all members were prepared to assist the enemy. The agency had intercepted letters, overheard conversations and received regular police reports. The means by which Fascists were arrested was through the Emergency Powers (Defence) Bill, regulation 18b which came into force on the first of September 1939. It allowed arrests and internment on political grounds. As well as Fascists, IRA members were detained.

On May 22nd 1940 the government decided to sanction internment of Mosley's Fascists and the arrests began the following day. The first group was based on a list made by Mosley he had hidden for safekeeping. This was supplemented by more detailed information from Chief Constables across the country with the result 350 British Union officials were arrested at the end of May and early June. Altogether nearly 800 men and women were interned.[54] They included a considerable number of men, and at least one woman, from Devon. One of the main figures at the Home Office was Alexander Maxwell, Permanent Under-Secretary during the second world war. He was a Devon man, educated at Plymouth College.[55]

By 19 September 1940 the country's chief constables had reported the internments led to the cessation of any organised pro-Nazi activity, the British Union had ceased to exist and there was a 'marked decrease in rumour-mongering'. The only chief constable who disagreed was based at Bath and he thought local members were merely 'lying low'.[56]

On May 23rd Sir Oswald Mosley was arrested and sent to Holloway Prison. Then in early June there were arrests throughout the country. One of those taken into custody was H. S. L. Knight, the former Exmouth Urban Council Surveyor who had been employed in the town from 1937 to 1939. The thirty-six year old married man was arrested at Guildford.[57] There were also arrests of Fascists in at least three parts of Devon. One of them was Frederick Samuel Hooper of Hartnoll Farm outside Tiverton. Hooper had been a leading Fascist involved in the Tithe War seven years previously and had lectured on behalf of fascism throughout Devon. When he was arrested Hooper was in the midst of working at this farm. A fellow internee later recorded his impressions of Hooper then being processed at the prison. He remembered:

> *As we stood waiting our turns, packed tight in the reception block, prisoners continued to arrive. If some took their arrest in feigned light-heartedness, others were seething and contained themselves with difficulty. There was one Devonshire farmer in particular, Frederick Hooper, a strong, stout, hale man of middle age, who greatly resembled John Bull; like his prototype he had broad, ruddy features adorned with what are now called 'side burns'.*
>
> *This typical yeoman was seething, firstly that he was an ex-Serviceman who was also a South American volunteer, should be suspected of intending treachery, secondly that he should have been apprehended by the police in the middle of his sheep-shearing, and given no opportunity to arrange the working of his farm in his absence.*[58]

In 1945 Hooper was still bitter about his arrest.

One fascist who was arrested was C. Hill who was in Exeter Prison by November 14th 1941. He was subsequently sent to the Isle of Man and his case was discussed early in 1942. Hill was described as 'comparatively harmless' on one occasion and on another as being an intelligent twenty-six year old man who had been an active and 'militant' district leader. He had been involved in disturbances on the island but the lead official reported he was convinced of Hill's sincerity in wanting to keep within the law.[59] His connections with Devon have not been discovered although there were fascists with that surname at Colyton and Woodbury.

A number of other local fascists were also arrested.

Branscombe

Life in the small coastal village of Branscombe was interrupted on June 3rd by the arrests of Rafe Temple Cotton, his mother Lucy Temple Cotton and an employee, John Edwin Pococke, at the Fruit and Flower Farm. The two Sidmouth newspapers failed to report the arrests although *The Sidmouth Observer* carried an interesting, albeit restrained, editorial:

> *We hope there are no Fifth Columnists in Sidmouth. There may be some Fascists and Peace Pledge adherents, but while we appreciate freedom of thought and speech yet this is not the time to advocate principles which are inimical to the State and anyone giving utterance to such should be restrained. Just now we want to show a united front to the enemy. The most ardent Peace Pledge member would hardly care to be governed under similar conditions to those in Germany where certainly 'silence is golden' as far as the ordinary individual is concerned.*[60]

There was a Sidmouth Group of the Peace Pledge Union which was active in the resort. One of its meetings was at Willow's Café on the previous Armistice Day.[61] The East Devon newspaper, *Pulman's Weekly*, had a short report on the arrests. It noted the three were detained overnight at Sidmouth Police Station and the following morning taken to other parts of the country. Cotton was described as being well-known through his open-air meetings throughout East Devon. The paper also carried a story of two itinerants who were arrested in nearby Bridport that week for failing to have proper identity papers and attempting to conceal their true names. One of them claimed 'I am no spy or Fifth Columnist'.[62] The story shows the heightened state of public anxiety in the weeks following Dunkirk and during the Fall of France. A week later there was an editorial entitled 'East Devon Chatterbugs'. The paper noted 'the appeal asking persons to report activities of a suspicious nature has caused untold distress and annoyance to innocent people and has resulted in the police investigating the 'tittle-tattle' of irresponsible people who have nothing better to do than make frequent telephone calls to their nearest police station. Defamatory rumours have become so rife that persons have had to consult their solicitors and issue warnings against such talk'.[63]

At this time, from the 2nd of May to the 16th, the Globe Hotel in nearby Colyton was advertising in *Action* for Fascists to visit.[64] The following day the evacuation of Dunkirk began and some of these servicemen were billeted at the hotel. It is not known if, when they arrived, Fascists from other parts of the country were also staying. It is also not known whether they realised their host was a member of British Union.

The Cotton's employee, John Edwin Pococke, had arrived from Eastbourne to Branscombe shortly before he was arrested. He placed an advert in *Action* on March 7 1940 seeking work; he was an 'active member, 1933, aged 38, good driver, worker, interested in market gardening, fruit farming, etc., desires work with B. U. farmer. Box 878'. The Cottons employed him shortly afterwards and he was arrested only three months later. Pococke, according to the subsequent MI5 report, had been engaged to a German girl in 1933 and became deeply impressed by Germany which he visited the following year. He joined the British Union in 1938. The case against Pococke and the Cottons charged Pococke with being a 'rabid pro-Nazi' who was said by the police to be a man who would sow discord amongst the troops. Pococke registered as a Conscientious Objector but an assessor in MI5 felt 'his avoidance of military service appeared for reasons other than conscience. By temperament and political conviction he could be regarded as a subversive influence given liberty'. During Mrs Cotton's interview she was asked of Pococke 'was he rather a keen man?' 'Yes, very keen.' 'Was that the reason you employed him?' 'He wanted to do national work without having to fight. That is why we employed him.' Rafe Temple Cotton said during his questioning he remembered Pococke's advert stating he was 'willing to tackle any work, however hard'. Cotton knew Pococke was a Conscientious Objector but was short of labour. Pococke did all the accounts and 'he lived up to his word, he worked very hard and very well'. Mrs Cotton said 'he is very interested in Germany. He is rather too pro-German for me. I do not want to say anything against him. He is quite a nice fellow.' Something of Pococke's personality comes through in another comment she made. She said she heard him say Crowle and Duvivier, the two Devon men recently imprisoned, were 'such fools as to express themselves too plainly on paper – a couple of prize bloody idiots I think'. On his arrest Pococke was sent to Liverpool Prison. He was interned and although the Home Office wanted his release MI5 did not immediately agree.[65] In early July the Conscientious Objectors' Tribunal recommended he serve in the military. Pococke objected on the grounds he saw no reason for war. He explained, in writing, he was a patriot 'at heart and in practice' as well as eager and willing to work for his country but his political views were National Socialist and incompatible with fighting Germany. He wrote:

> *I am engaged to a German girl and I abhor the thought of my taking part in any effort which aims at removing the system by which she chooses to be ruled, and from which she had benefited. The British Empire is strong enough and great enough if properly organised to care not a rap for any foreign Statesman – our territories could be made impregnable – and I like any true Britisher, would spring at once to the colours if our interests were attacked.*

The Tribunal could not find reasons to keep him off the Military Service Record.[66]

Pococke might not have been arrested had he not been employed by the Cottons. It was the two of them, particularly Rafe Temple Cotton, the police were most interested in securing because his name was on a list of eight Fascists empowered by Mosley to continue the party's work in the event of his own arrest. This led MI5 to believe Cotton was one of the most dangerous men in the country. Several years later they reassessed their position: Lucy Temple Cotton was seen as the driving force. Strong and unambiguous descriptions of her were made by a number of people

The camp for internees set up under the stands at York racecourse painted by Rafe Temple Cotton, 1940. On his watercolour Cotton noted 'the friendships we have made here and in jail have brightened the darkest days of these dreary months. These friendships and the high ideals, the firm resolve we share, will endure' (private collection).

during the course of the war: she was described as 'a very strong-minded woman but not very well informed', 'an ardent Fascist', 'evidently a convinced and somewhat truculent Fascist', 'a lady of immoderate enthusiasms', 'a lady of a vigorous and determined character' and 'a very eccentric person of a hysterical nature'.

The Cottons had come to Branscombe by 1930.[67] His horticulture studies at Reading prepared him for his Fruit and Flower Farm business. He later said 'I started there with a boy and myself and mother with a turnover, on a plain open field which had never grown anything but weeds and grass before'. Cotton was asked about becoming a Fascist and whether he or his mother joined first.

'I think it was fairly simultaneous. A friend persuaded us to go to a meeting.'

'Mrs Cotton was at the same meeting, was she?'

'Yes.'

'You joined together more or less?'

'We both thought there was something in it. We did not actually join at the meeting. We took books home and read them & discussed the policy, and seemed to agree most things between us.'

Mrs Cotton claimed she joined the party in 1933 'when I heard Sir Oswald Mosley and read his first book *Greater Britain* which I consider the best book he has ever written. I was interested in agricultural policy'.[68] Interestingly, in March 1936 Robert Saunders wrote 'the District Treasurer from Exeter and another man and his mother from Devon' came to a meeting in Dorset.[69] Presumably they were the Cottons. If so, it appears until then they had a low profile. Many years later Cotton's widow Enid recalled 'Lucy was very friendly with Lady Mosley and she thought her son should be embroiled in it, and Rafe couldn't resist her. Paul [Rafe's brother] said it's ridiculous Mother and would have nothing to do with it, and poor Rafe had to carry the can.'[70]

The case against the Cottons and Pococke was made in a statement marked Secret. It noted 'these people form a little group of members of the British Union residing at Hill Arrish . . .' It recorded the Cottons had twice visited Germany, that Cotton had first come to MI5's attention when he became District Leader at Honiton in 1936, that the Cottons were friendly with Duvivier and Crowle, and that one or both of them had communicated in code with the national headquarters of the British Union. It claimed their home was on an eminence 'said to be ideal for communicating with ships in the channel and that both mother and son sleep on the veranda at night'. An account of their last visit to Germany was given. It recorded the two of them, along with Philip Temple Cotton, had left in May 1939 for Ostend 'wearing Fascist badges expressing pro-Nazi sympathies'. Mrs Cotton claimed 'she wore the British Union badge but was accustomed to wearing it at all times'. She had only stopped on official instructions. There was also a curious allegation their home had been attacked by local people on account of their political views.

Rafe Temple Cotton was imprisoned at Liverpool, Brixton and the Isle of Man. While at Liverpool Prison in June 1940 he portrayed himself in a letter as being interested in mountain climbing, 'ski-running', bird life and wild flowers.[71] Four months after his arrest, on the first of October, Alexander Maxwell, Permanent Under-Secretary at the Home Office, wrote to Lord Swinton that he was:

> *a young man who lived with his mother in Devonshire and ran a farm. He and his mother are both ardent Fascists. He was the prospective British Union candidate for Exeter. His father was a colonel and a DSO. He had reached military age while under detention and says he is willing to fight in defence of the country and the committee are satisfied that both he and his mother, despite their misguided ideas, are patriotic people. In this particular case, where the two individuals have occupied a rather prominent position, it is proposed to ask them whether they are prepared to give a formal undertaking not to engage in activities of the British Union or similar.*

He thought they should report to the police on a weekly basis and report any change of address.[72] On October 15th 1940 the Advisory Committee recommended his release and that he join the forces or have restricted freedom.[73]

Cotton had several letters written in his support. One was written by T. E. Lloyd from the Royal Glen Hotel in Sidmouth. He wrote Cotton had been a neighbour 'but I have no direct knowledge of his political activities which, I believe, were largely inspired by his mother, a lady of immoderate enthusiasms.' He thought Cotton was

Photograph of interned fascists at the Isle of Man from the national press entitled 'this is how we treat our Fascist thugs!' (Sunday Pictorial, 1941).

'an honest and rather simple-minded man, who has never fully realised the serious implications of the policy advocated by the Fascist party' and 'a decent, honest fellow who has been very sadly misled'.

A more surprising one was written by Septimus Burra of Sidmouth on the 15th of August 1940.

> *I & my wife & daughters have been friendly with Mr Rafe Temple Cotton and his family since I first came to Sidmouth about 12 years ago . . . During the last few years I frequently discussed his politics with him and I know one reason for his*

interest in so-called fascism was his desire to end unemployment, with particular reference to increased employment under better conditions on the land in this country. I am certain he was and is very interested in this subject and that in common with many others he regarded it as a serious national danger. At the beginning of the present war, I had a conversation with Mr Cotton when he told me that he would like to join the Air Force but that he probably would not be allowed to do so owing to his occupation on the land. I am sure that he really meant this; in fact I am convinced that he is intensely earnest, that he joined the Fascist movement because he really thought it provided a remedy for certain social difficulties (not appreciating in the least what I regard as its threat to personal liberty) and that he never would have done so if he had believed that it was aimed against this country. I consider that he has really high standards of personal conduct and that he is entirely trustworthy.

What makes this letter extraordinary is Burra failed to mention he himself was a member of British Union and District Leader of Honiton. Perhaps such an admission would have made the Advisory Committee look more closely at his statements.

Cotton was still imprisoned in January 1941 when more letters were sent including from Ivy Abbot of Branscombe whose husband 'had worked for him for many years'. An unusual letter of support was written by Ida Shortland of Bickley in Lustleigh. She wrote she had known Cotton and his mother since November 1938. Mrs Cotton had been released but it was claimed she was working very hard 'and the worry and anxiety is telling upon her very much, she is sixty two but has plenty of pluck and is a real worker'. She also included an unusual history of herself in writing of her work in the Red Cross during the first world war and of local feeling against her as a Fascist in 1940.'[74]

Temple's brother, a pilot in the RAF, wrote from Cairo in support in May 1941 but by then Cotton was free. There was discussion in the Advisory Committee as to how dangerous he was. A note on his confidential record noted 'MI5's suggestions that the man has been concerned with codes and will be passing on secret information are,

I believe, groundless and this, as in some other cases, they over-colour the charges.' The valid points of his case, the folder noted, was he was an important and active member of the British Union until his arrest. However the committee felt Cotton was patriotic and would help rather than hinder the war effort.

There were restrictions: he had to report each week to the local police. In April 1943 Cotton had a hearing in an attempt to have the restrictions lifted. He said 'I find that a small but talkative section of the community regard me with suspicion because this is still in force. It therefore becomes definitely irksome & a hindrance to my work and trade.' It was pointed out Cotton had to walk a mile each week to report to the local constable.[75]

The main campaigner for Cotton's release had been his aunt, Kate Clutton. She wrote in December 1940 that she had travelled to Branscombe where she overheard village gossip about her relations including their home was 'plastered with portraits of Hitler and Mussolini', that 'they were using their sailing boat to help the enemy' and that 'Mrs Temple-Cotton is a German'. Miss Clutton ran her relations' affairs while they were imprisoned even though she lived near Reigate. The main reasons for interning Mrs Cotton were, according to an MI5 report, that she was a member of the British Union, had assisted her son as a District Leader and had supported Mosley in his demand for a negotiated peace. Another report noted, in addition to the points raised against her son, she had been awarded a Bronze Distinction by Mosley for her Fascist work. Cotton appears to have been conciliatory during the hearings for his release. His mother had another approach.

Cotton was asked about his mother's unpopularity in Branscombe and answered 'I think my mother rather exaggerates that. She is a very shy person and if someone does not say 'Good morning' to her she feels very hurt.' The transcript of her questioning in July 1940 confirms a strong personality.

> *'How do you think the local police would view your return?'*
>
> *'I think they are undoubtedly very friendly. The police are, not our gentry neighbours, not the people who are supposed to be gentle people, all the workmen are exceedingly friendly.'*

'Why are the gentlefolk not friendly?'

'Because they are not gentlefolk. . . . Because they think we are not British. They have not asked us what we thought, they have simply gone by the papers and the BBC and they said we were anti-British.'

'You would have some difficulty in stating your exact position to them?'

'Not in the least. I am perfectly clear I am for Britain and Britain alone.'

She made no attempt to alleviate the concerns of the Advisory Committee unlike Claude Duvivier and admitted having a Fascist badge and wearing it on the day she went to prison. However, when asked about her recent German trip she denied meeting Nazi leaders and said she had no desire to. But Mrs Cotton also told them the war was 'a fight for Jewish finance'. Other comments were equally alarming.

'Would you like to see Hitler destroyed?'

'I think he is a very good man for Germany but not for England.'

'You would not like to see him destroyed?'

'Certainly not, because the Germans love him.'

'Do you think the people in the concentration camps love him?'

'I cannot speak for the people in the concentration camps. I am speaking of Germans.'

'Do you think they would?'

'What interests me are the working men of Germany?'

Mrs Cotton was asked a great many questions on a number of issues.

'Did you ever listen to Haw Haw?'

'Yes, naturally we have.'

'Why naturally?'

'I thought everybody did.'

'Did you?'

'Oh, yes.'

'Did you like him?'

'I detest the man myself.'

'Did you know him before?'

'I have met him.'

'When a member of the British Union?'

'Yes.'

'Why did you detest him because he left the British Union?'

'He was a detestable man.'

'He was?'

'Yes, and I hate his voice too.'

'Did you listen to the New British Broadcasting Station?'

'I have never listened to it.'

'Why did you listen to Haw Haw if you detest his voice and he is a detestable man?'

'He is very amusing so is the other man. I like the other man better, the German. I always like to hear both sides of a question.'

'He only gave one side.'

'You hear the English first and the German afterwards.'

When Mrs Cotton was asked her thoughts of the British Navy being attacked and of the losses in ships and men she answered 'That was our own fault for going to war.'[76] Nevertheless, Mrs Cotton was given her freedom on the third of September 1940 but does not appear to have left until the 8th of November. According to the police report, she then travelled to Reigate, presumably to see her sister at Dover's Farm, and left for Branscombe the following day.

On November 15th Mrs Cotton was given her restrictions: she was not allowed to travel more than five miles from her home without permission from the police. On 13 January 1943, then aged 63, she appealed and claimed she was doing important work in growing food for the war effort but she felt she was being treated 'more like an alien'. Mrs Cotton stated 'why should I be treated as an alien. I have not done anything against the country at all' and suggested the only charge against her was she had helped her son in efforts for a negotiated peace. Her questioned asked:

'Of course you had been a member of British Union?'
'Yes, I do not deny it for a minute.'
'And you were a fairly keen member?'
'Oh yes, I went to all my son's meetings.'

The report from the Chief Constable of Devon noted she was still an ardent Fascist and 'during the early days after her release from internment she was known to have had sudden outbursts, when she did freely express such views'. Mrs Cotton was 'a very eccentric person of a hysterical nature'. He felt the restrictions should be kept because she continued to move in Fascist circles. Mrs Cotton had written to Mrs Muriel Whinfield who had also been interned at Holloway Prison, was a friend of the Mosleys and had been the British Union's prospective parliamentary candidate for Petersfield. She was also the mother of Peter Whinfield who was suspected by MI5 of being a Nazi agent and had visited Germany after war broke out.[77] Mrs Cotton tried to arrange to meet her as well as the wife of Admiral Domville. Lady Domville had a high profile in right wing and Fascist circles and had also been interned at Holloway Prison.[78] It was the Chief Constable's view Mrs Cotton would be drawn back into fascism. A supplement to the committee's report noted her as 'a lady of vigorous and determined character. The Appeal committee gave her an opportunity to modify her Fascist views but she did not take it.' It was their opinion she was untrustworthy and 'she is a person who requires a certain amount of watching and control'. In April the Committee recommended restrictions should be maintained.

There is one further note to be made of the Branscombe Fascists at this time. Not all were interned.

Only a few days after the arrests on 3 June 1940 there occurred another incident. There was an assault between LDV Leader Captain Frank Masters and James Stevenson of Sunbank in Branscombe. Masters had allegedly said Stevenson was not in the Local Defence Volunteers (later known as the Home Guard) because 'I suggest it may be your friendship with the other side'. Masters, who was 58 years old, five foot eight inches in height and who had only one arm, was then viciously attacked by Stevenson, who was twenty years younger, stood six feet four inches high and was described as 'powerful looking'. Stevenson knocked him to the ground and 'pummelled nearly unconscious'. One witness said to him 'You are a blackguard to knock down a man with one arm'.

The subsequent court case made reference to a 'small clique of Fascist sympathisers in Branscombe' and Stevenson was found guilty and sentenced to four months' imprisonment. It was a fact said the prosecutor 'known to everyone that Mr Temple Cotton and Mr Stevenson were great personal friends and visited one another's houses and that in the house of Mr Temple Cotton photographs of Hitler and Mussolini were stuck all over the place. Witnesses would say that they had seen Stevenson use the Fascist sign to people as he went along'. Stevenson and the Cottons, it was said in court, had lived 'cheek by jowl'. G. I. P. Knott, retired horse dealer, had said to Stevenson 'I am not anxious to speak to you because of the things that have come to my notice. You are a great friend of the Cottons and it is said you meet Cotton continually and give each other the Nazi salute'. Stevenson replied 'it is not Nazi. It is Fascist.' Knott had replied 'Don't talk such – nonsense. There is no difference in the present day.' Stevenson denied being a Fascist but other villagers had seen him salute.[79] The arrests of Pococke and the Cottons exposed tensions in the small coastal village in the first year of the war.

Exeter

On June 4th the police raided the headquarters of British Union at 19 South Street and arrested Harold John Forward of Jubilee Road and Cecil George Brooker of Union Road.[80] Forward had been the party's District Leader of the Exeter branch for only a short time but was interned until autumn 1943. In a letter marked Secret, Hugh Elles at Regional Headquarters in Bristol wrote to Sir Alexander Maxwell at the Home Office on 17 September 1943.

> *My dear Maxwell, I have had before me today the cases of five late detainees for inclusion in my Suspects List. It has been explained that the Government's policy is a gradual process of release of these creatures. Naturally I bow to a*

decision of this nature, but I venture to suggest that in one or two cases we are running undue risk in having certain individuals at large yet.

2. Attached you will find the names of the five persons whose release from detention has come to my notice, and I suggest that two of them at least should go back to gaol. We are entering a period of the war which will [torn] and the utmost patience and good will of everyone, and the presence and vocal activity of still disaffected persons is most undesirable, if not dangerous.

3. Of the five rogues and/or imbeciles on the list, I recommend to your especial attention Harold John Forward and Elspeth Elizabeth Thomas nee Rottman neither of whom should be at large.

1. *Harold John Forward, 24, student type. Still a violent Fascist.*
2. *Joyce Tregear, 40, possibly just a neurotic.*
3. *Uwe Karl Heinz Markmann, 27, a pure German naturalised 1939.*
4. *Elspeth Elizabeth Thomas nee Rottman, a pure German.*
5. *Robin Pinckard, 29, possibly just a 'bloody minded' man.*

Forward and the others were added to the list on September 28th. Then, on 14 October, Maxwell responded and noted Forward was 'according to our records, a young fanatic who joined the British Union when he was fifteen. I cannot find anything in the fairly full information we have about him to support your view that he is either 'a rogue or an imbecile'. Apart from his British Union ideas he would appear to be a decent fellow. His headmaster of the school at which he was brought up gave him a very good character and so did his employer. The case came before the Home Secretary in July last and he decided that Forward might be released. I have no information to justify me in suggest that he should reconsider that decision.'[81]

From Camp M on the Isle of Man Forward wrote to Robert Saunders. In one letter he signed it Wishing you all the best, H.M. Jack Forward'. 'H. M.' signified Hail Mosley.[82]

Everything is just the same here, except that Scotty and JD are working on a farm, and I, even I, did a week at Glen Laugh! No, it was not the hard work which frightened me away, the idea was to have a change from studying and the sight of barbed wire from the inside. Hope you are well and keeping the old flag flying, yours in the usual, Jack Forward.

Ps Scotty who's sitting on my bed, at the moment and munching bread loudly, sends his regards.[83]

He was freed sometime in late summer 1943. In October he wrote to Saunders:

I don't think I have written you since my release, if not it is high time. I was at home for nearly 2 ½ months, leading (disgustingly enough) quite a life of wine, woman and song!! Still it was nice. Now all that is changed as since Monday last it has been potato harvesting at 50s a week!! I was 'directed' to this Devon War Agricultural Committee's hostel by the Ministry of Labour and in spite of going before an appeals board, getting letters of recommendation, etc. I had to go. However the place is simply fowl so I shall get out as soon as possible, either by joining something or simply walking out and taking the 3 months in jail penalty.[84]

On December 12th Saunders passed the news. He wrote 'Jack Forward is working for the Devon War Agricultural Committee and has been living a very rough life in one of their hostels. When I last heard he was expecting to change his job for that of a lorry driver, with better conditions and better pay.' Earlier in the year Forward became engaged to a woman he met while potato harvesting and they settled in Exeter. Forward was to take up the cause of fascism again after the war.[85]

Edward Ronald D'Alessio of Plymouth

Edward Ronald D'Alessio was active as a Blackshirt in several other parts of the country as well as in Devon. He was dismissed from work in the summer of 1940 because of his British Union work, arrested on 29 September 1940 and released nearly two years later on 26 June 1942. It was his activities in Plymouth where he worked in the Naval Ordnance that caused concern to the authorities as well as an implausible scheme for starting his own colony.

D'Alessio was born in 1904 at Poona in India where his father was a government chaplain. He was educated at prep schools in Budleigh Salterton and Cheltenham before, at the age of 13, becoming a cadet at the Royal Naval College in Dartmouth. In 1922 he entered the Royal Naval Engineering College at Devonport, passed his exams, became a Lieutenant in 1926 and then was bought out of the navy the following year. He claimed he left the navy because he was seasick but also because he was temperamentally unsuited. He said 'I might say that as a Mid-Shipman I sowed my wild oats with rather more enthusiasm than I suppose I should have done and that got me into a certain amount of trouble'. He had a series of jobs including a stint at Nottingham in motor repair but returned to Plymouth in 1937. In October 1939 he attempted to be an A.R.P. ambulance driver but became ill and went to Naval Ordnance. He was dismissed the following summer for being a Fascist.

D'Alessio had joined the Fascists in Cheltenham in 1934 and became District Leader there at the age of thirty. He was also active in Gloucester. His business suffered as a result and he returned to Plymouth in 1937 where he became involved with the British Union of Fascists. He was questioned about this during his internment. 'That was risking the business again?' 'Yes, it was but I am afraid I simply could not help myself.' Headquarters asked him to be active. He said of this 'They had . . . a huge branch in Plymouth which had gone smash involving a great deal of trouble and scandal; and they asked me whether I could try and get things going again. But my attempts at getting things going I am afraid were absolutely hopeless.' He added 'there were no members there at all. There were a number of ex-members who were best left well alone.' There is another indication D'Alessio was a supporter: in February 1937 he contributed to national funds of the British Union as did his sister.[86]

Among the jobs D'Alessio had when out of Plymouth was working in cinemas. There he met a number of Jews and it was possibly then that he became Anti-Semitic. Later, during questioning over his interning, D'Alessio was asked 'You say your main interest had always been anti-Communist?' 'I have been anti-Communist since I reached 21, I think.' Then he was asked 'Anti-Jew?' to which he replied 'Yes, I am not one of those people who believe in persecution. I have had one or two Jewish friends but only one or two.' In February 1940 he was employed as an Inspector of Supplies at Holman Brothers, Admiralty Contractors, at Camborne in Cornwall. D'Alessio continued to espouse his political views. He admitted stating of the Jews 'I have expressed my dislike of them and the hope that in the new future we would provide them with a nation outside of this country.'

D'Alessio resigned his membership of the British Union in the autumn of 1939 and this was accepted in February 1940. He did this because of Hitler's treaty with the Soviets but he also claimed to have been angry over the affair of Crowle and Duvivier. His account paints a very isolated position in Plymouth at the start of the war. D'Alessio said 'there were no actual members in Plymouth although there had been a very large number of members and there were a number of sympathisers who avoided me like the plague as soon as hostilities started.' He was asked during questioning 'you also say *I also informed the county propaganda officer, Rafe Temple Cotton, that I was unable to do anything further*. Did you ring up Mr Temple Cotton or meet him at Plymouth?' D'Alessio answered 'No, I wrote to him. I very seldom saw him. He never kept an appointment and when he came down, he came down without notice, in a frightful hurry and excitement. We were not on very good terms actually and he dashed off away again.' He explained he fell ill, heard about the convictions of Crowle and Duvivier and was instructed by British Union headquarters to tell them they were expelled. D'Alessio claimed to have been annoyed that as District Leader of Plymouth he had been given no knowledge of the existence of Crowle although he had been in the dockyard 'for quite a long time'. He admitted knowing Duvivier because of his letters to the *Western Morning News*.

After his dismissal from Holman Brothers in Cornwall D'Alessio went to Marigold Holme at Timberscombe near Minehead in Somerset. His parents lived there and D'Alessio had been married for some fourteen years. His wife was Cornish and D'Alessio felt uncomfortable while living in Camborne. He informed his interrogators during his internment questioning 'I do not know whether you know Cornish people? My wife is Cornish, so that I shall not be giving any offence to anybody by saying these things, Cornish people will very often talk in a very anti-British manner without being in the least anti-British, but simply because they regard everybody else as foreigners. I have heard things said in Cornwall which I would not have dared to say myself, but I know they do not mean it.' His time in Somerset was not much happier. By this time, early 1940, a great number of urban people had moved into rural parts. D'Alessio wrote to a fellow Fascist in Cheltenham, who was he explained a 'practically illiterate joiner', 'Dear Steve, here we are for the time, in the best part of England, at present defiled by the presence of aliens and war funks'. They were 'people who, instead of trying to do something had scuttled into the country and were hiding in every possible direction, not children or evacuated mothers, but adult people well able to do something useful. There were any number of them about'. More importantly was a hare-brained notion of stealing a fishing boat in order to start a colony on an island either off Africa or in the Pacific.

D'Alessio was arrested on 29 September 1940 and sent to Liverpool Prison. He later served time in the internment camp on the Isle of Man and released on 12 June 1942 when he went to 91 North Road in Plymouth. By 6 January 1943 he was resident at Olive Farm in Orchard Hill near Bideford.[87] During this time he was on the Suspects List and his movements were tracked to 1 South View Terrace also in Bideford in February before moving only two months later to Brent Tor in Westward Ho!.[88]

William Milligan, Devon & Cornwall Propaganda Officer

Among those interned was William Milligan, a member of the party since 1934. He was listed in his Home Office file as having been the Devon & Cornwall Propaganda Officer but little of his activities in the region have been found besides organising in Plymouth in the summer of 1934. He was first Joint Organiser for Southampton and then in 1935 Secretary of Worthing Branch. He was on the payroll of party workers but later claimed to have left it around 1937. When his case was reviewed the Committee 'were not satisfied with his answers and were of the opinion that although open participation in British Union affairs was less apparent, this in no way indicated a lessening of interest'.[89]

The Duke of Cornwall Hotel, Plymouth, and the Welsh Family

An extraordinary story lies in the intelligence records of MI5 which relates to the running of the Duke of Cornwall Hotel in Plymouth, one of the port's most prestigious hotels during the war. It has since become well-known as one of the buildings which escaped being bombed unlike those nearby which were destroyed. The family who ran the hotel were forced to leave immediately before the Allied invasion of France in the spring of 1944. They had been watched from at least August 1939 but it was not until 1944 that they were removed from Plymouth.

The Welsh family ran the hotel for most of the war. According to one report, dated 28 April 1944, Joseph Ferdinand Welsh was born of Hungarian parents at Pozsony on the Austrian/Hungarian border on 18 November 1871. He came to England in 1900, was naturalised in 1912 and changed his name by deed poll in 1916 from Wellisch. From 1937 to March 1944 he managed the hotel but from August 1939 was suspected of pro-German sympathies. In October 1940 he was on the Suspects List.

Welsh had previously managed the Haymarket Hotel, London, and while there, it was alleged, was closely associated with the German Embassy. Among the claims were he was a friend of Ribbentrope, regularly received messages by couriers from the embassy and entertained German diplomats in private at the hotel.

The Duke of Cornwall Hotel, Plymouth (private collection).

Welsh, it was said, was a holder of the Order of Isabel the Catholic which he says was awarded to him by General Franco for composing a march for him. Another allegation was Welsh had been in touch with the Japanese Embassy regarding the specification and sketch of an invention of his allegedly used by the Italian Air Force in the Spanish Civil War.

Some information came from an unnamed informant who had stayed at the hotel. On one occasion Welsh allegedly invited him to listen in private in Welsh's room to a broadcast by Lord Haw Haw.

Mrs Welsh was also under suspicion. According to a report by Buckinghamshire County Constabulary Mrs Louise Welsh née Hollischer was born in England in 1884 of German parents and was educated in Germany where she lived for a considerable time before her marriage. She first came to notice in October 1939 when she and her husband were running the Duke of Cornwall Hotel

> *from 1937 until March of this year. In December 1941 the Plymouth City Police reported that they had information in their possession that Mrs Welsh had spoken with intense*

bitterness against the Jews in Austria just before the outbreak of the war and had stated that she did not blame Hitler for punishing them. She had also expressed her intention of returning to her own country, in the event of war breaking out between England and Germany but in fact she did not appear to have many any attempt to do so.

On the 8th October 1943 Mrs Welsh expressed anti-British sentiments to a reliable informant who was staying at the Duke of Cornwall Hotel. These were to the effect that England was not fighting this war for freedom but rather to subjugate Germany. She at this time stated that she considered the English were the biggest liars and they never kept their word to anybody. She suggested to the informant that possibly the Japanese did not bomb Pearl Harbour but that the English did it to bring America into the war.

Mrs Welsh is strongly anti-Semitic, and declared in October 1943 that Hitler did a good thing in clearing the Jews out of Germany. At the same time she said that she hated both Roosevelt and Churchill. She also said that she hated the English, and that all they liked were sports and drinking.

In October 1943 she made derogatory remarks regarding the visit of the King and Queen to America before the war and said that this was done to influence American public opinion when in fact the English hate the Americans . . .'

She was placed on the Suspects List in January 1944. Another report was made on her that month. She 'and husband were reported to be pro-German. Mrs Welsh speaks Hungarian and German with an Austrian accent. Commonly tells people she is Swiss so that it would not hurt her socially or business.' It was noted she and her husband had run the German Court Hotel in London – now the Winston Hotel. It went on:

She appeared in 1943 to be very well versed in the movements and locations of various units of American troops. Mrs Welsh is known to have said that the drunkenness and bad behaviour of British and American servicemen would never happen in Germany where they were altogether more sensible . . . although conversant with the movements of American units, there is not evidence to show that she [had] been passing on this information or utilising it in any way against this country. In her position as manageress of the Duke of Cornwall Hotel, which is frequented by large numbers of servicemen of all nationalities, however, she is able to learn a great deal of information which would be of use to the enemy... in view of this woman's anti-British sentiments and her foreign background, it is considered that she is a potentially dangerous woman, and should be carefully watched and placed on the list of persons to be detained in the event of invasion.

On February 10th 1944 Mrs Welsh and her daughter-in-law Bebe were placed on the Suspects List. In March she and her husband had a restriction order which prohibited their presence in an aliens protected area. They were forced to leave Plymouth. Not long after, on the 30th of April, MI5 recommended their detention.

Henry Theodore Joseph Welsh, the son of Mr & Mrs Welsh, was also under surveillance along with his wife Bebe. He first came to the attention of Plymouth's police in August 1939 when it was reported he took photographs of a field with a searchlight battery. For a short while he was in Wiltshire and at Littlecote at Widemouth Bay near Bude in north Cornwall but returned to the Duke of Cornwall Hotel in October 1942. His Home Office report noted his appearance before the Conscientious Objector Tribunal at Bristol. He had stated:

I have no ties of any kind with this country, other than superficial ones, nor indeed am I politically attached to any one country. I cannot and will not carry on even in self defence or in any way directly assisting in the slaughter of the enemy . . . While I am a British citizen subject I am in no sense British racially, traditionally or temperamentally.

His wife, Bebe, was the daughter of Augustus Franzel, a Hungarian who became a naturalised British citizen and was employed at the B. B. C. as a musical director but was said to have extreme political views. She was born in Manchester in 1913 and married Welsh in 1936. Her brother Emmerich was a prominent member of British Union and she was reported to the Home Office as also being active in it. Her Home Office file noted Welsh frequently attended hotel dances and:

> *On the arrival of American troops she showed a marked preference for these, and was nearly always in company with members of the U.S. forces. She was known to show particular interest in naval personnel. In September 1943 Bebe Welsh made a habit of taking an average of two officers, preferably U.S., to her room each evening. She is not a prostitute, and it was suggested that she might be doing this in order to extract information from them. Bebe Welsh was friendly with other men, and her husband appeared to countenance this, and she seemed to be on good terms with him. In October 1943 she was in the advanced stages of pregnancy and avoided the public rooms to a large extent, but it is known that she was on extremely intimate with a member of the U. S. forces. She is known to have said that she had been onboard a mine-sweeper and an American submarine about eight months previously. Bebe Welsh is reported to have said that although born in England she was not proud of it, but evaded stating her exact nationality.*

On 23 May 1944 Joseph Ferdinand Welsh, Louise Welsh, Henry Theodore Joseph Welsh and Bebe Welsh finally left the South West region.[90] Two weeks later the invasion of France began.

Torcross and the Watling Family

For a short period during the war, in 1941, one extended household in Torcross was the centre of concern by the authorities. Oxford City Constabulary reported the movements of Robert Hammond Watling, then aged about 40, of Newberry. He had been Assistant District Leader, Treasurer and Propaganda Secretary of the West Lewisham branch. In March 1941 'when Watling and his father, the Reverend Gilbert Watling, were leaving London for Torcross, Devonshire, their luggage was examined and a Fascist uniform, membership and subscription cards of the British Union, a large quantity of British Union publications and Fascist and pro-Nazi books and pamphlets were found. Some of these belonged to Robert Watling and some his brother Cyril Watling, who was also a member of the British Union.'

Torcross is situated along an unusual stretch of South Devon's coastline. It lies between Dartmouth and Salcombe but its main distinguishing feature is its position at the southern end of Slapton Lea, the long freshwater pool separated by the sea by a raised bank of shingle and sand. Two years after the Watlings arrived the local population was forced out and the villages taken over by American forces who used it to practice for the French landings in June 1944. Many years later it became known that immediately offshore there occurred a great naval disaster when several hundred American servicemen were killed during a training exercise. Neither of these events had yet occurred when the Watlings were accused of improper dealings with local British servicemen. The family lived at Golden Meadow in the hamlet of Widewell in Torcross, about half a mile from the sea.

An MI5 file dated 21 December 1941 contains a statement by Sergeant Archibald Forrest. He said on May 18th 'shortly before when he had been stationed at Torcross, Devon, he had on several occasions visited the house at which Watling was living with his father, his sister-in-law Mrs Cyril Watling and a housekeeper. On one occasion the Watling household all criticised the Jewish MPs and said it was a capitalistic war and the capitalists could stop it at any time, Mrs Cyril Watling adding that 'Haw Haw is the only man that tells us the truth.' On another occasion they criticised the Prime Minister, the government and capitalists and then Robert Watling told Forrest and another soldier to listen to the 'Freedom Station' adding the truth came from this station. The station was one of the German propaganda stations.

On May 24th Gunner William Patrick Gordon, who was also stationed at Torcross, stated on about the 10th of April he had visited the Watlings. Robert Watling said 'I wish the whole population of the British Empire and buildings were burnt to ashes.' 'All works, mines, factories etc. should strike at once and it would stop the war.' 'The British rule is worse than the Nazi rule; they (the Nazis) have more freedom.' 'Hitler's mechanised army is unbeatable and our navy will be ruined within a few months.'. . .

On 12 June Watling was placed on the Suspects List. Shortly afterwards he moved to Wiltshire and then to East Court Farm at Bickleigh in Devon on the 10th of October. By December 5th he was out of the region. It had been the opinion of a Special Branch officer that:

> *Neither Robert Watling or his father intend to raise a finger to help this country against Germany, and they have evacuated into the country merely to escape from the present bombing of London. They appear to hate bitterly anything savouring of democracy and would openly welcome a new system of government, even at the hands of a victorious enemy. Robert Watling particularly, appears to be imbibed with the Nazi doctrine, and it seems that nothing will ever change his views.*

The housekeeper referred to was Mrs Florence Lyon. The entire household appears to have been Fascists. A case was made against Mrs Lyon. She had been born in 1887 and was, while at Torcross in 1941, about 54 years old. Before the war she lived at Sydenham with her son Kenneth Lyon. Both were British Union members. She joined in 1938 and while there became familiar with the Watling and White families. They were already on the Suspects List. In September 1940 she left Sydenham and went to Hertfordshire where she lived next door to the Watlings. She later moved in with them. Mrs White, a German by birth, had also moved down and lived with the Lyons. An anonymous informant said an attempt was made to convert him (or her) and stated:

> *Indeed, it was on account of their becoming the subjects of local gossip that in March 1941 their lodging housekeeper gave them notice. Together they went to Torcross in Devonshire, where they lost no time in getting into conversation*

> *with soldiers stationed in the district and giving tongue to violently anti-British expressions; as there is reliable evidence that a number of gunners were entertained at various times; sometimes at the Watlings' invitations and sometime at the invitations of Mrs Lyon. On these occasions Mrs Lyon, who was the prime mover, made anti-government, anti-Jewish, anti-capitalist, defeatist and pacifist remarks, e.g. to a sergeant Mrs Lyon said 'why don't you stop the war, you are carrying on to make money for the capitalists, and will get no thanks for it', during March last when arrived at her present address which is the home of Mrs White to whom reference has already been made.*

A second report, dated 1 July 1941, recorded Lyon had moved to Resthaven, Riverside Bungalow in the village of Bishopsteignton near Teignmouth also in South Devon. It noted in April 1941 she had gone to stay with Reverend Gilbert Watling and his son Robert and daughter in law to Torcross, Devonshire, where she remained until 14 June as housekeeper. The report also noted according to Sergeant Frank Arthur Gibson on 11 April 1941 while he and other soldiers were engaged in fixing barbed wire Mrs Lyon and Mrs Watling approached them and engaged them in conversation, during the course of which Mrs Lyons said 'Churchill is living on the fat of the land while I am being starved to death . . . Churchill, Eden and members of Parliament ought to be put in a row and shot down.' Sergeant Gibson said 'what about Hitler?' Mrs Lyon replied 'no.' When one gunner said our gun would be fired again one day Mrs Lyon answered 'then don't forget to put Churchill in front of it . . . so that he gets blown to hell'.[91]

An order was issued to detain Mrs Lyon at Bishopsteignton and she was placed on the Suspects List 'for words which had recently been spoken'. She moved in Bishopsteignton to Coombe Cottage and then in July 1942 to Romford in Essex.

Other Fascists: in exile in Devon?

A number of individuals were on the Suspects List who may not have been Fascists but were pro-German or pro-Nazi. For example Eric Victor Blackmore lived with his sister at Berry Hill in Moreton Avenue at Crownhill in Plymouth when he was placed on the list on 11 December 1940. His boss at National Fertilisers Ltd stated he was pro-German. Blackmore had hosted German youths and was a member of an Anglo-German group. It was claimed that if German parachutists landed on Dartmoor Blackmore would drive out from Plymouth to help them. A similar report was given by another employee who was a special constable.[92]

A number of Fascists arrived in Devon for various reasons. I have found little information regarding Gertrude Grace Sharp alias Scholpp of the Wise Monkey Club, Hartland. She moved on 1 June 1942 to the Royal Hotel in Teignmouth, was on the Suspects List on May 18th 1942 and subsequently moved to London. Alma Runge was on the Suspects List for 'words recently spoken' by October 1941. Her address was then in care of Mrs Rowe of Rosedown Cottages, also in Hartland, but she moved frequently and by 13 November 1944 had left for Peckham. Why they were in Devon has not been determined. No other information on Rudolf Algernon Steinmetz of 36 Wolborough Street and later of 57 Brownhills Road in Newton Abbot has been found other than that he was on the Suspects List on 11 October 1941.

John Roland Smeaton-Stuart was another Fascist in Devon. He was born in Singapore in 1893, educated in England and worked in Kenya. He joined the Fascists in 1934, worked throughout the country and after he joined the national headquarters he quarrelled with Mosley and left the movement. He was arrested on August 1940 and released in November. By 26 August 1942 he had moved to the Grange in Plympton in South Devon. Within three months he had moved to Mount Pleasant in nearby Newton Ferrers and only nine months later, by 19 August 1943, he had moved to Southcott in the distant North Devon parish of Landkey near Barnstaple. He was still there on December 11th. He was excluded from Norfolk, where his home and employment was. His reasons for being in Devon were probably employment with the National

Savings Committee. Smeaton-Stuart remained on the Suspects List because it was thought he was still committed to fascism.[93]

In 1941 J. G. Potter James was on the Suspects List when he lived at Mrs Alford's home at Low Green in Bondleigh near North Tawton. A year before he had come to the attention of the Home Office by reportedly saying Britain would be better off under Nazi rule. While working as a London librarian he made clear he was pro-German in his politics and wished for a change of government to fascism.[94]

Robert Bryan Luke found his way from Kent to 74 Sterage Valley in Berrynarbor near Ilfracombe in 1941. He was born in 1920 and joined British Union at Bromley in April 1939. Luke became an active member in outdoor meetings and selling Fascist literature. He was arrested for being the lookout man while a Fascist painted street slogans but the prosecution was dropped for lack of evidence. Luke was called up in April 1940 but continued to attend Fascist meetings in uniform. He was arrested in June and interned. MI5 resisted calls for his release but he was freed in February 1941. Luke subsequently found agricultural work in north Devon. Letters revealed he continued to hold Fascist beliefs writing such phrases as 'occupied England', 'Hail Mosley' and 'Perish Judah'.[95]

Francis Tong moved throughout the South West including living at the Cleveland Hotel and Knapp House in Northham as well as 80 The Esplanade in Fowey. He was born in 1910, independently wealthy through his grandfather's estate, and joined Blackpool Branch in 1938. Tong was a frequent visitor to Germany and met Julius Streicher, the notorious Jew-hater, for whom he wrote several anti-Semitic articles. He continued to hold pro-Nazi views in the West Country and was placed on the Suspects List. Tong returned to Lancashire in 1943.[96]

In September 1940 Miss Haldine Violet Beamish moved to Little Crawley in Membury for employment with Henry Grey Thornton as his private secretary. She was then thirty-six years old and had an Irish father and a Swedish mother. Her Home Office report noted 'this woman was included in the list of persons to be detained in the even of invasion for this region in October 1940 on account of her expressions of pro-German sympathies. Since that date Beamish has moved about the country after leaving this region in January

1943'. The local vicar, who had known her for three years, reported Beamish supported Nazism. Other villagers said she claimed Britain would lose the war, Hitler would hang Churchill and local children would soon be learning German. Beamish claimed to be descended from Swedish aristocracy, to be a cousin of Herr Georring's first wife and to have kept his photograph in her bedroom. She moved to Redditch but was back in Membury by August 1944.[97]

Ernst Kellis also known as Keller was born on 12 March 1915. His father was German-born and he was British by naturalisation. He joined British Union in 1936 and became District Leader of Willesden, was detained June 1940, released in September 1943. He moved to Hampshire and then to Westbrook Farm in Bampton on 27 June 1944.[98]

Mrs Olive Evelyn Baker was on the Suspects List and moved to Ravenswood, Cliff Road, Paignton, on 9 February 1944. She was born in Canada in 1900 and had worked as a schoolmistress in Germany. Baker was a member of British Union as well as the Link. It has been suggested she was the mistress of Admiral Domville. On June 12th 1940 she was prosecuted for advertising the New British Broadcasting Station, the German propaganda media service, in Bath. At this time Baker had written to a German friend praising Hitler for being divine and suggesting he had been sent to make the world 'a cleaner and better place'. While waiting trial she cut her wrist and wrote, in her own blood, 'Hail Mosley' and 'Heil Hitler' on the walls of her cell. She was convicted at Bristol on the 5th of July and sentenced to five years' imprisonment. After her release in 1943 she moved to Paignton.[99]

On 4 January 1944 Roy Fritz Smith alias Schmidt was placed on the Suspects List. He was living at the Imperial Hotel in Torquay. He was born just before the first world war in London but raised by his German father in Germany where the family moved in 1919. Anonymous sources in Southampton reported him and his brother Ernest as active Fascists. Smith was also described as being 'thoroughly Germanised in every respect, loving the Fatherland and hating England and never missing a chance to belittle England' and as 'a real bad lot'. Smith was in Paris at the start of the war, returned to England and was arrested on suspicion of being a German agent. He joined the Pioneer Corps but was released on medical grounds in January 1943. The security forces continued to monitor him on account of his pro-German and pacifist views. In August 1942 he asked Special Branch to intern him as a German citizen on account he was being employed on anti-tank traps which he regarded as not non-combatant work. The authorities viewed him as having a history of trying to avoid military service including feigning mental instability however a medical report showed he suffered from conflicting loyalties. Upon his arrival in Torquay the local police felt he could not be trusted in the event of an invasion.[100]

William Thomas Clarke of 23 Queen Street, Torquay was added to the Suspects List on 21 March 1941, left the region and returned later that year. He moved to 4 Melville Road, Torquay on 10 November 1944. Clarke's file at the Home Office recorded he was aged forty in 1939 and had been employed by the post office in London until he was convicted of stealing packages. He then found employment in cafés and hotels mostly along the south coast. Clarke became a Fascist in 1936 and in 1940 was reported to have urged a Fascist friend to join the armed forces and cause 'subversive sabotage' by spreading pacifist propaganda. Clarke himself joined in April 1940 and claimed to have destroyed his photographs of Hitler, Mussolini and Mosley but retained his Fascist uniform and photograph of himself wearing it. Clarke had allegedly said he would prefer to shoot a refugee rather than Hitler and expressed such delight at the Fall of France that he was placed in protective custody to avoid 'being lynched' by his fellow soldiers. While in Ramsgate Gaol he told a soldier Mosley was a marvellous man who should be in charge of the country. Clarke was discharged on medical grounds early in 1941 and moved to Torquay. A Special Branch officer interviewed him and determined he continued to attend Fascist meetings and had paid for anti-Jewish materials.[101]

Mrs Nellie Abinger Pawle of Sevenash in Trentishoe Town at Combe Martin was listed for 'words recently spoken'. In 1940 she lived at Babbacome in Torbay but by the following year moved to the north Devon resort. In 1943 she moved to Blackcleave at Heddons Mouth in Parracombe. She was a British citizen, educated in Belgium and Germany, lived apart from her husband and spent much of her time on the continent. Her loyalty was under suspicion because she was an active Fascist, interested in the Link, supported Nazi Germany and kept a portrait of Hitler in her home. Her behaviour was reported by members of the public.[102]

Gilbert Henry Collins, was listed for 'words recently spoken' when living in London in July 1941. Three months later he moved to 4 Factory Row in Torquay. There years later he was still in Torbay living at Glynoarth, Vicarage Road, Chelston. Collins was a former civil servant who turned to journalism and writing detective stories but suffered from 'acute melancholia' after the failure of his novels. Collins was questioned by police and stated he had joined British Union in mid-September 1939 because he was against the war. His support for Mosley would not allow him to fight for Britain until Mosley was released. Collins also stated he could not predict his own behaviour if Britain was invaded and might assist the Germans.[103]

The case of Mrs Dorothea Duff reveals a small clique of Fascist sympathisers in Bovey Tracey. She was placed on the Suspects List for 'being a member of and active in the furtherance of the objects of the British Union' on 11 October 1941. Her Home Office file noted Duff as having some distinction as a pioneer airwoman and a 'woman of considerable force of character'. She was a widow and an enthusiastic and active member of British Union in Folkestone. Duff was arrested and interned in June 1940 and MI5 insisted she remained under arrest until April 1941. She was not able to travel more than five miles without police permission and had to report her movements each week. Duff had planned on living with her mother, Mrs Pyton, in Bovey Tracey but a shortage of accommodation forced her to have lodgings at nearby Slackwood. With Mrs Pyton was living Miss M. E. Riley, a woman noted by the Home Office as 'having British Union and pro-German sympathies'. Riley was employed by Captain R. F. R. McNeil who was also suspected of similar loyalties. MI5 had been interested in McNeil since 1932 when he was involved with the Duke of Manchester and complicity in arms trafficking to Portugal. McNeil lived at Colehays, situated near other properties in the parish where Fascists lived such as Soldridge and Parke.[104]

Hubert Sydney Maddocks lived at Skaigh View in Sticklepath near

Okehampton and was placed on the Suspects List by 28 February 1941. He was a single man aged 36 and had worked all his adult life at the Phoenix Assurance Company. He joined British Union in 1936 and was a member of The Link. He served on the latter's council and was described by the Home Office as 'one of the most active organisers and propagandists of this society'. He had founded a branch at Southend-on-Sea. Maddocks was reported to have met Hitler twice, visited Germany frequently, including a month before the start of war, and admitted to anti-Semitism. Maadocks was described by Admiral Domville as 'one of Mosley's best men'. He was interned in 1940 and released in January 1941. Shortly afterwards Madocks moved to this remote part of Devon. He remained restricted in his movements.[105] Another person apparently at this address was Jean Gordon Johnstone, a Scottish woman born in 1909 described as being 5 foot high with brown eyes, dark brown hair, slim build and having a sallow complexion and untidy appearance. She married Charles Johnstone, her cousin. Her Home Office report noted she was closely associated with a District Leader of British Union and that they attempted to infiltrate the Fellowship of Services, a group of ex-servicemen. She was a shorthand typist and assisted him in publishing propaganda. An informant reported she said of Germany's bombing of London 'personally I call it a damn good effort on the part of the Nazi airmen.'[106]

In 1941 Adolph Christian Carl Schultz of St Olaves, Petitor Road, Torquay was 71 years old, a naturalised British subject since 1907, and according to his Home Office file 'undoubtedly a man of considerable wealth and a former shipbroker and stockbroker, stated to have large interests in Germany'. MI5 kept him under surveillance during the first world war and since the beginning of the second noted he had loudly praised Hitler whose photograph Shultz kept on his mantelpiece. He later claimed to two local ladies that Hitler ('the saviour of the world') was his friend, that he was friendly with Rudolf Hess and had entertained Ribbentrope. The two women, who first met Schultz at the Moorland Hotel at Haytor, informed the police as did other local people. He was well-known to MI5 for his pro-Nazi views. Schultz was placed on the Suspects List in 1941.[107]

On 23 October 1940 Adolph Markham of Hollydale in

Teignmouth Road in Torquay was listed 'on the grounds that his conduct and words recently expressed or spoken expressing sympathy with the enemy indicate that he is likely to assist the enemy.' A year later he was noted as being 'of hostile origin and associations'. In July 1939 Markham lectured to the Torquay Rotary Club and stressed the German people all wore uniforms but many did not know what they represented. He spoke about the desire for peace and that in spite of the benefits of modern Germany its people 'would give a lot to be living in a free land like ours where one could call a spade a spade and not be afraid to do so'. Even so, the Home Office noted the police believed his talk was mild Nazi propaganda. Markham was born in 1891 in Edinburgh and was the son of Adolph Schulz. He changed his name by deed poll in 1914. Torquay residents reported he shared his father's pro-Nazi views.[108]

Henry John Newcombe Richards of 2 Pentillie Road in Mutley at Plymouth was a clerk in the National Provident Bank in Bedford Street but his pro-German comments brought threats of physical violence from his colleagues. The Home Office noted he and his wife had visited Germany before the war, that they were in favour of the Nazis, owned photographs of Hitler, had entertained Nazi officers and were members of The Link, the extreme anti-Semitic organisation. Richards was a member of the British People's Party, the Fascist organisation created by the Duke of Bedford. He was placed on the Suspects List for 'words recently spoken' in October 1941. His wife Beatrice lived at Loft Cottage in Poundsgate near Widecombe-in-the-Moor on 1 July 1941 and was also on the Suspects List.[109]

Norman Hart alias Sidney Hart lived in Montpelier Road in Torquay. He was a photographer for the Westminster branch of the St George Society, a Fascist organisation, and active in British Union. Hart left Torquay for London when Mosley was arrested. From there he sent a list of the names and addresses of British Union members in Devon and Cornwall to one Miss Marjorie Romo of Flat 6, Middleton Hall in Torquay. Unfortunately it does not appear to have survived. Romo later admitted to police she was a British Union member. Hart asked her to keep the list safe until he returned from London but it was seized by the police. It was the opinion of the Home Office that Hart had travelled to London to try to circumvent Mosley's arrest and keep the British Union party active. Hart returned to Torquay and then left for London in August 1941. By then he was on the Suspects List.[110]

Mrs Constance Norah Falls, formerly Pearson, née Ilieve lived at Tregonwell, Lynmouth in March 1944. She was born on 24 January 1896, joined British Union in autumn 1937 and previously belonged to Imperial Fascist Party in York in 1921. She was the women's team leader in Bournemouth and helped run the branch once the men left. She was detained on 3 June 1940 and the order was suspended on 1 July 1941. The Home Office noted nothing was heard of her until she wrote to A. E. Day, a Fascist printer of Taunton, soliciting funds for the 18b detainees fund. In July 1943 she married William de Boudry Falls, a member of Bournemouth British Union.[111]

Mrs Margery Lister, of Southgates, St Efrides Road, Torquay, was born in 1909. She married in 1929, visited Hamburg where she learned hairdressing and separated from her husband in 1939. She claimed she joined British Union at the behest of her husband, a musician, and 'to please the Fascist customers of the public house she managed in Lincoln with her husband before the war'. But the Home Office thought she succeeded her brother Leonard Jarvis as temporary District Leader of Normanton Branch in Yorkshire. She was detained on 30 May 1940 and released on November 2nd. The Home Office noted on May 1944 she had expressed pro-German, anti-Semitic and anti-Russian views and associated with former Fascists. Also, 'an agent who was in touch with this group reported in November that Mrs Lister had little real knowledge of politcs and did not take much part in discussions, except to give expression to her violently anti-Semitic views. She appears to have no morals and is generally more interested in collecting 'beaux' than in the political activities of her friends.'[112]

Mrs Caroline Mary Johannesen moved to Hawkchurch near Axminster in May 1941 when her husband Maurice obtained work with the Ministry of Supply. They moved to Stoke Abbot at Beaminster in Dorset in November. The Home Office recorded they joined British Union in 1934 and were active members. She was a member in Cobham in Surrey, was interned and released from Holloway

Prison on 13 August 1940. He was born in Aberdeen and his father was Norwegian. In April 1941 the Home Office discovered they were living in Launceston with Dr Claude Gouldesbrough of whom it was suspected had Mosley's confidence. Letters between Mrs Johannsen and Gouldesbrough showed their anti-Semitism. In one she noted he had written on Hitler's birthday and added 'did you hear Winnie the Poop on Sunday? He depressed me terribly – he spoke as if we were winning.'[113]

Florence Emily Hayes was a schoolmistress in Exeter where she lost her job after being interned at Holloway Prison. She had been Women's District Leader in Bournemouth and Women's County Officer for West Hampshire. Hayes later stated 'my nerves have never recovered from Holloway you know, and even now, the least overstrain has its effects . . . All I am fit for now is to potter about the garden, feed the hens and dream of days gone by'. Although she attended the 18B Social and Dance at the Royal Hotel on December 1st 1945 she temporarily withdrew from fascism and embraced spiritualism. Robert Saunders of Dorchester later wrote 'whatever may have happened to her physically, her spirit is as fanatical as ever. I always feel that she will consider her life imperfect if she does not end her days being burnt at the stake for her ideals.'[114]

Notes

1 *Action*, No. 194, 16 November 1939.
2 *Torquay Times*, 15 September 1939.
3 *Action*, No. 192, 2 November 1939.
4 Sheffield University, 119/A8/31.
5 Sheffield University, 119/A4/82.
6 National Archives, HO45/23672.
7 National Archives, HO45/23673.
8 *Action*, No. 41, 28 November 1936. She wrote from Holly Bush Farm, Frithsden, Hemel Hempstead, Herts.
9 *Western Morning News*, 5 August 1947.
10 Sheffield University, 119/A8/30.
11 *The Times*, 31 January 1940; *Express & Echo*, 30 January 1940.

12 Martin Pugh, *Hurrah for the Blackshirts* (2005), 232 ; Dorril, *Black Shirt*, 424.
13 *The Exmouth Journal*, 20 January & 3 February 1940.
14 *The Exmouth Journal*, 20 January 1940.
15 *The Exmouth Journal*, 3 February 1940.
16 *The Times*, 31 January 1940; *Express & Echo*, 30 January 1940.
17 *The Exmouth Journal*, 3 February 1940; *The Exmouth Chronicle*, 3 February 1940.
18 *The Times*, 1 February 1940.
19 National Archives, Ho45/23672.
20 National Archives, HO45/23673.
21 National Archives, HO45/23672.
22 National Archives, HO45/23673.
23 National Archives, HO45/23782.
24 For example, see *Western Morning News*, 4, 11, 16, 23, 28 January & 14, 20, 25 April 1939.
25 National Archives, HO262/8.
26 Information supplied by Arthur French.
27 Guy Mansell, '18b: one man's story', *Comrade*, April 2006, 13.
28 West, *MI5*, 129, 265.
29 Simpson, *Odious*, 80.
30 Sheffield University, 119/A4/20 & A8/29-30; Action, No. 216, 25 April 1940.
31 National Archives, HO262/8.
32 *Western Independent*, 9 June 1940.
33 *Dartmouth Western Guardian*, 8 August 1940; *Pulman's Weekly*, 30 July & 6 August 1940.
34 *Dartmouth Western Guardian*, 13 & 20 June 1940.
35 National Archives, HO45/25570.
36 National Archives, HO45/25570.
37 National Archives, HO45/25570.
38 National Archives, HO45/25570.
39 National Archives, HO45/25570.
40 Claudia Baldoli, *Exporting Fascism* (Oxford, 2003), 1.
41 *Western Independent*, 9 & 16 June 1940.
42 Gray, Exeter Remembers The War, 140-1.
43 National Archives, HO45/25570.
44 National Archives, HO45/25570.
45 National Archives, HO45/25568.
46 National Archives, HO45/25570.

47 National Archives, HO45/25569.
48 National Archives, HO45/25570. Fullaford was owned by Leslie Gladstone Shiner in 1939: Devon Record Office, Buckfastleigh East Voters' List, 1939.
49 National Archives, HO45/25570.
50 National Archives, HO45/25570.
51 *Dartmouth Western Guardian*, 1 August 1940.
52 National Archives, HO144/21538.
53 *Western Independent*, 9 June 1940.
54 National Archives, HO45/25754; Simpson, *Odious*, 50-3, 105-114.
55 Simpson, *Odious*, 41.
56 National Archives, HO45/25754.
57 *Pulman's Weekly*, 4 June 1940.
58 Simpson, *Odious*, 230; Sheffield University, Bellamy manuscript, 948-9.
59 National Archives, HO45/25752.
60 *The Sidmouth Observer*, 5 June 1940.
61 *The Sidmouth Observer*, November 1939. The honorary secretaries were M. Moral and A. Dalton of Sid Road in Sidmouth.
62 *Pulman's Weekly*, 11 June 1940.
63 *Pulman's Weekly*, 25 June 1940.
64 *Action*, No. 217-19, 2-16 May 1940.
65 *Western Morning News*, 7 June 1940; National Archives, HO45/25754; National Archives, HO45/23673.
66 *Pulman's Weekly*, 9 July 1940.
67 Devon Record Office, Voters' Lists, 1930, for Branscombe.
68 National Archives, HO45/23673.
69 Sheffield University, 119/A5/167-97, letter of 8 March from Saunders to Fitzgerald.
70 Interview at Branscombe, 1998.
71 National Archives, HO45/23672.
72 National Archives, HO45/25754.
73 National Archives, HO45/25754.
74 National Archives, HO45/23672.
75 National Archives, HO45/23672.
76 National Archives, HO45/23673.
77 Dorril, *Blackshirt*, 478; Gottlieb, *Feminine Fascism*, 347.
78 Gottlieb, *Feminine Fascism*, 294.
79 Derek Stevens, 'The view from the Country', *Marshwood Vale Magazine*, January 2006, no. 82; *The Western Times*, 7 & 21 June

1940; *The Sidmouth Observer*, 26 June 1940; *Pulman's Weekly*, 25 June & 9 July 1940.

80 *The Western Times*, 7 June 1940.

81 National Archives, HO45/25570, southwest division file 864023/12.

82 Sheffield University, 119/C10/168.

83 Sheffield University, 119/C10/171.

84 Sheffield University, 119/C10/167.

85 Sheffield University, 119/C10/165i; Robert Saunders, *A Tiller of Several Soils* (1987), letter to Jeffrey Custance, 12 Dec. 1943.

86 *Action*, 13 & 27 February 1934.

87 National Archives, HO45/23782.

88 National Archives, HO45/25570, southwest division file 864023/12.

89 National Archives, HO45/25754.

90 National Archives, HO45/25570, South West division file 864023/12.

91 National Archives, HO45/25569.

92 National Archives, HO45/25570.

93 National Archives, HO45/25714 & HO45/25570, Southwest division file 864023/12; Simpson, *Odious*, 266.

94 National Archives, HO45/25570.

95 National Archives, HO45/25570.

96 National Archives, HO45/25570.

97 National Archives, HO45/25570, 864023/12b, 'reports – cases still on list'. The house in 1936 was owned by the four Miss Leesons, Kate, Edith, Margaret and Dora: Devon Record Office, Membury Voters' List, 1936.

98 National Archives, HO45/25570.

99 Simpson, *Odious*, 169, 220; Gottlieb, *Feminine Fascism*, 281; National Archives, HO45/25570.

100 National Archives, HO45/25570.

101 National Archives, HO45/25570.

102 National Archives, HO45/25570.

103 National Archives, HO45/25570.

104 National Archives, HO45/25570; Simpson, *Odious*, 210. Ronald Frank Rouse McNeill and Dallas Kathleen McNeill lived at Colehays in 1939. Slackwood was the home of James Langworthy but no evidence has been found to link him with fascism other than having Dorothea Duff as a lodger: Devon Record Office, Bovey Tracey Voters' List for 1939.

105 National Archives, HO45/25570; Simpson, *Odious*, 143.

106 National Archives, HO45/25568.

107 National Archives, HO45/25570.

108 *Torquay Times*, 14 July 1939; National Archives, HO45/25570.

109 National Archives, HO45/25570.

110 National Archives, HO45/25570.

111 Alfred Ernest Day was placed on the Suspects List on 10 February 1944. He then lived at 62 Alma Street, Taunton: National Archives, HO45/25570.

112 National Archives, HO45/25570; Gottlieb, Feminine Fascism, 318.

113 National Archives, HO45/25568; Gottlieb, Feminine Fascism, 313.

114 Gottlieb, *Feminine Fascism*, 309, 251. It has not been possible to trace her school. It does not appear that she was employed outside the city by the county of Devon nor whether she was in a private or state school: Devon Record Office, 2227C/ES14, 15 & 26.

Epilogue

Post-war Fascism

Moves were made to revive the cause of fascism in Devon not long after winning the war against Germany, Italy and Japan in the summer of 1945. While the British public moved politically to the left and elected a Labour government a considerable range of far right parties were formed. Many of them competed for members. In 1945 Mosley's own plans for a party began to take shape. One of his key considerations was to ensure it distanced itself from German associations. In the late 1940s the British political climate was shaped by the gradual dismembering of the Empire, a dominant United States, concerns over the spread of Soviet Communism through Eastern Europe and a gradual awareness and horror of the Holocaust. The old Fascists had to adapt to a new political climate but Mosley's new organisation, the Union Movement, comprised many of the old members and had similar policies except Mosley envisioned Europe as one nation. In a press interview after the launch in 1947 Mosley announced Jews would be deported and he denied the Holocaust had happened.[1] Those former colleagues attracted to the racist policies of the British Union were, no doubt, satisfied if not delighted.

After their internment Robert Saunders, former District Leader of West Dorset, and Harold John 'Jack' Forward, his counterpart in

Exeter, had remained in close contact. In early January 1945 Forward wrote a chatty letter to Saunders with news of Fascist colleagues and friends. They lived under suspicion ('it seems everyone has been given an unendorsed identity card. I had had one for ages which rather worried the cops. Rather suspected foul play – as usual with them – but my honour was finally vindicated.') but he managed to see friends such as Claude Duvivier every Friday in Exeter. Of others he wrote:

> *Whilst at a ploughing match I met Farmer Hooper of Tiverton who was released from Ascot. Still farming and still very bitter. He said his friend Down has died. He has visited Joe Beckett of boxing fame. Also me, who do you think? Bill Bailey! Dow drives Devon General buses and lives at Sidmouth. Still bags of talk of course. 'Same as I've always said, we shall win'. 'Don't be downhearted Jack' etc etc. George Pownall was staying with him some time back. George visited me several times. He works on the land for the Surrey WAEC but seems fairly contented with the job (I shouldn't be), ever hear from Wally?*[2]

Forward married in June and his best man was a former Exeter Fascist. Saunders was invited to the wedding.[3] Social reunions of former internees were held in London and Forward and his wife went to one on October 6th with Mr & Mrs Duvivier.[4] Of the reunions he wrote:

> *Meeting so many old friends was a real tonic – too many to name, though I was sorry not to see Scotty and Nommie. Crewe, George Pownell and Mr & Mrs DV were there . . . Ken Browning, an Exeter member whom you may recall, has just been demobbed from the RAF. News a month or two back of one Yeatman, also Exeter member, that he was killed at Arnhem.*[5]

In 1946 there were moves to start Fascist book clubs. Saunders instigated the Wessex Book Club. Its stated aims were to supply books, act as a lending library, provide a discussion club and arrange meetings, outings and other social activities.[6] Forward suggested to him:

> *Have received your information about the Wessex Book Club, it would seem better to have local people join this instead of forming our own club in view of the small numbers involved? Shall get in touch with Major Hammond, Mrs Fraher, Mr Duvivier, John Rowe, Rowe (senior), Marshall Jose, K. Browning, the farmer from Tiverton who was at Walton but whose name I can't recall. Frank Bailly (of house 3) now living near here.*[7]

Forward circularised fellow Fascists details of the book club. He had already suggested a lending library but there was little response except from a Miss Griffin. There was also a poor response to the Book Club, only Claude Barrett had joined. He had targeted:

> *Major Hammond, Kennerleigh, Lapford*
> *C. Duvivier, Sanctuary Farm, Woodbury*
> *J. Rowe, Portland Street, Exeter*
> *W. Rowe, Senior, Honiton*
> *Mr K. Browning, Reading*
> *C. Barrett, 9 Fairview Terrace, Pinhoe*
> *D. Elworthy, 40 Regent Street, Exeter*
> *Marshall Jose, Devonshire Place*
> *Regrets at incomplete addresses temporarily lost in the confusion of house moving. I also want to get in touch with these two gentlemen when I can get their addresses from somewhere – a farmer near Tiverton, (Bill) Frank Bailly, Sidford.*[8]

The aim in establishing book clubs was that from these would grow Mosley's new party.[9] Rafe Temple Cotton turned down Saunder's offer to run the book club. He wrote in July:

> *If your club is an attempt to revive British Union on all its old lines, I am not with you. We need something much larger in conception. We have got to get Christ, Mohammed, Buddha,*

> *Confucius and a few others right into politics and science and everyday life. We should have learnt too a lesson about trying to force ideas down peoples' throats. Even if those ideas are right you can't make people swallow them, they will come back in your own face unless people are ready to receive them.*[10]

Forward was also uncertain. He felt he had to disguise his continued commitment to fascism. From his home at 1 Manstone Road in Exeter he wrote a lukewarm letter to Saunders in November 1946.

> *Dear Bob, Thanks for newsletters. Am afraid however that I don't much like the idea of having MP send out letters giving my name and address as a local centre. You see, I hope one day to join my father in the dairy business, that being the only profession left to me after having internment stop me going to a university, and should there be any hostile publicity in the Jewish press – mentioning names – and there well may be – it would hardly do business any good. My politics are half forgotten in this neighbourhood now and I want things to stay like that. Other people in Devon such as DV* [Claude Duvivier of Woodbury] *or* [Rafe Temple] *Cotton* [of Branscombe] *have an established position and in any case are not dependent upon the goodwill of their neighbours to the same extent. Three years internment and three years compulsory lorry driving are 6 years wasted as far as a career is concerned and who can waste the years between 20 and 27 and expect to get anywhere? Actually I think to have anything at all to do with MP may be unwise. Maybe all this is being selfish. If you think so write and say so. I regret that this is the situation.*

Even so, he became the chief organiser although he found it difficult to restart interest. In March 1947 Forward wrote 'nearly everyone I contact seems to write *Thanks for calling or writing. I must see about it* – but they never do!' He had failed to contact some members, such as Dundas of Littlehempston, but had success with others such as Cotton who 'wants to join the Wessex Book Club so will send him membership forms etc immediately. Offers to do anything he can to help'.[11] Shortly afterwards Forward had tea with A. C. Woodgate, a former Fascist who had been interned. Forward described him as a former:

> *speaker in Exeter, and quite good too, ex 18b, tall fellow about 40, is back in Exeter with wife and son, is in the National Fire Service. They were at our place to tea a little back. I gave him the usual literature which he seemed to know little of. His wife is not too keen on his getting enthusiastic about British Union again (says the least little things will start him off again) but then she had a rough time when he was inside.*[12]

In 1948 Woodgate began farming at Coryton in East Devon.[13]

In November 1947 Mosley started a new political party, the Union Movement.[14] Cotton brought a new contact to a meeting in Salisbury. He wrote to Saunders in October on one occasion 'we should like to bring with us a Mr Mathews of Sidmouth who I believe is an old London & Birmingham member, a friend of Irving and others, he seems quite sound and discrete and useful.'[15] By the end of the year Saunders and Forward were planning on holding a conference in Exeter.[16] Forward saw this as a test of local enthusiasm amongst former British Union members. He had moved to 27 Park Road and thought 'a conference could be held at my house – neighbours wouldn't know what it was all about and I can't think of anywhere better.'[17] Forward wrote to Saunders:

> *I have for some time felt that Exeter supporters were not as keenly interested in Union Movement affairs as they should be. However, the amount of interest can be assessed by the number who attend this conference or send letters of apology for absence – an alternative which you or I would feel compelled to observe.*
>
> *the following have received letters of invitation individually written or duplicated:*

Major Hammond	*Kennerleigh*
Mr Rowe sen.	*Combe Raleigh*
Mr Long	*Exeter*
Mr Hooper	*Tiverton*
Mr & Mrs Cotton	*Branscombe*
Sidmouth supporters via Mr Cotton	
Mrs Fraher and Mr John Fraher	*Exeter*
Mr Rowe junior	*Exeter*
Mr Jose	*Exeter*
Mr Bailey	*Sidford*
Mr Gill	*Exeter*
Mr Elworthy	*Exeter*

The following have been told:
Mr Barrett, Mr Browning
I also wrote to yourself, Mr Sheddick (twice), Mr Pocock and Mr Rawlinson.[18]

Saunders subsequently thought it was 'quite a successful conference in Exeter on Sunday. Fourteen of us turned up, in spite of the usual travelling difficulties. Pat Sheddick is taking over the whole of Devon and Cornwall for the time being.'[19]

Sheddick lived at 3 Lipson Hill Terrace in Plymouth and had started the Mayflower Book Club. He wrote to Saunders asking for a list of contacts because he was new to Plymouth and did not know British Union members from before the war. In March 1947 Sheddick thought he was gaining ground but by June wrote 'the Mayflower is still plodding along though we don't make much headway'. He found the political constraints wearying and was 'looking forward to the day when 'book clubs' are no longer necessary!!' Not much is known of Sheddick's views except those regarding race; he wrote to a colleague 'all the fat, greasy Asiatic parasites who have fattened on our country for so long will find the day of reckoning has arrived and Britain will once again be British'.[20] Sheddick did not last in Plymouth: he moved to Horsham in February 1948[21] at which point E. R. Lee took over.[22]

The following month events in Exeter took an eventful turn for Forward. He wrote to Saunders on May 21st 1948 'just a line to let you know that a Mr Jameson Dixon living at Silverton (about 8 miles from Exeter) has written to me saying he wants to start a branch in Exeter. He was once DDL of Dover'. Forward planned to meet him to see if he was 'the man Exeter has been waiting for'.[23] Saunders needed an active figure and hoped he had found one. He should have been apprehensive when in May he received two letters in which Jameson-Dixon complained of the poor organisation of Mosley's new party and then wrote 'if you have a member at Poole by the name of Mrs Latham beware. It is quite a private matter between her and me, and another member of ours a Miss W. Roberts at Taunton. I don't want to meet her as it very nearly came to a law case some 2 years ago.'[24]

Jameson-Dixon was not being honest about his familiarity with Miss Roberts. In about 1945 Jameson-Dixon and his wife Lilliam had moved to Silverton after short stints in No-Man's-Land near Tiverton and at Torquay. They acted as housekeepers for the Reverend Ellis Roberts and his middle-aged daughter Winifred at Silverleigh at 8 Fore Street. The Roberts had been living in Ipplepen for more than ten years and the Reverend had little or no sight and had been in a wheelchair for some time. On the day he arrived he was carried upstairs to his bed where he remained until his death in January 1947. He was buried in Silverton. How these two pairs of Fascists had met and arranged to live together at Silverton has not been discovered. In August 1947 Jameson-Dixon gave away a bride at what was an unusual wedding in Silverton: in the Methodist chapel Eugenie Le Poidevin of Guernsey married Deputy Leader Werner Petri, a German at 92 POW Hostel in the village. The reception was held at Silverleigh. The three later moved to 2 Shute Orchard Cottages, now known as 15 High Street. In about 1950 they moved once more to Somerset.[25]

Forward wrote to Saunders in 1948:

> *Jameson Dixon certainly seems to be moving fast, according to this letter he has been dashing about seeing all sorts of people such as Lee at Plymouth and Mathews at Sidmouth. He has also been to London and brought back a lot of literature. Now that I have seen him I know that he certainly is not too old for the job and he writes a very good letter*

which is a great advantage. Despite this I am still not sure how to weigh him up but perhaps the reason is a stick in the mud's mistrust of too much hustle! Was glad to hear you were able to go up to town for the big rally.[26]

Within days Forward realised Jameson-Dixon was not the solution. He wrote that month:

We have something of a problem in Jameson-Dixon! He called at the DAEC office to see me a couple of days ago (wearing British Union badge boldly). Before this he had called at home to see if I was there and worked up considerable heat talking to Ruth about Lee arranging a meeting to conflict with his. Dixon has called a meeting at the Top Hat Café in South Street, Exeter, for June 5th and Lee a meeting at a hotel in Plymouth the Saturday or Sunday following. Lee, in a letter received this morning, says he regards Dixon as a fanatic interested mainly in hearing his own voice and that Jack Pococke agrees with this estimate.

Dixon wants me to be his treasurer saying that he would be more comfortable with someone else handling the cash, which is fair enough. I'm afraid I couldn't work with the chap though. We can't stop Dixon organising a branch anyway, can we, if he is really determined? The question is, is Dixon better than no active organiser at all? I think perhaps he would be, but the situation where members 'on the fringe' are asked to go to Exeter one week and Plymouth the next is to be avoided. Bad feeling between Dixon and Lee has had a beginning and will develop unless some compromise is arrived at. One can't help siding with Lee a little. He seems very competent, and distributes 40 Unions in Plymouth alone which would show that considerable progress has been made there recently.[27]

Rafe Temple Cotton also had reservations. He wrote to Saunders:

You mention Jameson-Dixon, well we met him in the old days in Torquay and formed a very poor opinion of him. This is of course merely my opinion. I think he is the sort of self important fool who having the most unsound ideas himself would lead people to think that his ideas were the official policy of whatever movement he was working for and I think he is a thoroughly bad advertisement for any movement. He came to Sidmouth yesterday and interviewed Mrs Mathews (Pat being away) and she was very much disgusted at him generally. (Mathews is the man I brought to Exeter and Salisbury). I presume he (young Dick) had Mathews' address from Lee which I think was a pity.[28]

Forward boycotted the Exeter meeting and instead travelled to Plymouth and brought others with him.[29] In July it was clear to Forward there was a better solution to their problems.

Ruth and I have had a weekend at Plymouth during which we visited Lee (had been intending to do this for a long while) I now regard him as an excellent man doing very good work, in fact just the right sort of sane chap the movement requires. He has made some good contacts (according to his correspondence) and distributes 78 Union *each week, which, considering the reputation of the old Plymouth branch is not bad. He showed me letters he has had from Jameson-Dixon containing statements, some insulting and others that can only be described as downright untruths. Jameson-Dixon is still a menace. He was written complaining that he sent out 30 letters to supporters and received not a single reply. I think that in a little while he will be so disgusted that he will throw the whole job in and that will be a very good thing. Speaks of Lee having 'double-crossed' him which of course was not at all the case. Jameson-Dixon's meeting in Exeter was cancelled through lack of support. I am acting as you suggested in your last letter i.e. supporting Lee and being an interested spectator only . . .*[30]

It appears that by Christmas Jameson-Dixon had given up the idea of an Exeter Branch. Lee remained active and later lived at 35 Fountains Crescent in Pennycross at Plymouth.[31]

In 1949 Lee organised meetings in Exeter with the assistance of Forward.[32] The party had attracted former members such as John Pococke and others who are not known to have been British Union member such as Mr & Mrs C. Parsons.[33] Rafe Temple Cotton and his mother were also active. He resumed his public speaking and was holding meetings as late as 1950. Saunders thought he had improved from his pre-war meetings.[34]

1950s

The 1950s opened yet another chapter in British fascism. In 1951 Mosley left the country to live in Ireland and his Union Movement struggled on but it lacked the force of his British Union party.[35] Many former Blackshirts maintained their Fascist interests in the 1950s.

The two main Exeter leaders were no longer young men able to devote their energy to promoting fascism. Both had reached middle age and had other responsibilities. Even so, a letter by Jack Forward of 1951 shows becoming a parent had not diminished his political beliefs. He wrote:

> *Young Geoffrey is quite a good baby and hasn't so far kept us awake much at night. Shall try to bring him up sanely, appreciating the valuable things, and putting Yiddisher culture (whether from British people or otherwise) in its proper place. Training of children however, if overdone, is liable to result in the opposite result to the one intended.*[36]

He wrote of former colleagues he had not:

> *Seen Rafe for ages and did not know of Mrs Cotton's illness. Hear from Bill Bailey from time to time and of course see Johnny Rowe frequently (you will just remember him in the Exeter branch I expect). My movement activities are limited I*

> *am afraid to distributing* Union *locally and sending a very rare donation to Raven-Thompson. For the rest I feel too disgusted with the intelligence of people around me to attempt to reason with them. Results of the war here knocked a little of the stuffing out of them, I imagine. Wartime 'Defeat Hitler and or Germany and all will be well with the world' idea, I mean.*[37]

As late as 1958 Forward had kept his Fascist beliefs. That year he discussed a trip to Bournemouth to hear Mosley.[38]

Rafe Temple Cotton remained in Branscombe and married not long before his dominating mother died. The Cottons had remained active in fascism for nearly twenty years but also developed interests in spiritualism.

Henry Jameson-Dixon was in 1950 an elderly man and unable to be an effective organiser even if a party would have taken him. He maintained his anti-Semitism views. By 1950 he had moved to 174 Lower Merridge at Courtway in Bridgwater in Somerset from where he congratulated a Coventry politician on his stand on defence. He warned him of a Jewish threat and of a world dictatorship by 1955. He thought 'what a bunch of stupid idiots our politicians are. All of them are chained to the Jewish Task of World Conquest and in the end they will perish in the great purge that is to come'.[39]

After the war Henry Williamson supported yet another Fascist party, the National Front After Victory.[40] His death in 1977 revived speculation about his motives. Williamson's interest in fascism has been attributed to having been traumatised by his experiences in the first world war. In the 1930s he visited Germany, wrote in praise of Hitler ('I salute the great man across the Rhine') but singularly failed to take into account the brutality against political opponents, widely reported in the British press, and a range of other people notably the Jews. It is hard to understand how an individual driven by a horror of war would embrace Hitler's Nazis who were widely recognised as aggressively militaristic in the 1930s. It would have been more logical for his being repulsed by the overt militarism of German fascism and to have become a pacifist. Instead he embraced it.

One man who defended Williamson was Ernest Martin, a

research fellow at the University of Exeter. He wrote 'one has heard all sorts of wild statements about this writer . . . in London and in the area around Georgeham and Braunton. Always there's some reference to his defence of Hitler, his devotion to a politician like Mosley. He was suspected of all sorts of things during the war'. Martin thought it was appropriate to feel unease about Williamson's political postures and 'occasional follies' but nothing more. In contrast, the war correspondent Negley Farson thought of Williamson as that 'horror on the hill' while his son Dan considered Williamson to have merely been politically naïve. He excused Williamson as being 'like most boys he could not resist the boom of the big parade'. He also noted Williamson's enthusiasms for Mosley and Hitler.[41] In 1950 Williamson declined an offer to reengage in Fascist politics. He did this not from a lack of conviction but because he was told the public would not buy his books. Williamson planned to focus on writing and explained 'I have had to retire from all such things and here in isolation on this hilltop hut and caravan to try and become again an objective writer as I was years ago, outside any conflicts or politics or dreams of saving the world.'[42]

From 1944 the former Torquay resident A. K. Chesterton edited *Truth*, a newspaper owned by several members of the Conservative party. In the 1950s he formed the League of Empire Loyalists and his party, along with British National Party, the Racial Preservation Society and the Greater Britain Movement merged in the late 1960s to form the National Front. Chesterton became its head. His Fascist journey had taken him from curiosity at Torquay in 1932 through more than thirty years of devoted commitment to become the Father of the National Front.[43]

Devon's contribution to fascism was, far from being inconsequential, was varied and diverse.

Conclusion

Why did fascism fail in Devon? Many reasons were shared with the rest of the country. Mosley began his party in the depth of the Great Depression but a slight economic revival stopped the anticipated political crisis. One great factor was adopting the name Fascist after there had already been the use of the Italian *Fascisti* in Britain. The British public were wary of the movement because of its continental origins and saw in German fascism, with its increasing violence and aggression through the 1930s, a taste of what would lay in store for Britain. Also, Mosley promised to deal with the Jews and after the Second World War this was remembered with revulsion. It was difficult to promote fascism in the 1930s but those attempting to do so after 1945 found the going that much harder. Mosley's Blackshirts had tried to carve out support at the expense of existing parties and each of these existing competitors was active in different ways in trying to diminish the new movement.

In Devon local opposition, particularly in Plymouth and to a lesser extent in Exeter, resulted in violent disorder and the manner in which the Fascists responded forced the police to restrict and then thwart the movement. In towns and villages across Devon, in places as far apart at Seaton, Okehampton, Braunton and Salcombe, the Fascists were remarkably active and in some places successful. The sight of 80 Blackshirts in uniform marching through the streets of Exmouth in 1933 must have caused many locals to stop and wonder at the spectacle and potential consequences of such a party. In rural communities recruitment amongst farmers was high, particularly in North Devon, but it was the Fascists themselves who killed off that support. The reason was intervention by national headquarters and it could be argued London was almost single-handedly to blame for the collapse of fascism in Devon. The order to withdraw from the Tithe War and to initiate violent tactics used in the East End of London lost the party the Plymouth Branch in 1935. The Fascists never recovered there and this loss of momentum was never overcome in the rest of Devon even with the vigorous efforts of Rafe Temple Cotton who revived Exeter from 1935 through into the Second World War. On public order grounds

Plymouth's police shattered fascism in the port and several years later their counterparts in Exeter used the same reason for limiting fascist campaigning.

The national party, and particularly Sir Oswald Mosley, was also responsible for turning the *Western Morning News* from a passive supporter to a harsh critic. It is possible the editor had been searching for a reason to withdraw the paper's support but it was the ineptness of Mosley that supplied him with one. Some independent newspapers continued to publish positive news stories but the loss of the *Western Morning News* starved the Fascists of the publicity they needed.

In one other way the national party had a tremendous influence on the course of local events. There was an erratic level of financing: periodic gluts of money were followed by stringent cuts. This was responsible for branches opening and closing as well as rural campaigns being initiated and probably being cancelled.

It is difficult to assess local membership. There were at least two thousand in Devon but we know the names of less five per cent of them. Some were native-born while others had moved to the county. Perhaps amongst many farmers the support came from a single-issue, the Fascist policy on tithe reform. But others were clearly interested in the party in a wider sense. In Plymouth and Exeter there were many young members, many were men but in the former particularly there was a significant number of women. Devon produced two of the country's most prominent Fascists in Henry Williamson and A. K. Chesterton but both were more influential outside of Devon than in it.

Some members were clearly anti-Semitic, such as Claude Duvivier, Jack Forward, Henry Jameson Dixon and Lucy Temple Cotton. Many were also pro-German, notably Winifred Roberts and William Crowle, and a portion even wanted Germany to win the Second World War, including William Tillotson, but it is not possible to define the majority as unpatriotic. Indeed, a great number were highly patriotic but their natural sympathies with Fascists from other countries divided loyalties. It is only possible to ponder how Mosley would have governed Britain had he come to power. Would British fascism have followed the German, Italian or Spanish model? Certainly had Hitler successfully invaded Britain and set up a Mosley government, not a clear certainty by any means, life under German rule would have been like that on the continent or at least like the Channel Islands.[44] It is unlikely Mosley could have spared Britain the horrors experienced by others under German occupation. A negotiated peace might well have brought the same conditions. These thoughts dominated British perceptions of Mosley's movement after the war and overrode the fear of communism that ran through the 1930s. Perhaps one common thread amongst Fascists was a hatred of communism and the refrain 'better fascism than communism' was commonly said and used before the war. The revelations after 1945 of the evils of Nazism has coloured the popular perceptions of British fascism in a way which has not happened to communism although Stalin was equally guilty of extraordinary levels of mass murder.

It would be unfair to dismiss Fascists as cranks or misfits although this clearly applied to some individuals. Many were driven by high ideals and some were drawn to fascism by Mosley's own considerable charisma. A dislike of party politics and distrust in democracy drove some individuals. The granting of the vote to women contributed to a feeling in some that effective government could only be achieved by other means. The post 1914–1918 generation also questioned the validity of the Great War, was dismayed by the Great Depression and worried about losing the British Empire. The political atmosphere was volatile and in it local Fascists spread the word about fascism in the most unlikely remote villages of Devon.

The rise and subsequent decline of fascism in Devon is as much a story of how the other political parties fought it in different ways across the county. Agitation in Plymouth was very different from that in Barnstaple, Torquay or Exeter. It must be kept in mind that even with the hundreds of public meetings and marches fascism remained a minority interest. The party achieved considerable public attention but not one candidate was put up for public office; the public were never given the opportunity to vote for a Fascist in Devon. Most of all, the arrival and disappearance of Mosley's Blackshirts is a tale of how an extreme party suddenly appeared in a remote corner of England and galvanised tremendous support. It is commonly said in Devon this would not happen today, but it has once before. It could easily again. History can repeat itself and it is also possible to overlook and forget it.

Notes

1 Dave Renton, *Fascism, Anti-Fascism and Britain in the 1940s* (Basingstoke, 2000), 26-32.
2 Sheffield University, 119/C10/164i.
3 Sheffield University, 119/C10/163 & 161.
4 Sheffield University, 119/C10/157
5 Sheffield University, 119/C10/155i. Forward later wrote that Browning was once A/D/L Sales, Exeter: 119/C10/154. Yeatman may have lived in Little Hempston.
6 Sheffield University, 119/C10/4.
7 Sheffield University, 119/C10/147.
8 Sheffield University, 119/C10/142i.
9 Renton, *Fascism*, 51.
10 Sheffield University, 119/C11/52.
11 Sheffield University, 119/C11/127.
12 Sheffield University, 119/C11/126.
13 Sheffield University, 119/C12/120.
14 Renton, *Fascism*, 28.
15 Sheffield University, 119/C11/48 & 119/C11/124.
16 Sheffield University, 119/C11/122.
17 Sheffield University, 119/C11/121.
18 Sheffield University, 119/C11/120.
19 Sheffield University, 119/C15/115.
20 Sheffield University, 119/C11/312-13, 319ii, 320.
21 Sheffield University, 119/C11/165 & 191.
22 Sheffield University, 119/C11/119.
23 Sheffield University, 119/C11/118.
24 Sheffield University, 119/C12/80 & C15/149.
25 Devon Record Office, Silverton Voters' Lists, 1948; *Express & Echo*, 11 August 1947. I am grateful to Mrs Sylvia Tree for her memories of the Roberts' arrival in the village.
26 Sheffield University, 119/C12/120.
27 Sheffield University, 119/C12/119.
28 Sheffield University, 119/C12/63.

29 Sheffield University, 119/C12/119.
30 Sheffield University, 119/C12/117.
31 Sheffield University, 119/C15/221 & C13/113.
32 Sheffield University, 119/C12/115-16.
33 Sheffield University, 119/C12/169.
34 Sheffield University, 119/C16/136.
35 Renton, Fascism, 41.
36 Sheffield University, 119/C13/99.
37 Sheffield University, 119/C13/99.
38 Sheffield University, 119/D3/22.
39 Devon Record Office, Silverton Voters' List, 1950; Warwick University Modern Archives Centre, MSS 24/3/1/1/72.
40 Renton, *Fascism*, 26.
41 University of Exeter, Special Collections, Martin Collection as yet unlisted.
42 Robert Saunders, *A Tiller of Several Soils* (1987), letter dated 9 May 1950.
43 Dorril, *Blackshirt*, 636.
44 See Madeleine Bunting, *The Model Occupation* (2004), for a chilling account.

Index